The Crown and Canadian Federalism

The Crown and Canadian Federalism

D. Michael Jackson

DUNDURN
TORONTO

Editor: Andrea Waters
Project Editor: Cheryl Hawley
Design: Courtney Horner
Printer: Webcom

Library and Archives Canada Cataloguing in Publication

Jackson, D. Michael, author
        The crown and Canadian federalism / by D. Michael Jackson.

Includes bibliographical references and index.
Issued in print and electronic formats.

ISBN 978-1-4597-0988-1 (pbk.).--ISBN 978-1-4597-0989-8 (pdf).--ISBN 978-1-4597-0990-4 (epub)

1. Monarchy--Canada. 2. Federal government--Canada. 3. Constitutional history--Canada. 4. Canada--Politics and government. I. Title.

JL15.J32 2013   320.471   C2013-900894-2   C2013-900895-0

1 2 3 4 5   17 16 15 14 13

We acknowledge the support of the **Canada Council for the Arts** and the **Ontario Arts Council** for our publishing program. We also acknowledge the financial support of the **Government of Canada** through the **Canada Book Fund** and **Livres Canada Books**, and the **Government of Ontario** through the **Ontario Book Publishing Tax Credit** and the **Ontario Media Development Corporation**.

Care has been taken to trace the ownership of copyright material used in this book. The author and the publisher welcome any information enabling them to rectify any references or credits in subsequent editions.

J. Kirk Howard, President

Printed and bound in Canada.

VISIT US AT
Dundurn.com
@dundurnpress
Facebook.com/dundurnpress
Pinterest.com/dundurnpress

Dundurn	Gazelle Book Services Limited	Dundurn
3 Church Street, Suite 500	White Cross Mills	2250 Military Road
Toronto, Ontario, Canada	High Town, Lancaster, England	Tonawanda, NY
M5E 1M2	LA1 4XS	U.S.A. 14150

This book is dedicated to

The Honourable Lynda M. Haverstock, CM, SOM
exemplary vice-regal representative

l'honorable Serge Joyal, PC, OC, OQ
Sénateur, grand défenseur de la Couronne canadienne

Dr. David E. Smith, OC, FRSC
pre-eminent scholar of the Crown

Table of Contents

Preface

The Crown in Canada — the institution of constitutional monarchy — all too often has been treated in the media or in academe as an archaic relic which has no place in a modern democratic society, despite abundant evidence to the contrary. Or it is decried as a foreign institution, which Canadian history demonstrates is not the case. Or again, the Crown is assumed to be the property of the federal government to do with as it pleases, whereas the Canadian Crown belongs to the provinces too and is an integral part of their constitutional existence.

Like parliamentary democracy itself, the Crown suffers from a widespread ignorance about how Canada is governed. A co-founder of the Dominion Institute, Rudyard Griffiths, called us "a nation of amnesiacs." "Not only do Canadians have relatively low levels of civic literacy," he said, "we seem to be fast shedding, with little concern, the remaining knowledge we do possess about the country's proud democratic history, its basic political customs and many of its key institutions."[1] Ontario teacher Nathan Tidridge has deplored the failure of secondary schools in the Canadian provinces, especially his own, to educate young people about their country's political institutions. "In the Ontario curriculum," he says, "there is no mention of the words Sovereign/monarch/Queen, governor general, prime minister, Cabinet, or responsible government."[2] Law professor Ian Holloway observes "a strand of anti-historicism" in Canada, evidenced by the trend to teach Canadian history as only beginning in 1867, ignoring its millennial roots in Britain.[3] Worse still, says Tidridge, in Ontario "high school history begins in 1914 with the start of the Great War […] such things as the 1939 Royal Tour of King George VI and all other mention of the Crown (whether it is the Queen, members of the Royal Family or any of the vice-regal representatives) have been removed from the curricula." Noting egregious errors and outright anti-monarchical statements from several Ontario civics textbooks, Tidridge concludes "we are currently educating our schools to be illiterate, ambivalent or even hostile toward our constitutional monarchy, an institution that requires an educated population in order to work effectively."[4]

Another educational failure is equally evident: a lack of knowledge about how the traditions of our Aboriginal peoples influenced European settlers and their subsequent building of a society and an economy in a new land. Indeed, John Ralston Saul contends that these traditions are more significant than the others.[5] Certainly the ongoing and crucial role of the Crown in Aboriginal, especially First Nations, affairs has been only dimly understood by most Canadians and has contributed to the tendency to dismiss the institution as irrelevant to modern Canada. The provincial dimension of the Canadian Crown has similarly suffered from lack of appreciation and understanding, which moved former Ontario vice-regal representative Hilary Weston to say "[d]espite its historic roots and symbolic importance, the office of the lieutenant governor is a fragile institution, constantly threatened by misunderstanding, outdatedness or mockery."[6]

A staunch defender of the Canadian Crown, Senator Lowell Murray summarized the situation at the Golden Jubilee of Queen Elizabeth II in 2002:

> When, in the past thirty years, has a Prime Minister — or for that matter, a Governor General — been heard speaking of the central place of the Crown in Canada's parliamentary democracy? When has the representative of the Crown been heard speaking of the office as the transcendent, continuing symbol of our existence as a nation, above the political fray, the ultimate safeguard of our constitutional liberties? Governors general speak eloquently of the values that unite Canadians, but never about the significance of their office as the embodiment and defender of those val-

ues [...] The office has been held by dedicated and highly respected Canadians. Yet its significance in our parliamentary democracy is unappreciated and misunderstood by the mass of Canadians. Most people wrongly believe it to be completely ceremonial and utterly powerless. That is the fault of successive generations of politicians, of an educational system that has never given the institution due study, and of past vice-regal incumbents themselves.[7]

Following a successful Golden Jubilee celebration, however, the Crown started to make a comeback, aided by a Conservative government elected in 2006 with a more sympathetic attitude to the monarchy than its Liberal and Progressive Conservative predecessors of the previous four decades. Appropriately, the Queen presided at the ninetieth anniversary of the Battle of Vimy Ridge in 2007, before the spectacular monument inaugurated by her uncle, King Edward VIII, in 1936 on territory given to Canada by France. The Prince of Wales and Duchess of Cornwall made a long-postponed tour in 2009, the same year as there appeared the federal government's new citizenship guide for immigrants, which featured the Crown among key Canadian institutions.

The constitutional issues of dissolution and prorogation in the federal Parliament in 2008 and 2009 brought home the unfamiliarity of Canadians with their own mode of governance. Reactions to the governor general's prorogation of Parliament ranged from wild allegations of a *coup d'état* to surprise that the monarch's representative had any role to play at all. If any good stemmed from these episodes, it was an increased public awareness of the purpose of the vice-regal office and an acceptance of the role by the political players. Then, in 2010, a highly successful tour by the Queen and the Duke of Edinburgh took place, soon followed by the installation of David Johnston as governor general. Public statements by the prime minister and the new governor general placed considerable emphasis on the constitutional monarchy as a fundamentally Canadian institution and on the historic, beneficent role of the Sovereign — a refreshing change from the negative, deprecatory attitude to the Crown of the past four decades in official Ottawa. The 2011 marriage of Prince William and Catherine Middleton, Duke and Duchess of Cambridge and future king and queen, and the brilliant success of their tour of Canada soon thereafter aroused intense curiosity and positive feedback about the monarchical institution among Canadians, going far beyond the trivia of a celebrity cult.

The Diamond Jubilee of Queen Elizabeth II in 2012, celebrating her sixty-year reign, revealed a genuine widespread and enthusiastic appreciation of and affection for the monarch, not only in the United Kingdom but in her realms around the world. Canada mounted a substantial celebration across the country, including a high-profile Diamond Jubilee Medal program. Media commentary was positive and upbeat, even in outlets usually negative on the subject, suggesting that the monarchy had rebounded in public opinion.

At this timely juncture, we set out to explain the Canadian Crown, especially with respect to federalism, with the aim of drawing attention to its unique contribution to Canada's political culture and heritage. We are neither a political scientist nor a historian, although we emphasize the political and historical importance of the Crown. Nor do we have a legal background. In spite of this, we devote considerable attention to the constitutional evolution of the Canadian Crown, in the hope of explaining and demystifying this oft-cited but usually not well understood dimension of the topic. While this book addresses the whole of Canada, the majority of the case studies focus on the Province of Saskatchewan, which is the jurisdiction the author knows best. Saskatchewan is a province where the office of lieutenant governor reached a low ebb in the second half of the twentieth century, yet by the new millennium it had found new vigour.

Our study contains modest original research and only occasionally have primary sources been consulted. Instead, we have constantly referred to and copiously quoted the leading authorities in the field. For one of our purposes is to draw attention to both historic and contemporary analyses of the Crown. After a long period during which the monarchy in Canada did not engage scholars, in 1977, year of the Silver Jubilee of Queen Elizabeth II, Frank MacKinnon published a comprehensive study, *The Crown in Canada*.[8] Two years later, *The Canadian Crown* by Jacques Monet[9] appeared, together with its French version, *La Couronne au Canada*,[10] providing a more general, illustrated portrayal of the monarchical institution in Canada. These important books were precursors to the revival of academic interest in the Crown that began nearly two decades later with David E. Smith's landmark

The Invisible Crown in 1995[11] and his many subsequent publications on Canada's governance. We owe a particular debt to Dr. Smith, Canada's outstanding scholar on the Crown and parliamentary government. We also gratefully acknowledge Peter Boyce of Australia for his perceptive analyses of the Crown in the three "senior" Commonwealth realms, Noel Cox for his insightful study of the Crown in New Zealand and other realms, John Saywell's pioneering work on the office of lieutenant governor and his masterful study of the judicial impact on Canadian federalism, and Janet Ajzenstat for her lucid explanations of Canada's political culture. Our intent is to communicate this work to a wider public, providing a readily accessible exploration and explanation of the Crown and Canadian federalism. In Canada's other official language, the term *ouvrage de vulgarisation* appropriately describes this approach; we are pleased to act as a *vulgarisateur*!

We wish to thank the Honourable Lynda M. Haverstock, former lieutenant governor of Saskatchewan, for suggesting that this book be written. Dr. Haverstock was a model vice-regal representative. She demonstrated that the Queen's representative could not only exercise considerable non-partisan influence but also inspire widespread respect, affection, and loyalty for the Crown and Sovereign. We thank Christopher McCreery for his advice and assistance throughout the project and Robert E. Hawkins and Peter Neary for reviewing portions of the text, in the process correcting errors and making valuable suggestions for improvement. The shortcomings that remain are, of course, the responsibility of the author.

Michael Jackson
Regina, 2013

Note:
Parts of this book have been adapted from previous publications, as follows:

D. Michael Jackson and Lynda M. Haverstock, "The Crown in the Provinces: Canada's Compound Monarchy," in Jennifer Smith and D. Michael Jackson, eds., *The Evolving Canadian Crown*. Montreal & Kingston: McGill-Queen's University Press, 2012.

D. Michael Jackson, "Political Paradox: The Lieutenant Governor in Saskatchewan," in *Saskatchewan Politics: Into the Twenty-First Century*, 2001; and "The Crown in Saskatchewan: An Institution Renewed," in *Saskatchewan Politics: Crowding the Centre*, 2009; both edited by Howard A. Leeson and published by Canadian Plains Research Center, University of Regina.

Canada's Diamond Jubilee portrait of Queen Elizabeth II, by Toronto artist Phil Richards, was unveiled by the Queen in 2012.

Introduction: The Crown in Canada

The Crown has appropriate formal aspects but is more than just a formality. It is at the intersection of democracy, responsible government, the role of the state and the trinity of Canada's parliament — House of Commons, Senate and Crown. It reflects how we embraced accountability and shaped Confederation. It is not an afterthought. It is part of who we are.[1]

— Senator Hugh Segal

The roles of the Queen, governor general, and lieutenant governor in Canada are obscure to many citizens, as is the entire institution of the Crown. They defy simple explanations. They are, however, integral to the federal, parliamentary, monarchical democracy that is Canada.

Queen Elizabeth II is legally, constitutionally, historically, and by deliberate choice of Canadians the sovereign of our country. She is also Queen of Australia, New Zealand, Papua New Guinea, and eleven other small Commonwealth realms.* This is separate from her role in the

---

* "Realm" is the term used to describe the fifteen Commonwealth nations other than the United Kingdom of which the Queen is Sovereign. These are, in order of population: Canada, Australia, New Zealand, Papua New Guinea, Jamaica, Antigua & Barbuda, the Bahamas, Barbados, Belize, Grenada, St. Christopher & Nevis, St. Vincent & the Grenadines, Solomon Islands, Tuvalu. Some Commonwealth countries have their own monarchs: Brunei Darussalam, Lesotho, Malaysia, Swaziland, and Tonga. The other

The Queen reigns as Sovereign of sixteen Commonwealth realms, symbolized by her personal flags for each. Shown here are those for Australia, New Zealand, Jamaica, and the United Kingdom.

United Kingdom. The roots of constitutional monarchy in Canada can be traced back a thousand years. Winston Churchill, speaking in Winnipeg in 1929, said, "in the centre of our affairs is the golden circle of the crown which links us all together with the majestic past that takes us back to the Tudors, the Plantagenets, the Magna Charta, Habeas Corpus, Petition of Rights, and English common law."[2] Churchill was referring not only to the United Kingdom, where these legal milestones occurred, but also to Canada, which inherited them. Three generations later, in 2004, Michael Ignatieff, an internationally known Canadian scholar and writer who was leader of the Liberal Party of Canada from 2009 to 2011, made similar observations about Canada's institutions in a lecture entitled "Peace, Order and Good Government: A Foreign Policy Agenda for Canada":

> What makes Canadian values and identity distinc-
> tive is our particular history as a political community.
> We are British North America, a colonial fragment
> that remained loyal to the Crown, but which secured
> "responsible government" first among all the colonies

Commonwealth nations are republics. All fifty-four Commonwealth states recognize the Queen as Head of the Commonwealth.

of the Crown and which went on to create a transcontinental nation state, divided into five regions and two language groups. We have reason to be proud of our loyalty to British institutions, proud of our peaceful achievement of national independence [...] we are held together not by common myths of origin or shared ethnic or religious roots, but by political institutions [...] When we look for distinctive Canadian values [...] we should look at the history of our institutions and register the enduring commitments they represent.[3]

Former prime minister John Diefenbaker once pointed out that Canada not only inherited and adapted these British institutions but also further developed them:

The genius of British political institutions is that they have maintained tradition with the necessary flexibility. Magna Carta and other charters of freedom, and Parliament itself, though nurtured on English soil, have matured when their seeds have been planted in the far corners of the earth. They have grown and adapted themselves to meet the needs of countries and peoples and races everywhere in the world. In this process of adoption and adaptation, Canada was the first among the nations in the British Empire or Commonwealth to have religious freedom; the first to abolish slavery; first to have responsible government; first to bring about the establishment of free and independent nationhood while maintaining a democratic monarchy.[4]

Diefenbaker's phrase "a democratic monarchy" may appear paradoxical, if not contradictory, to those who equate democracy with republican government. Yet this paradox lies at the heart of what is indubitably a genuine Canadian democracy. What, then, is this perplexing Canadian "Crown"? In its simplest terms, the Crown is the democratic institution of constitutional monarchy. It incarnates Canada's Westminster-style parliamentary democracy, symbolized by the Queen, the governor general, and the lieutenant governors. This institution is subtle, complex, and perhaps even nebulous. But that does not mean it is not important — far from it. The Crown pervades Canada's constitutional order and political culture. The leading scholar on the subject, David E. Smith, entitled his definitive 1995 book *The Invisible Crown: The First Principle of Canadian Government*. Note the dual nature of the title. The Crown may seem invisible because it is so discreet. Yet Smith is unequivocal in stating that it is "an organizing principle of government" in Canada. True, the Crown is usually viewed as a symbol, and so it is, a rich and colourful one. However, Smith considers the Crown vitally important "because it determines the way Canadians govern themselves."[5]

New Zealand scholar Noel Cox echoes Smith's comments. First, he says, the Sovereign is the "legal head and linchpin of the executive branch of government" — a "practical role as the mechanism through which executive government is conducted." Second, the Crown is "a legal source of executive authority." Third, and most interesting, is the "conceptual or symbolic role of the Crown." Cox asserts that in countries deriving their constitutional systems from the United Kingdom, the Crown "fulfils the function exercised by a State in many jurisdictions, yet the Crown is not simply a metonym for the State."[6] Unlike the experience, for example, in post-revolutionary France, English common law never developed a theory of the State and was content to leave supreme executive power vested in the king. Thus the Crown "holds the conceptual place held by the State in those legal systems derived from or influenced by the Roman civil law."[7] Cox goes on to say that "this institution is more important than the person of the Sovereign. The Crown can be seen as a living thing, personified by the Queen and the Governor-General, and distinct from any obscure concept of governmental State."[8] (As we shall see in Chapter VI, this means that the term "head of state" is problematic for a constitutional monarchy.)

This supra-governmental dimension of the Crown is highly significant for Canadian federalism and for Canada's First Nations. David E. Smith says that, using the powers of the Crown, "the provinces have evolved a degree of autonomy unimagined by the Fathers of Confederation," which "led to a constitutional amalgam in Canada [...] called compound monarchy."[9] That compound monarchy may well be a key to the governance of the First Nations in the twenty-first century.

Emanating from this constitutional and political structure and tradition is the intriguing monarchical aura found throughout Canada, which reveals more about Canadians than they consciously realize. Our landscapes, streetscapes, and institutions are replete with royal and vice-regal names. Here are some examples:

The provinces of Alberta and Prince Edward Island. Prince of Wales Island, King William Island, Victoria Island, Prince Charles Island, King George V Mountain, and the Queen Elizabeth Islands in the Arctic. Mount Lorne, Yukon. The Queen Charlotte Islands and the Strait of Georgia in British Columbia. Mount Victoria, Lake Louise, and Princess Margaret Mountain in Alberta. Rupert's Land, still the name of an ecclesiastical province of the Anglican Church in northern and western Canada. Lake James in Manitoba. Mont-Royal, Lake Champlain, and Rupert River in Quebec. Lake Simcoe and Georgian Bay in Ontario. Lake George in New Brunswick. Victoria Cove in Newfoundland and Labrador.

The cities or towns of Victoria, Prince Rupert, and Prince George in British Columbia; Athlone and Willingdon in Alberta; Regina, Prince Albert, Earl Grey, and Aberdeeen in Saskatchewan; Victoria Beach, Louise, and Minto in Manitoba; Vaudreuil, Jonquière, Sherbrooke, Bagotville, and Victoriaville — and *le Chemin du Roy* — in Quebec; Amherstberg, Aylmer, Colborne, Kingston, Cornwall, Prescott, Georgetown, Guelph, Port Dalhousie, and Windsor, and the counties of Dufferin, Durham, Elgin, Frontenac, Grey, Haldimand, Simcoe, and York in Ontario; Charlottetown, Georgetown, and Lorne Valley in Prince Edward Island; Kingsport, Annapolis Royal, Kentville, and Stanley in Nova Scotia; Dorchester and Fredericton in New Brunswick; King's Cove, Grey River, and Athlone in Newfoundland and Labrador.

Historic sites such as Queenston Heights, Louisbourg, Port Royal, Fort Frontenac, Fort George, Fort York, and Prince of Wales Fort. The Connaught Tunnel on the Canadian Pacific Railway and the CPR's legendary steam locomotive, the Royal Hudson. Stanley Park in Vancouver and the Dufferin Terrace and Château Frontenac Hotel in Quebec City, and, to add more hotels, the Royal York in Toronto, the Reine Elizabeth in Montreal, the Lord Elgin in Ottawa, the Bessborough in Saskatoon, and the Empress in Victoria. The Queen Elizabeth Way in Ontario, Canada's first divided highway, was named after and

Canada's first divided highway, the Queen Elizabeth Way in Ontario, was named after and opened by the consort of King George VI in 1939.

Ontario Ministry of Transportation

opened by Queen Elizabeth, wife of King George VI, in 1939. And the Queen Elizabeth II Highway between Calgary and Edmonton in Alberta was named after her daughter in 2005.

The historic titles of the Royal Canadian Navy and Royal Canadian Air Force were restored in 2011. Every naval vessel is called "Her Majesty's Canadian Ship." The Canadian Army takes pride in storied royal names: Princess Patricia's Canadian Light Infantry, *le Royal 22e Régiment*, the Royal Canadian Regiment, the Royal Montreal Regiment, the Royal Canadian Dragoons, the Queen's Own Rifles of Canada, the Royal Hamilton Light Infantry, the Royal Winnipeg Rifles, Lord Strathcona's Horse (Royal Canadians), 8th Canadian Hussars (Princess Louise's), the Royal Regina Rifles, the Royal Canadian Horse Artillery, the King's Own Calgary Regiment, the Royal Newfoundland Regiment — and the list goes on. The Royal Canadian Sea Cadets, Royal Canadian Army Cadets, and Royal Canadian Air Cadets comprise the largest youth movement in Canada.

The cultural and community sectors are similar. Think, for example, of the Royal Winnipeg Ballet, the Royal Ontario Museum, the Royal Saskatchewan Museum, the Royal Tyrell Museum of Alberta, or the

Badges of Canadian Forces units feature their royal connections. Shown is that of Lord Strathcona's Horse (Royal Canadians), an armoured regiment based in Alberta.

Department of National Defence

Royal British Columbia Museum. The Royal Canadian Legion and the Royal Society of Canada. The Royal Conservatory of Music and the Royal College of Organists. The Royal Canadian Geographic Society and the Royal Astronomical Society of Canada. The Royal College of Physicians and Surgeons, the Victorian Order of Nurses, and the Vanier Institute of the Family. The Governor General's Literary Awards and Awards for the Performing Arts, and the Massey Lectures. Dalhousie University, Carleton University, Champlain College, Massey College, Victoria University, and Vanier College. The Royal Agricultural Winter Fair in Toronto — and the historic Queen's Plate horse races in the same city. The Royal Nova Scotia International Tattoo. The Duke of Edinburgh's Awards for young Canadians.

Additionally there are royal and vice-regal patrons of innumerable worthy causes and colonels-in-chief of many armed forces units. Iconic sports trophies are named after governors general: the Stanley Cup, Lady Byng Trophy, and Clarkson Cup in hockey; the Grey Cup and Vanier Cup in football; the Devonshire Cup and Willingdon Cup in golf; and the Minto Cup in lacrosse. Countless streets, hospitals, and schools across Canada bear royal or vice-regal names. The royal connection is highly visible in our currency and heraldry, our courts and police, and our annual Victoria Day/Queen's Birthday holiday; in tours of members of the Royal Family; in regional visits of the governor general and lieutenant governors; in the annual opening of parliament or legislature; in the conferring of national and provincial honours.

In 1909, Governor General Earl Grey donated the iconic Canadian football trophy, the Grey Cup.

Canadian Football League

Many Canadians may take all this for granted or consider it peripheral. On the other hand, there seems to be an innate awareness in the population that the monarchical dimension is something quintessentially Canadian, though perhaps intangible and elusive, which makes us different in the Americas. Of course, this was precisely the view of our predecessors in the eighteenth and nineteenth centuries.

I

Canada — Historically a Constitutional Monarchy

... Canada is a constitutional monarchy by *deliberate choice*. It is not by accident, nor from absentmindedness, or coercion, or the fear of coercion, that the *British North America Act, 1867, Section 9*, says "The Executive Government and authority of and over Canada is hereby declared to continue and be vested in the Queen." On the contrary, Sir John A. Macdonald, in the *Confederation Debates* in the Parliament of the Province of Canada, took pains to emphasize that the Quebec Resolutions on the subject [...] had "met with unanimous assent of the Conference."[1]

— Eugene Forsey

FIVE CENTURIES OF MONARCHY

A publication on the vice-regal office in Quebec emphasizes the historic roots of the Crown in that province, dating back to the earliest days of French settlement in *la Nouvelle France*: "Le pouvoir de cette haute figure d'autorité [le lieutenant-gouverneur] a des origines qui remontent bien avant la Confédération. On retrouve les racines de la fonction jusque dans la structure politique et administrative de la Nouvelle-France et de l'ancienne province de Québec."[2] Noting that "Canada is one the oldest continuing monarchies in the world today," an anglophone Quebec commentator points out, "[t]he white lilies of the Kings of France flew over the province of Quebec before the Union Jack flew over Canada, and that the lilies of the King of France — the fleur-de-lys — still fly over the province of Quebec is a fact that should not be forgotten by all monarchists in Canada."[3]

Indeed, monarchy has existed in Canada for half a millennium, since John Cabot landed in Newfoundland in 1497 and Jacques Cartier did the same at Gaspé in 1534, claiming these lands for their respective kings — Henry VII of England and François 1er of France. At that time, kings literally governed their countries. But by 1759 and the British conquest of New France, this was no longer the case in the United Kingdom. There, unlike France, monarchy had transmuted into its "constitutional" form, where the kings or queens reigned but did not rule. Government was carried out in their name by their advisers, the ministers of the Crown, led by the prime minister and responsible to elected representatives of the people in parliament — what came to be called "responsible government." While at first British monarchs retained some power and considerable influence, these dwindled through successive reigns, and by Queen Victoria's reign the royal role was essentially symbolic.

The system that the British brought with them to Canada in the eighteenth century could not be deemed "responsible government" at first. The colonial governors ran the government in the name of the monarch and not always with the support of the majority of the elected assembly. But at least there *were* elected assemblies in the British colonies: representative institutions were introduced in Nova Scotia as early as 1758, in Prince Edward Island by 1773, and in New Brunswick a year later. This was something the French colonists in Quebec had never enjoyed. They embraced this system quickly after it was introduced in 1792 under the terms of the *Constitutional Act* passed in the British Parliament the previous year, dividing Quebec into Upper and Lower Canada. They had a majority in the Lower Canada assembly and used it to push for responsible government, just as reformers did in Upper Canada and the British Atlantic colonies. Nova Scotia, led by Joseph Howe, was the first to secure full responsible government, in 1847–1848. Commenting on this gradual implementation of democracy in Canada, Senator Hugh Segal says "[o]ur democracy did not burst forth in an eighteenth-century revolt against each of our mother countries or the British Empire, of which we were then a loyal part. It was founded through an evolution from Crown-appointed governments to responsible legislatures and parliaments within the broad pre-Victorian outreach of the British Empire. American democracy revolted against the Crown; Canadian democracy evolved with the Crown."[4]

Some royal governors, in league with the ruling elites, such as the Family Compact in Upper Canada and the Château Clique in Lower Canada, tried to slow the inexorable move towards responsible government. This led to the rebellions of 1837–38 in both provinces. After the trauma of the rebellions, reformist Governor General Lord Durham recommended responsible government in a united Canada. This was put into effect in 1841, pursuant to the imperial *Act of Union* passed by the British Parliament in 1840. Some governors general of the new Province of Canada, like Lord Sydenham and Lord Metcalfe, were reactionary and tried to turn the clock back. Others, like Sir Charles Bagot, were progressive and in tune with the times.

Eventually, under the brilliant leadership of Reform politicians Louis-Hippolyte LaFontaine in French Canada and Robert Baldwin in English Canada, responsible government was achieved by 1849, a year after Nova Scotia. In that year, by giving his assent to the controversial Rebellion Losses Bill, the governor general of the united Province of Canada, Lord Elgin, courageously accepted, in the face of sectarian violence, advice from ministers who were backed by a majority in the assembly. Ironically, some of the same reactionary elements, whether anglophone or francophone, who opposed implementation of responsible government turned their backs on the Crown which had granted it and signed an Annexation Manifesto urging union with a different imperial power — the United States. Lord Elgin emerged serenely from the chaos as the prototype of the modern governor general — a symbol of unity representing a Crown and Sovereign above partisan politics, an emblem of civic virtue, a supporter of cultural initiatives.[5]

In the 1850s, frustrated with the political impasse between mainly francophone Canada East and anglophone Canada West in the United Canadas, the "Clear Grit" wing of the Reform movement called for a presidential system on the American model. Its chief spokesman was George Brown of the *Globe* newspaper, who articulated what he considered the failure of responsible parliamentary democracy. Fortunately, Brown concluded that the best option was to press for reform in the existing system, notably by dissolving the legislative union of 1841 in favour of a federal arrangement. This led to his initiative of the "Great Coalition" government in 1864, where the Reform leader joined with his Conservative opponents to seek a federation of the British North American colonies. Brown was to become one of the most influential Fathers of Confederation.[6] During the negotiations for confederation in the 1860s, one point was uncontested by all the colonial delegates, including those from French-speaking Canada: the new country would be a constitutional monarchy, with Queen Victoria as sovereign. The *British North America Act* (now the *Constitution Act, 1867*) stated at the outset that Canada's constitution would be "similar in principle to that of the United Kingdom" and that "the executive government and authority of and over Canada is hereby declared to continue and to be vested in the Queen." A governor general would represent the Queen for the dominion, and a lieutenant governor would serve similarly in each province.

Speeches by political leaders in the pre-Confederation debates in the colonial legislatures are instructive in this regard. The Fathers of Confederation were very conscious of the constitutional options open to them, primarily, of course, the republican, presidential system in the United States. Their analysis of the strengths and weaknesses of the monarchical and republican polities led them to the conclusion that they clearly preferred the former for the new nation. John A. Macdonald, speaking in the Legislative Assembly of Canada on February 6, 1865, said:

> I think it is well that, in framing our constitution ... our first act should have been to recognize the sovereignty of Her Majesty ... [at the Quebec Conference] the desire to remain connected with Great Britain and to retain our allegiance to Her Majesty was unanimous.
>
> ... by a resolution which meets with the universal approval of the people of this country, we have provided that for all time to come, so far as we can legislate into the future, we shall have as the head of the executive

Queen Victoria was the first sovereign of the Canadian Confederation.

Senate of Canada

power the sovereign of Great Britain. [...] No one can look into futurity and say what will be the destiny of this country. Changes come over nations and people in the course of ages. But, so far as we can legislate, we provide that, for all time to come, the sovereign of Great Britain shall be the sovereign of British North America. [...] By adhering to the monarchical principle, we avoid one defect inherent in the constitution of the United States. By election of the president by a majority and for a short period, he never is the sovereign and chief of the nation. He is never looked up to by the whole people as the head and front of the nation. He is at best but the successful leader of a party.[7]

The next day, Macdonald's francophone colleague, George-Étienne Cartier, recalling the reaction in Quebec to the American War of Independence, stated that the "French Canadians understood their position too well. If they had their institutions, their language, and their religion intact today, it was precisely because of their adherence to the British Crown." He went on to say, "[o]ur attempt was for the purpose of forming a federation with a view of perpetuating the monarchical element. [...] in our federation the monarchical principle would form the leading feature."[8] He further commented, "[u]nder the British system, ministers might be abused and assailed; but that abuse never reaches the sovereign."[9] Richard Cartwright, speaking a month later in the same legislature, said, "I had rather be the subject of an hereditary monarch, who dare not enter the hut of the poorest peasant without leave ... than be the free and sovereign elector of an autocratic president ..."[10] At the end of the Charlottetown Conference in September of 1864, during the portion held in Halifax, John A. Macdonald revealed his monarchist — and centralist — views when he said, "[i]f we can only obtain that object — a vigorous general government — we shall not be New Brunswickers, nor Nova Scotians, nor Canadians, but British Americans, under the sway of the British sovereign."[11] Appropriately, the steamship in which the Canadian delegates travelled to Charlottetown and Halifax was the *Queen Victoria*.

Indeed, the Fathers of Confederation wanted to call the new country the "Kingdom of Canada." This was evident in their discussions at the Quebec Conference in October 1864. Frances Monck, niece of the governor general, observing the conference, noted in her diary that the delegates had come to Quebec "to arrange about a united kingdom of Canada."[12] "Kingdom" was definitely the preferred term of John A. Macdonald, who was to become the first prime minister of Canada. As his biographer Richard Gwyn points out, during the Confederation debates, Macdonald went so far as to suggest "that the Queen be represented in the new nation by 'one of her own family, a Royal prince, as a Viceroy to rule over us.'"[13] Gwyn also recounts the intriguing story that Queen Victoria herself (crediting her late husband Prince Albert with the idea) had thought of such positions in the colonies for her sons. There was even an assumption that "the likeliest sibling to be sent to rule Canada as its King was the third son, Prince Arthur."[14] As it turned out, Prince Arthur, by then Duke of Connaught, did serve as Canada's governor general from 1911 to 1916. Prophetically, his sister, Princess Louise, wife of the Marquis of Lorne, governor general from 1878 to 1883, had written to her brother in 1878, "I think it possible you may come here one day. Canada is so loyal, so interesting, and with such a marvellous future that it really seems as if the Governor Generalship should always be filled by a member of our family."[15] The famous Connaught Tunnel on the Canadian Pacific Railway bears witness to this royal governor general. So do Connaught School and Connaught Crescent, not far from the Saskatchewan Legislative Building, opened by the Duke in 1912 in Regina, the provincial capital named after Prince Arthur's mother.*

In 1866, the governor general of Canada, Viscount Monck, informed the Colonial Secretary, Lord Carnarvon, of "a very strong desire that Her Majesty would be graciously pleased to designate the union a 'Kingdom' and so give to her representative the title of 'Viceroy.'"[16] To Macdonald's great chagrin, this was not to be. British officials were reluctant, partly because they considered the terminology pretentious, placing Canada on a similar footing to the United Kingdom. The main reason, however,

---

* The next street is named Leopold Crescent after Prince Arthur's younger brother, Leopold. Regina's two principal streets are called, appropriately, Victoria Avenue and Albert Street.

was a well-justified fear of American hostility, then, as now, a deciding factor in British foreign policy. One of the officials wrote that the terms "kingdom" and "viceroy" would be "too open a monarchical blister on the side of the United States."[17] The Legislature of the State of Maine passed a resolution expressing its opposition. The issue was raised in Congress. The British Minister in Washington, reporting on negative rumblings in the House of Representatives in Congress, advised that the title "Kingdom of Canada" had elicited "much remark of an unfriendly character in the United States."[18] As a result, early in 1867 the delegates at the London Conference had to content themselves with the term "dominion." Found in Psalm 72 and the Book of Zechariah, it was proposed by Leonard Tilley, premier of New Brunswick.* Queen Victoria was not even informed of the delegates' preference for "kingdom" and apparently showed a distinct lack of enthusiasm for the word "dominion," as did the British prime minister, Lord Derby.[19]

W.L. Morton, who entitled his 1963 general history *The Kingdom of Canada*, observed that "Dominion" was "a historic term, but one of little meaning in English and of even less when translated into French as 'la Puissance.' This failure to define accurately and with due solemnity what was in process, the establishment of a new nation under the British Crown, was to cost Canada much confusion of thought in the next two generations."[20] John Ralston Saul offers a very different interpretation. The United States, he says, did not want "a large, independent country on its northern border," which the term "kingdom" clearly meant; but "dominion" was not the second-rate alternative it has been made out to be. It means "power," and its French translation as "puissance" is entirely appropriate. Both were deliberate choices of the Fathers of Confederation, indicating their thorough grasp of the implications of Canada's emergence from colonial status. Saul regretted the abandonment of "Dominion" and "Puissance" in the mid-twentieth century as a "nihilist act" by the federal political leaders of the day.[21]

---

* Psalm 72: 5: "May he have dominion also from sea to sea, and from the River to the ends of the earth"; Zechariah 9: 10: "his dominion shall be from sea to sea, and from the River to the ends of the earth" (The New Revised Standard Version of *The Holy Bible*). This is the source of the motto on Canada's coat of arms: *A mari usque ad mare*, "From Sea to Sea."

In 1870, a federal cabinet minister, Christopher Dunkin, described the new Canada as comprising "three kingdoms" — the three distinct societies of Quebec, Ontario, and the Maritime provinces, no doubt an analogy with England, Scotland, and Ireland in the United Kingdom. These three kingdoms were reflected in the composition of the Senate. The analogy broke down with Canada's western expansion, and the Senate has been handicapped ever since by the imbalance of its regional representation.[22] Be that as it may, it was only at the accession of Queen Elizabeth II in 1952 that Canada's independent monarchical status was officially affirmed when the present royal title was adopted: "by the grace of God, of the United Kingdom, Canada and her other Realms and Territories, Queen, Head of the Commonwealth, Defender of the Faith."

"Thus," said W.L. Morton, "the intent of Macdonald and the Fathers of Confederation was realized at last, and Canada became the Kingdom of Canada its history had prepared it to be [...] when the Queen in 1957 opened Parliament, the new rank of Canada stood revealed in all its historic reality."[23]

INDEPENDENCE AND LEGITIMACY

The Crown in Canada and in the other dominions, far from being a hindrance to their independence, was a vehicle for achieving it. Responsible government had developed in pre-Confederation Canada through the judicious exercise of royal power by Lord Elgin and other governors. Similarly, after 1867 the delegation of royal power resulted in Canada's autonomy within the British Empire and then its independence as a monarchy distinct from the United Kingdom. The failure to gain the title "Kingdom of Canada" in 1867 was not the last word. As early as 1875, in a speech in Toronto, Sir John A. Macdonald made what is believed to be the first reference to Queen Victoria as "Queen of Canada."[24] During an exchange in 1901 between the British colonial secretary, Joseph Chamberlain, and the Canadian governor general(the Earl of Minto) and prime minister (Sir Wilfrid Laurier), Canada proposed "King of Canada, Australia, South Africa and all the British Dominions beyond the seas" as the royal style for King Edward VII.[25]

The record of Canada — and Australia, New Zealand, and South Africa — in the First World War, fighting for the same king but in their own national contingents, gave substance to the theory of separate Crowns. This was confirmed by their participation in the Versailles peace treaty process in 1919. With the Balfour Report of 1926, Empire became Commonwealth: the dominions were now "autonomous communities [...] equal in status, in no way subordinate to one another [...] though united by a common allegiance to the Crown and freely associated as members of the British Commonwealth of Nations." From this point, the governor general ceased to represent the British government, became solely the representative of the Sovereign, and was appointed by the Sovereign on the advice of the dominion prime minister.* The Imperial Conference of 1926 declared that "the Governor-General of a Dominion is the representative of the Crown and [...] is not the representative or agent of His Majesty's Government in Great Britain."

Even prior to the Balfour Report, an understanding had developed that the imperial government would consult the dominions on proposed appointees to the position of governor general. In 1916, Prime Minister Borden protested to the British government that he had not been consulted on their choice of the Duke of Devonshire to succeed the Duke of Connaught. This was the last such occurrence. In 1921, for the first time, a British prime minister consulted with his Canadian counterpart, Arthur Meighen, before recommending to King George V the appointment of Lord Byng as governor general. In 1926, the year of the Balfour Report, Prime Minister Mackenzie King chose Viscount Willingdon, to the pleasure of King George V, who had requested Willingdon's inclusion in the list of suggested names given to Canada. Willingdon was the first Canadian governor general to represent the King only and not the British government. The 1931 imperial conference formally stated that, in appointing a governor general, the King "should act on the advice of His Majesty's Ministers in the Dominion concerned." The same year,

---

* Canada did not recommend a Canadian national as governor general to the king until 1952, with Vincent Massey. Australia was the first to choose a national in 1931 (Sir Isaac Isaacs), but reverted to British appointees from 1936 until 1965; New Zealand did not make the move until 1972.

Prime Minister R.B. Bennett advised King George V on the appointment of Lord Bessborough as governor general. In 1935, Bessborough wanted to leave the position early. Opposition leader Mackenzie King, anticipating (rightly, as it turned out) that his Liberals would win the forthcoming general election, balked at any further vice-regal appointment proposed by Bennett. He suggested the popular Scottish writer John Buchan, well known as the author of the adventure story *The Thirty-Nine Steps*. King told Bennett that "scholarship and worth should now be more the criteria for governor generals and lieutenant governors, that Canada could not go on filling these offices with aristocrats and millionaires."[26] The comment was prescient. Bennett accepted the proposal and communicated it to Lord Bessborough. John Buchan, now Lord Tweedsmuir, was named governor general — the last such appointment by King George V.[27]

Independence of the dominions was formalized by the *Statute of Westminster*, passed by the British Parliament in 1931. The next year, the term "Kingdom of Canada" was again proposed in the Canadian Parliament. Noel Cox asserts that "the devolution of the Crown was the principal avenue through which independence was conferred upon the dominions," through "the transfer of the political control of the royal prerogative from imperial to dominion Ministers [...] with the growth of independence more authority was assumed by the Crown acting on the advice of local Ministers."[28] From the 1930s, the concept of the "divisible Crown" was gradually accepted, supplanting the original notion of common allegiance to one Crown, so that the Sovereign, while obviously one person, reigned separately in each realm. In 1936, the dominions gave their approval to the abdication of King Edward VIII each in their own way.[29] At his coronation in 1937, King George VI was the first monarch to refer to his role as king of the dominions. In 1939, the Canadian government ensured that the King declared war for Canada on Germany separately from the United Kingdom and did so one week later.

As we have seen, the separate Canadian kingdom came to ultimate fruition with accession of Queen Elizabeth II in 1952 and her coronation in 1953. The citizenship oath in Canada reflects the notion of multiple Crowns: "I swear/affirm that I will be faithful and bear true allegiance to Her Majesty Queen Elizabeth the Second, Queen of Canada, Her Heirs and Successors, and that I will faithfully observe the laws of Canada and

OFFICE OF THE PRIME MINISTER

CANADA

Approved

George R.I

The Prime Minister of Canada presents
his humble duty to His Majesty the King.

It is expedient that a Proclamation
should be issued in the name of His Majesty,
in Canada, declaring that a state of war with the
German Reich has existed in Canada as and from
September tenth.

The Prime Minister of Canada, accordingly,
humbly submits to His Majesty the petition of
The King's Privy Council for Canada that His Majesty
may approve the issuing of such a Proclamation in
His name.

The Prime Minister of Canada remains
His Majesty's most faithful and obedient servant.

W.L. Mackenzie King

Prime Minister of Canada.

Ottawa, September 10th, 1939.

In 1939, George VI declared war on Germany as King of Canada — separately from
the United Kingdom.

Library & Archives Canada, R219-100-6-E

fulfil my duties as a Canadian citizen." The oath in New Zealand is similar. Significantly, new citizens from other realms who have already sworn allegiance to the Queen in right of that country must take it again.

The legal authenticity of the separate Canadian Crown was clearly stated in 1982 by the leading judicial authorities in the United Kingdom. Opposing the terms of patriation of the Canadian constitution, some First Nations argued in 1981 in the Queen's Bench Division of the High Court of Justice of England and subsequently in the Court of Appeal that "treaty or other obligations entered into by the Crown to the Indian peoples of Canada are still owed by Her Majesty in right of Her Government in the United Kingdom." In rejecting the appeal, Lord Denning, Master of the Rolls, stated that, following the Balfour Report and the Imperial Conference of 1926, "it was recognized that, as a result of constitutional practice, the Crown was no longer indivisible. [...] As a result, the obligations of the Crown under the Royal Proclamation [of 1763] and the Indian treaties became the obligations of the Crown in respect of Canada." Lord Justice May added, "Although the Crown at one time was one and indivisible [...] this is no longer so. In matters of law and government *the Queen of the United Kingdom is entirely independent and distinct from the Queen of Canada* [our emphasis]."[30]

Symbolic initiatives since Queen Elizabeth's accession in 1952 have underscored the distinctive identity of the Canadian Crown. In 1962, Canada introduced a personal Canadian flag for the Queen. From the centennial of Confederation in 1967, an indigenous Canadian honours system under the Crown replaced British or imperial honours as formal recognition of achievement, bravery, merit, and service. A "vice-regal salute," composed of the first six bars of the royal anthem, "God Save the Queen," and the first four and last four bars of the national anthem, "O Canada," was introduced in 1968 to mark the arrival of the governor general and lieutenant governors at official functions. By 1988, a Canadian Heraldic Authority was created in the office of the governor general to exercise the royal prerogative of granting coats of arms, badges, and flags, which had previously been exercised through the heralds in England and Scotland. In 2011, on the occasion of the tour of the Duke and Duchess of Cambridge (Prince William and Catherine), Ottawa announced personal Canadian flags both for the Duke and for his father, the Prince of Wales, symbolizing their roles in the "Kingdom of Canada."

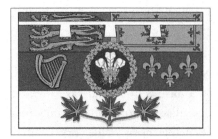

The unique Canadian flags for the Prince of Wales, the Queen, and the Duke of Cambridge (Prince William) symbolize Canada's independent Crown.

© *Her Majesty The Queen in Right of Canada, reprinted by permission of the Canadian Heraldic Authority*

Continuity in the Crown has conferred legitimacy on government through the governors general, first in their dual role of representing the British government and the monarch, then as surrogate for the Sovereign. This applies particularly to the First Nations in Canada and the Maori in New Zealand, for whom the treaty relationship is clearly with the successors of Queen Victoria. Legitimacy, of course, depends on other factors too, notably popular support. But the Crown is an important element: "Not only is the Crown above party politics, it is, to some degree, an independent source of legitimacy in a country, and control of the Crown thereby acts to confer some degree of legitimacy upon the political leadership."[31] That Crown has provided stability, continuity, authenticity, and validity to governance in Canada and the Queen's other realms.

THE MONARCHY AND QUEBEC

What does all this have to do with the Crown in Canada today, especially in Quebec? Simply this: it was under the umbrella of the Crown — it was thanks to the flexible, adaptable, evolving system of constitutional monarchy — that democratic government eventually prevailed in nineteenth-century Canada without the convulsions of revolution. Jacques

Monet, writing of the surrender of New France in 1760 by the last French royal governor (and the first born in Quebec), Pierre de Vaudreuil, to the first British governor, Jeffrey Amherst, said, "il lui légua l'idéal et les anciennes traditions de notre patrimoine monarchique." The second British governor, James Murray, "accepta ce legs de la Nouvelle-France," while the third, Sir Guy Carleton (later Lord Dorchester), "travailla à le faire passer dans l'Acte de Québec, lequel allait garantir la nationalité et les institutions du Canada français."[32]

At the time of the British conquest of New France there was no republican tradition in America (or, for that matter, in France). While the French-Canadian *habitants* remained attached to the French royal dynasty long after the conquest, "the clergy, seigneurs and merchants found the King of Britain acceptable as second best. Their fear was not of their new king but of his older American subjects who hoped to assimilate French Canadians as they were assimilating the German, Dutch, and French populations of the other American colonies."[33] King George III reciprocated the feeling, judging from his gallant comment to Madame Chaussegros de Léry, the first French-Canadian lady presented at his court after the transfer of Canada from the French to the British Crown: "Madame, si les dames canadiennes vous ressemblent, j'ai vraiment fait une conquête."[34]

Louis XV was the last King of France to rule over Canada.

Portrait of King Louis XV by Carl Van Loo; © Crown Collection, Official Residences Division, National Capital Commission

There is ongoing debate among historians about the results of the Conquest, the motives of the British in their policies towards Quebec, and what these meant to the *Canadiens*. One point of view among the late-eighteenth-century *Canadien* élite, especially the Church, was that the British conquest was providential, preserving them from the evils of the French Revolution: violence, republicanism, and atheism. Much early nineteenth-century French-Canadian opinion lauded the benefits of British liberal political institutions. The suppression of the rebellion of the *Patriotes* in 1837–38 disabused some of these proponents and reinforced the *nationaliste* school of thought, which viewed the Conquest as a catastrophe, redeemed only by the dogged *survivance* of the *Canadiens* in the face of anglophone hostility. Divergent schools of thought continued in the twentieth century, some emphasizing the basic entente between anglophone and francophone Canadians, others moving from the *nationaliste* approach to the sovereigntist option, culminating in the Parti Québécois and the Bloc Québécois.[35]

For the Crown, the results appear to speak for themselves. The Royal Proclamation of 1763 provided that English civil and criminal law would apply in Quebec, which presumably excluded Roman Catholics from public office. However, under Governor Murray, that simply did not happen. Local customs and French civil law continued, and *Canadiens* willingly served on juries, unknown to them under the French regime.[36] Then, in 1774, the British Parliament passed the *Quebec Act*, which undid the restrictive measures of the Proclamation of 1763. One of the constitutional foundations of Canada, the *Quebec Act* accommodated the principles of British institutions to the reality of the province. It allowed religious freedom for Roman Catholics and permitted them to hold public office, such as judgeships, a practice not then allowed in Britain.[37] While the *Act* established English criminal law, it retained French civil law. George III, who took great interest in Canada, personally supported the *Act*: "In terminating the [parliamentary] session [in 1774], the King applauded the Quebec Act, as founded on the clearest principles of humanity and justice, and calculated to produce the best effects in quieting the minds and promoting the happiness of the Canadians."[38] Senator Hugh Segal believes that the *Quebec Act* began the historic Canadian process of accommodation and "the resilience of loyalty to the Crown as an organizing principle of Canadian society."[39]

King George III was partial to French-speaking Canada and supported the *Quebec Act*.

Senate of Canada

The American War of Independence proved the point. The Thirteen Colonies resented the *Quebec Act*, which protected what was to them a foreign people with a rival economy and, worse still, restored Quebec's historic boundaries south through the Ohio Country to Louisiana. Their armies invaded Canada early in the war. But Quebeckers did not, contrary to the expectations of the rebellious colonists, see the American invaders as liberators from the yoke of the British Crown. Only a few joined the Americans. The majority carefully remained neutral, but a good number of *Canadiens* fought on the British side, helping repel the attack on Quebec City by Benedict Arnold's army on New Year's Eve, 1775. After the American invaders withdrew early in 1776, people in Quebec celebrated: "Le 8 mai [1776] … A la réception du succès des royalistes, les Dames Ursulines ont chanté ce matin un *Te Deum*, pendant la messe."[40]

Following the independence granted in 1783 to the Thirteen Colonies as the United States of America, thousands of Loyalists — those loyal to George III and the Crown — fled the new republic for Nova Scotia and

Quebec. As a consequence, the province of New Brunswick was created out of Nova Scotia in 1784, with its own elected assembly. Quebec, now bereft of its southern extension through the Ohio Country to Louisiana, took more time to reorganize. To accommodate the influx of Loyalists into the Lake Ontario area, the *Constitutional Act* of 1791 divided Quebec into the provinces of Upper and Lower Canada and provided French Canadians with their first elected assembly ever. Once again, King George III took a personal interest. "When Pitt was preparing his Canada Bill, the King stressed to him that the people whose welfare must first be considered were the original French-Catholic inhabitants."[41]

There is an intriguing vignette of Prince Edward, fourth son of George III, later Duke of Kent and father of Queen Victoria, who arrived in Quebec as military commander in 1791. Disturbances broke out in 1792 during the first elections to the assembly. Observing attempts at preventing voters from access to the poll in Charlesbourg, the Prince "sprang to the hustings. He addressed the angry crowd 'in pure French, and with a tone of affection and authority.' 'Part then in peace. I urge you to unanimity and concord. Let me hear no more of the odious distinction of *English* and *French*. You are all His Britannick Majesty's *beloved* Canadian subjects.'" This is believed to be the first use of the term "Canadian" for both French and English inhabitants and set a precedent.[42] Edward was the first member of the Royal Family to live in Canada. He served in Quebec from 1791 to 1794 and in Nova Scotia from 1794 to 1800, and was knowledgeable and supportive of Canadians and *Canadiens*. The latter relationship was undoubtedly facilitated by his mistress from France, Alphonsine Thérèse-Bernardine de Mongenêt, who accompanied him to North America, where she was known as Madame Julie de Saint-Laurent. Author Nathan Tidridge calls Prince Edward "Father of the Canadian Crown." He was to be father of Queen Victoria, first sovereign of the Canadian federation, after being required in 1818 to renounce his liaison with Julie de Saint-Laurent in order to contract a dynastic marriage with Princess Victoria of Saxe-Coburg-Saalfeld. In 1792, he undertook the first royal tour, an extensive visit through the newly created Upper Canada. As commander-in-chief of British North America, argues Tidridge, he was one of the first to anticipate the union of the British North American colonies, with the Crown as a unifying force.[43]

Prince Edward, Duke of Kent and a son of George III, was the first member of the Royal Family to live in Canada.

Communications Nova Scotia

Following the implementation of the *Constitutional Act*, prominent French-Canadian leaders saw this British constitution as a prime asset for their own governance. Pierre Bédard, first leader of the "French party" in the Lower Canada assembly and first editor of the journal of political opinion *Le Canadien*, vigorously opposed policies of British officials that, in his view, subverted democratic institutions and free speech. In 1811, he was imprisoned by the governor, Sir James Craig, for his outspoken opposition. Fortunately, Craig was succeeded by Sir George Prevost, lieutenant governor of Nova Scotia, who was French-speaking and, like Murray and Carleton, a francophile. He released Bédard and made him a judge. In spite of what had happened to him, notes Janet Ajzenstat, Bédard "never relinquished his confidence in British institutions. After his release from jail, he argued that what had happened ought not to diminish French Canadians' admiration for their Constitution." Bédard was, in effect, arguing for responsible government. In 1808, while "he was urging his constituents to stand firm on their rights under the Constitution to elect representatives who would foil the governor's political plots, he did not fail to remind them to honour and obey the governor as the king's representative."[44]

His counsel was followed in the War of 1812. Once again, *Canadiens* joined with Canadians, British, and the First Nations to repel an American invasion. After releasing Bédard and reconciling with the French-Canadians, Governor Prevost had formed a *Canadien* regiment, *les Voltigeurs*, commanded by Charles-Michel de Salaberry.* Salaberry had been one of the first French-Canadians to respond to an invitation in 1794 from Prince Edward, Duke of Kent, to join the British army[45] as Britain fought, first against the French revolutionary armies, then in the Napoleonic Wars. The latter precipitated the War of 1812. It began ominously in French Canada, when a riot over conscription occurred in Montreal. This was, however, dealt with judiciously by Prevost, who calmed the population. A leading historian of the war notes how Americans wrongly assumed that "French Canadians would welcome an American liberation. In fact most of the *habitants* regarded British rule as far better than an American conquest. In October 1812 a British officer reported that the Lower Canadian militia had turned out 'with the greatest alacrity, and altho' they abominate the War, they hate the very name of an American.'"[46] In October 1813, at Châteauguay, south of Montreal, Salaberry, leading 460 *Voltigeurs* and 22 First Nations warriors, defeated a 4,500-strong American army. A few months later, *Canadien* volunteers took part in the crucial battle of Crysler's Farm, near Morrisburg in present-day Ontario. In 1814, *Canadien* militia took the lead in capturing American warships at Île aux Noix, at the north end of Lake Champlain.

At the end of the war, in 1815, Canada remained in the British Empire. Its constitutional evolution resumed, leading to full responsible government under Lord Elgin. *Canadiens* were in the forefront of this process unfolding under a British monarch. Senator Serge Joyal notes the key role of the nationalist leader Louis-Joseph Papineau:

> Le témoignage le plus percutant des sentiments prévalant
> à l'égard de la Couronne, à cette époque, est le discours
> que prononça Louis-Joseph Papineau lui-même, alors

---

* Charles-Michel de Salaberry was made a Companion of the Order of the Bath in 1817 and appointed to the legislative council of Lower Canada in 1818.

président de la Chambre d'assemblée, à l'occasion du décès de George III:

« La nécessité de ce choix venant d'une grande calamité nationale, la mort du souverain bien aimé qui a régné sur les habitants de ce pays depuis qu'ils sont devenus sujets britanniques, il est impossible de ne pas exprimer nos sentiments de gratitude pour les bienfaits que nous avons reçus de lui et les sentiments de regret pour sa perte si profondément sentie ici et dans toutes les parties de l'empire. Et comment pourrait-il en être autrement, quand chaque année de son règne a été marquée par de nouvelles faveurs accordées à ce pays [...] tous ces avantages sont devenus pour nous un droit de naissance, et seront, je l'espère, l'héritage durable de notre postérité! Pour les conserver sachons agir comme des sujets anglais et des hommes indépendants. » *Gazette de Québec*, juillet 1820.[47]

How intriguing it is that Papineau, the great Quebec nationalist and future rebel against the Crown's authority in the 1837–38 rebellion of *les Patriotes*, should laud King George III as the worthy successor of King Louis XV.

Étienne Parent, writing in *Le Canadien* in the 1820s and 1830s, believed that "the British Constitution was the best possible form of government for Lower Canada [...] French Canadians were as capable as the British of appreciating the benefits of good political institutions, and as capable of using them to their own advantage."[48] French-Canadians, more than anyone, looked to the Crown as the protector of their minority rights, of their identity, language, legal system, and religion — and this despite the undoubted setbacks of the *Patriote* rebellion of 1837–38. As the Province of Canada moved towards full responsible government, *Canadien* leaders proudly proclaimed their loyalty to the Crown. Dr. Étienne-Pascal Taché, veteran of Châteauguay and a minor participant in the rebellion, made a famous speech in 1846 in the legislative assembly in Montreal. Pointing to the portrait of Queen Victoria in the chamber, he said: "Indeed we claim to be children of the same mother as you ... Be satisfied we will never forget our allegiance till the last cannon which is shot on this continent in defence of Great Britain is fired by the hand of a French Canadian."[49] Taché was to become premier of the Province of Canada and a Father of Confederation; he chaired the Quebec Conference in November of 1864. In 1849, another prominent Quebec leader, Hector Langevin (also to become a Father of Confederation), hailed Lord Elgin: "Il nous faut [...] approuver la conduite du noble Lord qui représente parmi nous notre auguste Souveraine, et qui se fait le gardien de nos droits constitutionnels."[50] After all, it was Lord Elgin who, in implementing responsible government, "en lisant le discours du Trône en français, a donné de sa propre initiative, dès 1849, une sanction toute royale à l'utilisation officielle de la langue française au Canada."[51]

Throughout the 1860s, French-Canadian leaders showed complete solidarity with their English-speaking colleagues in wishing Canada to remain a monarchy under Queen Victoria at Confederation. The leading francophone Father of Confederation, George-Étienne Cartier, was such a monarchist that he named one of his daughters Reine-Victoria. His own first name was George rather than Georges because his father had named him in honour of King George III. During the negotiations for Confederation in 1864, he said in Halifax:

> I am living in a Province in which the inhabitants are monarchical by religion, by habit and by the remembrance of past history. Our great desire and our object in making efforts to obtain the federation of the Provinces is not to weaken monarchical institutions, but on the contrary to increase their influence. We know very well that, as soon as confederation is obtained, the Confederacy will have to be erected into a Vice-Royalty, and we may expect that a member of the Royal Family will be sent here as the head.[52]

During the Confederation debates, Cartier reiterated the point: "In this country, we should have a distinct form of government, the characteristic of which would be to possess the monarchical element." For French-Canadians, he said, "[i]f they had their institutions, their language and their religion intact today, it was precisely because of their adherence to the British Crown." [53]

Quebeckers enthusiastically welcomed members of the Royal Family to the province. In 1860, the first visit of a Prince of Wales (later King Edward VII) was an occasion of great excitement. In Montreal the Prince opened the spectacular new Victoria Bridge and in Ottawa he laid the cornerstone of the Parliament Buildings. His successor as Prince of Wales, the future King George V, was just as enthusiastically received when he presided at the three hundredth anniversary of the founding of the City of Quebec in 1908. This was also the case with the first-ever visit of reigning monarchs, King George VI and Queen Elizabeth, in 1939. Premier Maurice Duplessis, in welcoming them to Quebec, stressed the loyalty of the province to the Crown: "Notre province a toujours été fidèle à la couronne britannique, elle s'est montrée aussi fidèle aux traditions héritées des ancêtres, au pacte fédératif de 1867 comme à la mission que les hommes d'État anglais de 1791 lui avaient donné: *To remain altogether French*. Ce passé nous tient toujours au cœur et nous ne cesserons de considérer le Trône comme le rempart de nos institutions démocratiques et de nos libertés constitutionnelles."[54] He repeated the sentiments twelve years later, when the daughter of the King and Queen, Princess Elizabeth, visited Quebec: "Notre province, peuplée en très grande majorité de Canadiens d'origine française, a toujours été fidèle à la Couronne britannique, symbole d'autorité et de liberté. Québec est synonyme de loyauté."[55]

Successive governors general, through their official residence, *La Citadelle*, in Quebec City, made their mark on the province. The Earl of Dufferin, governor general from 1872 to 1878, contributed enormously to the restoration of Quebec City as a true heritage site, the only walled city in North America. It was Dufferin who established *La Citadelle* as the Quebec equivalent of Rideau Hall. Earl Grey (1904–1911) — he of the famous Grey Cup — masterminded the three hundredth anniversary celebrations in 1908. General Georges Vanier (1959–1967), gallant soldier in the First World War and former ambassador to France, was the epitome of the vice-regal francophone. Since Vanier, there has been a custom that French-speaking and English-speaking governors general alternate, showing the special attention paid to Quebec and francophone Canada by the national Crown.

Unfortunately, much of this has been forgotten in Quebec. The rise of the sovereigntist movement from the 1960s weakened Quebec's historic links with the Crown. Separatists purported to see it as a symbol of colonialism and of Ottawa's ascendancy rather than as a vehicle for franco-phone particularity. The Queen's visit to Charlottetown and Quebec in 1964 for the centennial of the Confederation conferences of 1864 elicited protests from some Quebec nationalists; given concerns for the Queen's safety, there were calls for the cancellation of the tour. It was ironic that at the time of this unrest the governor general was Georges Vanier. One of the best governors general the country has had, Vanier was the very model of the bilingual, bicultural Canadian, a deeply spiritual person with innate dignity and sensitivity. During the 1964 tour, the Queen her-self acted with calm and courage, paying an eloquent tribute in French in the Quebec assembly to francophone culture in Canada. Vanier was dis-appointed and embarrassed by the excessive security measures taken due to a few hundred separatists, but admired the Queen's poise and persever-ance and applauded the decision of Prime Minister Pearson and Premier Lesage not to bow to pressure and cancel the tour.[56] Vanier had faced hostile demonstrators in Montreal at the annual St. Jean Baptiste Day parade, some waving insulting placards such as "Vanier vendu" and boo-ing the governor general. Vanier and his elegant wife Pauline remained serene throughout.[57] They made such an impression that Pearson asked Vanier to stay on as governor general well past the customary five-year vice-regal mandate. He did so until his death in 1967 — Canada's centen-nial year — at the age of seventy-nine.

Despite the 1964 episode, the Queen had successful visits to Montreal three years later for Expo 67 and, with all members of her immediate family, in 1976 for the Summer Olympic Games. In 1987, Queen Elizabeth the Queen Mother was well received in Montreal. Later that year, Queen Elizabeth II had her first visit to Quebec City since 1964. Premier Robert Bourassa welcomed Her Majesty "on behalf of the great majority of Quebecers," and in her reply the Queen referred to the recognition in the recent Meech Lake Accord "that Quebec constitutes a distinct society." Other members of the Royal Family visited Quebec from time to time without incident. Nonetheless, the federal govern-ment, apparently unnerved by separatist rhetoric, declined to invite the Queen to the four hundredth anniversary of Quebec City in 2008, despite a request to do so by the event organizers. Nor did they invite the Prince of Wales to replicate the role of his great-grandfather from 1908.

Georges Vanier, first francophone governor general, held office when the sovereigntist movement first made waves in Quebec.

Cavouk Studios, National Archives, neg. C-63530 © Cavouk Studios

As historian Margaret MacMillan has pointed out, history can be selectively used to portray a partial and often one-sided view of a nation, and she notes how this has been the case in Quebec. "French-Canadian nationalists," she says, "have depicted a past in which the Conquest by the British in 1763 led to two and a half centuries of humiliation [...] French Canadians — innocent, benevolent, communitarian, and tolerant of others — are the heroes of the story; the English — cold-hearted, passionless, and money-grubbing — the villains."[58] There are, however, francophone commentators who continue to appreciate the historic validity of the Crown. Commenting on the irony that the British conquest ensured the survival of the French on the North American continent in the face of the emerging and devouring giant of the United States, political scientist Christian Dufour wrote:

> … la tutelle anglaise a permis aux Canadiens d'échapper à ce qui semblait être leur destin obligé : l'annexion à la nouvelle république américaine voisine, vingt-cinq fois plus peuplée et convaincue que « son destin manifeste » est de prendre possession de la totalité du continent nord-américain. Commençant leur inéluctable ascension vers l'hégémonie mondiale, les États-Unis vont se constituer en vraie nation. Ils n'ont que faire des particularismes de l'Ancien Monde. Ils ne feront qu'une bouchée des 100,000 Allemands qui habitent la Pennsylvanie à l'époque de la guerre d'In-dépendance; ils folklorisent la Louisiane que leur cédera la France napoléonienne en 1803. Aux côtés du jeune géant yankee, le Canada naîtra déjà vieux, tourné vers le passé, de l'improbable mariage des Canadiens du Roi-Soleil avec ces Américains qui veulent relever du roi d'Angleterre.[59]

A final word: Prince William, the eldest son of the Prince of Wales and thus heir to the throne, is, through his mother, a descendant of King Henri IV of France (1589–1610), who sent Champlain to found Quebec. A daughter of Henri IV, Henriette Marie, married King Charles I of England; one of their daughters, Henriette d'Angleterre, married the Duc d'Orléans, brother of King Louis XIV. Diana Spencer was descended from this line. If Quebeckers were to look for a king who inherits the French monarchy, William is it![60]

THE MONARCHY AND THE FIRST NATIONS

Today, it is common knowledge that Canada's indigenous inhabitants were displaced and marginalized by European colonization. The ideal and intent of fair treatment for native peoples were always there, but thwarted by poor implementation and even interference. That ideal and intent could be found in the Crown. The Royal Proclamation of

1763 issued by King George III recognized Aboriginal ownership of their lands. It firmly stated the principle that European settlement could proceed only by treaty with the First Nations, which is why the American colonists to the south opposed it. The Proclamation of 1763 "is viewed by many First Nations as their Magna Carta for inherent rights: it protected First Nations lands and recognized First Nations peoples as nations. It established that a treaty with the Crown was the sole means by which the British could acquire land and excluded private interests from such transactions."[61] It established the notion of the honour of the Crown and its responsibility for the peace, welfare, and good government of all its peoples.

The Diamond Jubilee of Queen Elizabeth II in 2012, coinciding with the bicentennial of the War of 1812, was an opportunity for the First Nations to remind Canadian of their crucial role as allies of the Crown in that conflict — a role underscored by recent historical studies.[62] The positive attitude of the British towards Indians since the Royal Proclamation of 1763 paid off in spades, as the vast majority of the First Nations rallied to the Crown. With leaders of the calibre of Tecumseh, they were key to early British/Canadian victories, such as the capture of Michilimackinac and Detroit, the occupation of Michigan, and the repelling of invasion at Queenston Heights. While militarily a draw between the United States and the British Empire, the War of 1812 confirmed the distinction between the American republic and loyalist British North America and secured Canada's future existence as a nation under the Crown. A sad outcome, however, was the failure of that Crown to protect the First Nations who had so ably defended it. Dreams of an Indian buffer state in the lands west of the Mississippi River were dashed by the Treaty of Ghent in 1815, which abandoned the territory to the United States as Britain made concessions to secure peace.[63]

Americans had a lengthy history of violent conflict with the First Nations, whom they feared and resented. There was forcible occupation of the West through a series of wars, decimating the Indian tribes. Canada followed a different path under the Crown. Nineteenth-century treaties defined the relationship between the First Nations and the settlers. The treaties were and remain a solemn covenant, "the promise to reconcile differences between First Nations and the Queen through a treaty relationship made before the Creator in the name of the Queen and in the name of First Nations."[64] The direct, treasured relationship between the First Nations and the Sovereign stems from the treaties:

> ... the treaties created in the minds of the Indians a strong tie with the Queen and her heirs. Since it was in her name that the treaties were signed, and since the commissioners were considered Royal representatives, the Indians saw the treaties as pacts with Queen Victoria rather than with the government of Canada. [...] Crowfoot, a chief of the Blackfoot, saw the treaty as a pact of faith between the Blackfoot and the Crown.
>
> Queen Victoria was a very important person to the Indians, even though no one from the tribes had ever met her. [...] The symbol of the Queen remained as a positive source of strength throughout the succeeding years, and when her land — England — was threatened by war, many Indians wanted to help.[65]

In 1914, a chief from Ontario said that "[t]he Indian Race as a rule are loyal to England; this loyalty was created by the noblest Queen that ever lived, Queen Victoria."

"The Indians of Western Canada endorsed these sentiments, for they remembered their long association with the Crown, first through the North-West Mounted Police (whom they saw as representatives of the Queen sent to protect them), and secondly, through their treaties with Queen Victoria."[66] A number of First Nations today fly the Union Jack at their ceremonies. Says Jim Miller, a leading scholar on the First Nations, "the raising of Britain's venerable pennant is neither anachronistic nor out of place for First Nations, given their long-standing and still vibrant sense of kinship with the Crown."[67]

Miller has described how First Nations have always treasured their link with the Crown and since the eighteenth century have sought direct access to the Sovereign to defend their rights and remedy their grievances. Mohawk chief Joseph Brant travelled to London in 1775–1776 and again in 1785 to press for protection of their lands in accordance with the Proclamation of 1763, and was warmly received by King George III on both visits. In 1860, Nahnebahwequa, a Mississauga Indian woman, secured an audience with Queen Victoria to petition about land wrongly taken from her family and tribe. In 1906, after lobbying one of Queen Victoria's sons, the Duke of Connaught, governor general of Canada, a delegation of chiefs from the northwest First Nations of British Columbia — not covered by treaties — journeyed to London to present their land claims to King Edward VII. Iroquois leaders from Ontario made the case for their sovereignty to King George V in 1921. A delegation marking the centennial of Treaties 6 and 7 had an audience with Queen Elizabeth II in 1976. First Nations leaders tried to do the same over the patriation of the constitution between 1977 and 1982, but were rebuffed at the direction of the Canadian government.[68]

First Nations leaders have rarely been known to criticize the monarchy or the Crown. Their critical comments have almost always been directed at the Crown's ministers for their failure to respect and live up to the spirit of the treaties. Chief David Ahenakew of the Federation of Saskatchewan Indians, in an impromptu speech to the Queen at the centennial of the Royal Canadian Mounted Police in Regina in 1973, said that, while Indians were loyal to the Crown, "we are saddened to say that, over the years, some of your servants have not kept your part of the agreement."[69] Since then, however, several Supreme Court decisions have revived the crucial notion of the honour of the Crown in dealings with the First Nations. "Canadians have inherited the British tradition of acting honourably for the sake of the Sovereign," says David Arnot. "Appealing to the Honour of the Crown was recourse not merely to the sovereign as a person, but to a bedrock of principles of fundamental justice that lay beyond persons and beyond politics. It is precisely this distinction that rests at the heart of our ideals of 'human rights' today."[70]

Starting with *Guerin v. The Queen* in 1984, the Supreme Court held that the Crown's fiduciary duty to the First Nations went beyond legal, contractual technicalities; that Aboriginal oral tradition carried great weight in interpreting this duty; and that the Crown's responsibility rested on the bedrock of the Royal Proclamation of 1763. In a second decision, *Delgamuukw v. British Columbia*, the Supreme Court gave clearer scope to claims for Aboriginal title and Aboriginal rights.[71] In *Marshall #1* (1999), the Court specified that "the Honour of the Crown is always at stake in its dealings with Aboriginal people [...] Interpretations of treaties and statutory provisions which have an impact upon treaty or Aboriginal rights must be approached in a manner which maintains the integrity of the Crown."[72] Common themes in the recent court rulings are the notions of honour, fairness, and justice and the personal obligation of the Crown's ministers and officials to conduct themselves accordingly.

In New Zealand, the vitally important relationship of the Maori people with the Crown is enshrined in the landmark 1840 Treaty of Waitangi. This relationship is even more intense than that of Aboriginals in Canada, because a single treaty encompasses all the indigenous peoples. The Treaty of Waitangi is one of the constitutional building blocks of New Zealand, conferring legitimacy on the Crown — which, in turn, validates for the Maori people the legitimacy of the current legal and political system in their country. Says Noel Cox, "it continues to be the case, and in fact this appears increasingly imperative to Maori, that *the Crown is not only something other than the government of the day* [our emphasis], but also that the Crown is able to function in such a manner as to hold the government to the guarantees made under the Treaty of Waitangi."[73] Any move to eliminate the monarchy would very much impinge on the interests of the Maori in New Zealand, as it would on the First Nations in Canada.

John Whyte, a Canadian constitutional expert favourable to republicanism, nonetheless observes that "abolition of the monarchy would be seen by Canadian Indian communities as an immense threat to their special status within Canada. Indians understand their political commitment and fidelity to the Queen and, conversely, the obligations of protection and support that lie against the Queen." The treaty relationship with the Sovereign provides in their view "the clear textual basis for a direct and personal relationship. This is not an example of primitive literalism on the part of these communities; it is a shrewd tactic to maintain the original purity of the treaties and their implicit acceptance of inherent Aboriginal governmental powers."[74] Indeed, other writers believe that "[t]he Crown holds the promise of providing an institution that holds the political legitimacy upon which Canada can build a common future with Aboriginal peoples."[75]

II

Crown, Parliamentary Democracy, and the Royal Prerogative

In a system of parliamentary-cabinet government, the oath of the sovereign to do good becomes the obligation of her ministers, and her judges, to fulfil.[1]

— David E. Smith

A MONARCHICAL CONSTITUTION

The Canadian constitutional order has been described as follows: "As an institution, the Crown is a cohesive force for the three functions of government: legislative, executive and judicial. The legislative function (Parliament/Legislature) is 'The Queen in Parliament' and enacts the laws. The executive (cabinet/governments) is 'The Queen in Council' and executes the laws. The judicial (courts) is 'The Queen on the Bench' and interprets the laws."[2]

The Queen is one of the three components of Parliament. Canadian bills begin with the phrase, "Her Majesty, by and with the advice and consent of the Senate and the House of Commons, enacts as follows." Provincial legislatures comprise the lieutenant governor and the elected legislative assembly; provincial bills begin with the phrase, "Her Majesty, by and with the advice and consent of the Legislative Assembly of (province)." Bills in Parliament and Legislature only become law when they receive royal assent from the Queen's representative. Government orders-in-council, proclamations, and writs must be signed by the vice-regal person in order to have legal effect. Parliament and legislatures are summoned and prorogued and elections are called in the Queen's name by her representatives. They appoint prime ministers and premiers and swear in cabinet ministers.

Parliamentarians, judges, police and military personnel, and new citizens swear allegiance to the Queen of Canada. The constitutional validity of the oath of allegiance has been confirmed by two recent court rulings. In 1994, in *Roach*, the Federal Court of Canada ruled that requiring candidates for citizenship to swear an oath to the Queen accords with the fundamental structure of the Constitution of Canada as long as it is a constitutional monarchy. In 2008, *Chainnigh* addressed the obligation of military officers to honour and swear allegiance to the Queen in Canada. In so doing, the Federal Court outlined the nature of the relationship between the Sovereign and the armed forces, and found that oaths to the Queen flow from her being the pinnacle of the military command structure and the fount of military command authority.[3]

Governor General David Johnston reads the Speech from the Throne at the opening of Parliament in 2011. Next to him in the Senate Chamber is Prime Minister Stephen Harper.

Sergeant Ronald Duchesne, Rideau Hall. © Her Majesty The Queen in Right of Canada, represented by the Office of the Secretary to the Governor General (2011)

State enterprises are called Crown corporations. Public land is Crown land. Justice is administered by the courts in the name of the Queen. Criminal proceedings are undertaken on behalf of the Queen by Crown prosecutors (*Regina* v. name of defendant). In some provinces, the trial division of the superior courts is Her Majesty's Court of Queen's Bench. Senior members of the legal profession may be honoured as Queen's Counsel. Since 2011, after a forty-three-year lapse, the naval and air components of the Canadian Armed Forces are again called the Royal Canadian Navy and the Royal Canadian Air Force, while the Canadian Army has always had regiments with royal names (and members of the Royal Family as colonels-in-chief). The governor general is commander-in-chief of Canada. The Queen is commissioner-in-chief and the Prince of Wales is honorary commissioner of the national police force, the Royal Canadian Mounted Police. Canadian currency is the responsibility of the Royal Canadian Mint. The Queen is featured on the $20 dollar bank note, the most widely circulated bill, and on the obverse of all coins of the realm, as well as on many postage stamps.

This royal authority is mostly symbolic. Constitutional monarchy, as it evolved in the United Kingdom by the eighteenth century and in Canada by 1848–1849, means that most executive powers are exercised by the first minister and cabinet in the name of the Sovereign. This is the theory of "responsible government," which is fundamental to our parliamentary democracy. Cabinets and governments derive their powers from the Crown, but they can only exercise them with the support of a majority of elected representatives of the people in Parliament or Legislature. If they lose the confidence of the House, they must submit their resignations to the Queen's representative or ask that person to dissolve the House and call an election.

But there is more. The Sovereign and her representatives almost always act on what is called "advice," given by the "first minister" (prime minister or premier). This advice is very different from the usual meaning of the term, which is a suggestion that one is free to accept or reject: "When ministers offer advice to the sovereign, that advice is binding and the sovereign has normally no option but to accept it."[4] The ministers are using a potent power called the "royal prerogative." The constitutional powers of the Sovereign fall into two categories, both exercised "on advice": *statutory*, that is, by legislation; and *prerogative*. The royal prerogative goes back centuries when monarchs had a near-absolute right to do whatever they wanted. In A.V. Dicey's classic nineteenth-century phrase, it is "the residue of discretionary or arbitrary authority which, at any given time, is legally left in the hands of the Crown."[5] In a constitutional monarchy, this authority is wielded by the first minister and cabinet.

THE ROYAL PREROGATIVE — NO DEAD LETTER

The term "residue" in Dicey's phrase cited previously may imply that prerogative powers are vestigial, historic relics on the wane. However, far from being a dead letter, the royal prerogative powers are very much part of modern Canadian government. They include orders-in-council, writs, proclamations, and warrants signed by the Queen's representative, preparation of budgets and legislation, the prerogative of mercy, the creation of honours, a myriad of administrative decisions, and a vast range of appointments, ranging from deputy ministers and diplomats to judges, lieutenant governors, Queen's Counsel, and members of boards, commissions, and agencies.

In a revealing study, Philippe Lagassé notes that the prerogative gives the executive control over foreign affairs, defence and war, national security, and public order. He points out that, while prerogatives can be abolished or curtailed by Parliament through statute, or by conventions, or by the courts through judicial rulings, these have had a surprisingly limited effect in Canada. This reflects, he says, "an acquiescence that Parliament and the courts exhibit toward prerogative power."[6] Court rulings require that parliamentary statutes be very explicit if they are to supplant prerogative powers. Lagassé cites the Omar Khadr case in 2010,[7] where the Supreme Court unanimously ruled that the prerogative power over Canadian foreign affairs had not been replaced by legislation governing the Department of Foreign Affairs and International Trade. Lagassé goes on to say that "[p]rerogative powers, in effect, fill the gaps and silences left by statutes. They allow the executive to do what Acts of Parliament have not expressly forbidden."[8] Nor do political conventions greatly constrain the exercise of the prerogative. And the Supreme Court has been reluctant to do so. Lagassé concludes that "[f]ar from being mere residuals of monarchical rule whose importance is steadily declining, the prerogative powers of the Crown remain a resilient source of Canadian executive power precisely because of [their] ambivalences."[9]

Concern has been widely expressed in Canada that too much power is concentrated in the prime minister's or premier's office and that Parliament or Legislature is not in control. This reflects the exercising of the royal prerogative by the Queen's advisers. It is a key to Canadian governance. David E. Smith emphasizes that, in addition to its symbolism, the Crown makes a "practical contribution" to "the primary feature of Canadian government — executive dominance."[10] This is why study of the Crown is essential to understanding what "makes Canada tick." As we have said elsewhere, the "exercise of the lieutenant governor's theoretical royal powers by the government is far more significant than the reserve powers remaining at the discretion of the vice-regal incumbent."[11] Then do the Queen's representatives have any powers left? It was noted earlier that the vice-regal representatives *almost* always act on "advice." But there are still some parts of the royal prerogative that may, on very rare occasions, be exercised by the vice-regal representatives at their own discretion. These are the "reserve powers" of appointing the first minister, granting or refusing royal assent, proroguing and dissolving Parliament or Legislature, and ultimately dismissing a first minister and government. In normal times these powers, too, are exercised on the advice of the first minister, but in exceptional circumstances the reserve powers can be exercised at the discretion of the Sovereign or her representatives.

The reserve powers are among the basic conventions, not written in law, that underlie the Canadian constitutional order. These conventions include responsible government, which is the fundamental principle that the first minister and government must have the support of the majority in the House of Commons or Legislature; if they lose it in a vote of confidence, they must either resign or request dissolution and an election. The crucial role of conventions has been spelled out by the Supreme Court of Canada in two important decisions: the *Patriation Reference* of 1981 and the *Quebec Secession Reference* of 1998.[12] In the former, the court asserted that "constitutional conventions plus constitutional law equal the total constitution of the country. [...] while [conventions] are not laws, some conventions may be more important than some laws. Their importance depends on that of the value or principle which they are meant to safeguard."[13] As such, conventions are an integral part of the constitution, although they are not normally enforceable by the courts. "Rather than relying on the coercive force of law, convention encourages good behaviour through self-restraint and moral obligation out of respect for the constitution and parliament."[14] While conventions may have had a limited effect on the exercise of the prerogative powers, they are nonetheless a potent force.

What is the role of the Crown's representative in maintaining these conventions? Brian Slattery explains:

> [Responsible government] requires the active participation — indeed intervention — of the governor general. She has the responsibility of identifying the person who will occupy the office of the prime minister. [...] the governor general has the constitutional responsibility to ensure that the prime minister possesses and continues to hold the confidence of the House of Commons and does not attempt to govern in the absence of such confidence. [...] In other words, the governor general has a grave constitutional responsibility. It is her role to ensure that the principle of responsible government is observed and not flouted. [...] In the final analysis, it is the governor general who stands in the breach against unprincipled political action that threatens to bring about a virtual coup d'état. *She is the ultimate protector of the constitutional order* [our emphasis].[15]

The latter comment echoes one made by Joseph Trutch in a pre-Confederation debate in British Columbia's legislative council in 1870: "We, as servants of the crown, are directly and immediately responsible to the governor, and the governor is responsible to the queen, who is the guardian of the people's rights."[16] Janet Ajzenstat made a trenchant observation on the relationship between Sovereign and ministers: "The monarch (or his/her representative) *has* the power but does not *wield* it, except on advice. What's the point of this convoluted piece of constitutional mumbo-jumbo? Is it just a leftover from the past? I would argue that it's much more important than that! And if ever lose it we'll be very sorry."[17]

THE RESERVE POWERS:
DISSOLUTION AND PROROGATION

If a minority government is defeated in the House soon after an election, without having won any votes of confidence, the governor general or lieutenant governor, rather than agreeing to yet another election, could call on another elected member of the House to try to form a government. Given the frequency of minority governments since the 1980s in Canada, both in Ottawa (for example, from 2004 to 2011) and in the provinces (Ontario, Saskatchewan, Manitoba, Nova Scotia, and Quebec), this may occur more often, especially if Canadians eventually adopt proportional representation.

Reserve Powers of the Governor General and the King-Byng Affair

Canadian governors general have very rarely declined to accept the advice of their first ministers. In 1864, Lord Monck, last governor general of the united Province of Canada and first of the Dominion of Canada in 1867, asked the just-defeated Taché-Macdonald Conservative government to find an alternative to yet another election, although he was prepared to grant dissolution if they insisted. They did not insist, and Monck's intervention proved positive. It was one of the factors contributing to the "Great Coalition" government with George Brown, which ultimately led to Confederation.[18] In 1896, Governor General Lord Aberdeen refused to agree to a number of appointments, including senators and judges, proposed by Prime Minister Sir Charles Tupper after his defeat in a general election by Wilfrid Laurier's Liberals. This unusual exercise of vice-regal authority did not elicit much criticism, as the appointments patently lacked credibility.

On the other hand, the refusal of dissolution in the Canadian Parliament in 1926 by the governor general *was* controversial. Following the October 1925 election, Prime Minister William Lyon Mackenzie King's Liberals had fewer seats than the Conservatives led by Arthur Meighen, but a number of seats were held by Progressives, Labour, and others. The governor general, Viscount Byng, discussed the options with King: another dissolution, which he ruled out; King's resignation and calling on Meighen to form a government; or the Liberals carrying on.[19] Mackenzie King, believing that Meighen would not be able to command a majority in the House, chose the third option. The Liberals were able to continue as a minority government and survive several confidence votes with the support of the Progressives. However, the government was facing major charges of corruption in a customs scandal. In June 1926, eight months after the election, the prime minister asked Governor General Byng for dissolution no fewer than three times, in order to avoid a non-confidence vote in the House, which he knew would be supported by the Progressives. Byng refused the requests for dissolution, on the grounds that King "had had the opportunity to govern, and that it would be most unfair to call another election without giving Meighen and the Conservative Party, which had the most seats in the House, a chance to form a government."[20] Thereupon, King resigned and Byng called on Meighen to form a government. The new government was defeated in the House three days later and Byng granted dissolution to Prime Minister Meighen. The Liberals won a majority in the ensuing election, partly by claiming that the governor general — and Meighen — had acted unconstitutionally. This King-Byng Affair thus became a controversial political issue.

The majority of commentators were of the view that Governor General Byng was right on the grounds of constitutional principles, although Mackenzie King won politically.[21] Others, however, held that the governor general should have accepted the first minister's advice, even if it was bad advice; the prime minister would have borne the electoral consequences.[22] One observer commented that if Byng had granted dissolution, the Liberals would very likely have been defeated due to the customs scandal; ironically, Mackenzie King ended up better off with Byng's refusal of dissolution.[23]

Viscount Byng, the governor general who refused dissolution of Parliament to Prime Minister Mackenzie King in 1926 during the "King-Byng Affair."

Portrait by Ernest Fosbery; © Crown Collection, Official Residences Division, National Capital Commission

The *Manual of Official Procedure of the Government of Canada*, drafted four decades after the King-Byng Affair, commented on its consequences:

> On dissolution the Governor General retains a certain degree of discretion and is entitled to satisfy himself that dissolution recommended by the Prime Minister is justified under Canadian constitutional practice. A decision by the Governor General not to accept the advice to dissolve Parliament would, however, amount to a withdrawal of his confidence in the Prime Minister and could involve immediate and serious problems, as was demonstrated in 1926. In regard to dissolution the preponderant constitutional opinion appears to be that in certain circumstances the Governor General still retains some discretion, *even after the 1926 crisis* [our emphasis]. Those events did not eliminate the Governor General's discretionary right to decline the advice to dissolve but served to bring out the extremely limited circumstances in which the possibility of declining the advice of the Prime Minister could be entertained.[24]

As a sequel to the King-Byng Affair, the refusal of dissolution on the grounds that an election had been held eight months previously no longer applies. In 1958, Governor General Georges Vanier granted dissolution to Prime Minister John Diefenbaker eight months after the 1957 election, where the Conservatives had won a minority government. After the June 1962 election, the Conservatives were again in minority situation and their government in crisis mode. In February 1963, fewer than eight months since the election, Diefenbaker apparently considered asking Vanier for dissolution, rather than facing a non-confidence vote in the House. The Vaniers had been close friends with Lord and Lady Byng since the 1926 events; it was therefore a great relief to the governor general that the government was defeated in the House and the prime minister then asked for dissolution. Interestingly, like Lord Aberdeen in 1896, Vanier balked at Diefenbaker's request to appoint senators after his defeat and before the election.[25] He had already reserved approval of an order-in-council proposed by Diefenbaker making a bizarre change to the Canadian table of precedence; the government dropped the idea.[26]

In the 1963 election, Lester Pearson's Liberals won the largest number of seats but not a majority. Diefenbaker, in what his biographer Denis Smith called "mischievous talk designed to keep the Liberals on edge," mused about meeting the House to test its confidence, although his senior ministers urged him to resign. However, Smith recounts, "in mysterious circumstances, six Créditiste MPs delivered a sworn affidavit to the governor general and to Mike Pearson declaring that the Liberal Party had the right to form the next government and promising their voting support to that government."[27] The Liberals could now command a majority in the House. Diefenbaker called on Vanier to offer his resignation, and Pearson became prime minister. Here, said Peter Neary, "the role of the Governor General was to accept the resignation of one prime minister and swear in another — *after the politicians had sorted out the matter themselves* [our emphasis]."[28]

The possibility of an alternative government in waiting (like Meighen's in 1926) also no longer precludes dissolution on the defeat of a minority government. Dissolution was granted in these circumstances in 1963, 1974, 1979, and 2008. However, quoting none other than Arthur Meighen, "[a] dissolution very manifestly should not be granted when its effect is to avoid a vote of censure." Constitutional expert James Hurley has said that "if a Prime Minister were to seek to prevent a House of Commons from exercising its fundamental and defining power — to grant or to deny confidence to the Government of Canada — there would be a strong case for the Governor General to use his or her discretionary powers to protect parliamentary democracy."[29] Robert E. Hawkins, for his part, acknowledges that "there is no question that the role of the governor general is to protect parliamentary democracy in these circumstances." However, says Hawkins, "in this difficult situation the safest course is to grant the request for dissolution and let the people decide. That is democracy. Otherwise, the governor general will be the issue in the election which will eventually arise." Still, he adds that if the prime minister attempts to hang on without either meeting the House to test its confidence or recommending dissolution, the Queen's representative should require the prime minister to do one or the other, failing which the governor general should dissolve the House and let the voters sort it out.[30]

The Issue of Dissolution in 2008

There was debate over the potential use of the reserve power of dissolution when Prime Minister Stephen Harper called an election in September 2008. This was in spite of not having been defeated in the House of Commons and contrary to his own government's legislation setting a fixed election date. Should Governor General Michaëlle Jean have considered refusing her first minister's request for dissolution? Patrick Monahan, dean of Osgoode Hall Law School at York University, maintained that she should not, indeed could not. "While the formal legal power to trigger an election rests in the hands of the governor-general, there is a firm constitutional requirement that she will exercise her powers only on the advice of the prime minister," he wrote. "Thus when the prime minister asks the governor-general to dissolve Parliament and fix the date of the election, the governor-general is expected to automatically grant the request without making an independent assessment of its merits."[31]

Monahan stated that, although it may be a political issue, the "fixed election date" legislation is not constitutionally relevant. The law in question has an escape hatch: nothing in it affects the "powers of the Governor-General, including the power to dissolve Parliament at the Governor-General's discretion," which is, of course, normally on the advice of the prime minister. Any attempt to change those powers would have been unconstitutional. Indeed, in a 2009 ruling, *Conacher*, the Federal Court of Canada found that the Crown's power was not bound or limited by the legislation.[32] The constitutional five-year limit for Parliament (and legislatures) remains.

Former governor general Adrienne Clarkson speculated on the reserve power of dissolution in her 2006 memoir. Recalling the King-Byng Affair of 1926, she said:

> The question arose during Paul Martin's minority government of whether or not I as Governor General would grant dissolution and allow an election to be called if the prime minister requested it. After considering the opinions of the constitutional experts whom I consulted regularly, I decided that, if the government lasted six months, I would allow dissolution. To put the Canadian people through an election before six months would have been irresponsible, and in that case I would have decided in favour of the good of the Canadian people and denied dissolution.[33]

Patrick Monahan dismissed Clarkson's view on the grounds that "it is surely for the elected prime minister, and not the unelected governor-general, to decide what is in the best interests of the Canadian people." He pointed out that "even if the governor-general has a 'reserve power' that would entitle her in exceptional circumstances to refuse a prime minister's request for an election," the circumstances of 1926 were totally different from those described by Clarkson. In that case, an election had occurred eight months before; Prime Minister Mackenzie King was about to be defeated on a confidence vote, suggesting that he had lost the confidence of the House; and the opposition Conservatives had won significantly more seats than the governing Liberals. This was not the situation in 2008.[34] However, Monahan's opinion was challenged by other commentators. Said Andrew Heard, "[t]he governor general has a duty to act on any *constitutionally valid* advice, not any and all advice a prime minister might offer. [...] Certainly, the governor general should leave most constitutional problems to either the courts or the electoral system to sort out. Yet there are still some matters that are perhaps best dealt with by the governor general refusing to act on unconstitutional advice."[35]

Monahan was less categorical about the vice-regal reserve powers when he wrote about the prorogation that occurred soon after the 2008 election. "Are there circumstances in which it can be said that a governor general is justified in refusing to act on the advice of the prime minister?" he asked — and replied, "[d]espite the principle of democratic accountability [...] the answer to this question must be 'yes.'" In the highly unlikely event that a prime minister who had lost the confidence of the House refused to resign, "the governor general would be justified in refusing to accept advice from the prime minister and could, instead, dismiss him or her and appoint a new first minister, or else dissolve Parliament and call an election on her own motion." Monahan then addressed the complex situation where a prime minister has not yet been defeated in the House but it is unclear whether or not the prime minister has the confidence of the House. The King-Byng Affair was the last case where a governor general did not accept advice in these circumstances. Monahan noted that "[m]ost commentators are of the view that a prime minister seeking two dissolutions within a space of less than six months is not automatically entitled to a second dissolution"[36] — which supports Adrienne Clarkson's opinion. The authors of the *Manual of Official Procedure of the Government of Canada* had come to a similar conclusion forty years earlier:

> Dissolution leads to a general election with the consequent interruption of the routine of government. So the basic argument is that in certain circumstances the Governor General need not accept the advice *if a general election would not be in the public interest* [our emphasis]. This implies that an alternative Government could be formed which could command a majority in

the House of Commons so that the government of the country can be continued without resorting to an election, and that no new major issue of national policy has arisen which should be put before the electorate.

The Byng-King crisis and the subsequent election results did not bring to an end the Governor General's discretion regarding dissolution; it remains to be used *in those rare and almost indefinable circumstances* [our emphasis] when it is necessary for the protection of the constitution.[37]

The Issue of Prorogation in 2008–2009

The vice-regal reserve powers were profiled even more sharply in December 2008, when Prime Minister Harper's Conservatives, having been returned in the October election with another minority, albeit a stronger one, were faced with a non-confidence motion by the combined opposition. This followed a provocative economic statement by the government, which came shortly after the government had won a confidence vote on the address in reply to the speech from the throne — a significant issue of timing which the government quickly realized. The proposed non-confidence vote was premised on a coalition government to be formed between the opposition Liberals under Stéphane Dion and the New Democrats, led by Jack Layton, with parliamentary support promised by the Bloc Québécois. The opposition was thus able to present a cogent alternative to yet another election only two months after the previous one. Although editorial reaction was mixed, the consensus appeared to be that while the proposed coalition was politically questionable, it was constitutionally proper. The *Globe and Mail* put it this way: "Contrary to silly Conservative claims of a coup d'état, coalition-making is entirely within the boundaries of parliamentary democracy. There is no constitutional impropriety here. But there certainly would be a political one."[38] Indeed, some Conservative politicians made intemperate statements about "going over the head of the governor general" and even asking the Queen to intervene, showing either their disregard for, or their ignorance of, the constitutional order. Conservative political adviser Tom Flanagan asserted that the people, rather than parliamentarians, should decide through an election who should form the government.[39] On the other hand, a coalition government led by Dion, whose status in his own party was shaky, with support from the Bloc Québécois, would likely have been a recipe for political disaster, especially in Conservative-dominated western Canada.

Governor General Michaëlle Jean granted a controversial prorogation in 2008 to Prime Minister Stephen Harper, but the two had an uneasy relationship.

Government of Saskatchewan

The issue was temporarily resolved by yet another use of the royal prerogative, that of prorogation. Interrupting an official visit in Eastern Europe at the request of the prime minister, Governor General Michaëlle Jean returned to Canada to deal with what was termed by some a "constitutional crisis." To avoid facing a motion of non-confidence in the House of Commons, which he would surely lose, Prime Minister Harper requested prorogation of the House. This was a mere two weeks after the throne speech and after very little other business had been transacted. Once again, opinion was divided. There were those who believed that the governor general should refuse what appeared to be an unprecedented, premature prorogation and leave the government to its fate.[40] Others believed that she had no choice but to accept ministerial advice; indeed, not to do so would have forced the resignation of the prime minister. Still another view was that Harper would not have resigned but would have continued his political battle through and after a non-confidence vote, with negative repercussions for the national vice-regal office.[41] Whether or not he resigned, there would have been a destructive effect on the institutions of the Crown and Parliament and the legitimacy of the office of governor general would have been drawn into the fray. In the end, Jean did grant prorogation, knowing that Parliament would resume seven weeks later with another throne speech, immediately followed by a budget. In February 2009, following much sabre-rattling by the opposition, the budget was approved by the House with the support of the Liberals under their new leader, Michael Ignatieff, who had replaced Stéphane Dion.

What were the implications of this unusual exercise of the royal prerogative of prorogation? While some observers decried it as a trick to avoid a vote of non-confidence, others pointed out that refusing advice of a first minister to prorogue would have been even more controversial. Its last use in the Commonwealth realms had been in the Australian state of New South Wales in 1911. It had never been done in Canada. Indeed, the 1968 *Manual of Official Procedure of the Government of Canada* stated categorically that the "Governor General does not retain any discretion in the matter of summoning or proroguing Parliament, but acts directly on the advice of the Prime Minister."[42]

There is one historical precedent. In August 1873, the governor general, Lord Dufferin, was faced with a prorogation request by Prime

Minister Sir John A. Macdonald. This was to avoid a non-confidence vote emanating from the infamous Pacific Scandal, where it was alleged that Macdonald and some of his ministers had accepted money for the 1872 election campaign from financier Sir Hugh Allan, who was lobbying for the contract to build the Canadian Pacific Railway. The governor general was reluctant to grant prorogation in these circumstances, and the Liberal opposition and its supporters in the press vociferously urged him not to. Lord Dufferin, says Barbara Messamore, "wrestled with the constitutional dilemma posed by the scandal and his ministers' advice" before concluding that he would grant prorogation.[43] He did so after agreeing with Macdonald that a royal commission of inquiry would be appointed and that Parliament would resume in ten weeks. This occurred on the day Parliament was to reassemble. Dufferin had to deal at the last minute with a delegation of both Liberal and Conservative members who protested his decision; he pointed out in response that to refuse prorogation would amount to dismissing his ministry. Parliament resumed in October, the commission reported, and Macdonald resigned. The governor general then called on the Liberal leader, Alexander Mackenzie, to form a government, which won an election in January 1874.[44]

More than 130 years after Macdonald's resignation, Barbara Messamore asked, "Was the Governor-General correct in accepting Harper's advice to prorogue Parliament?" She responded to her own question, "[t]he answer is an unqualified yes." The prime minister was "entitled to use this manoeuvre to buy a little time to see if he can garner sufficient support."[45] C.E.S. Franks also concluded that "the governor general made the right decision." He noted that "[d]espite the constitutional and parliamentary legitimacy and correctness of the governor general's decision to refuse prorogation and allow the installation of the coalition government that enjoyed the confidence of the House, the rhetoric of illegitimacy and anti-democratic behaviour would have prevailed. The King-Byng dispute of 1926 would have been replayed all over again, only worse."[46]

There were some significant outcomes for the vice-regal office and the Canadian Crown in this episode. First, the Canadian public was exposed as seldom before to the powers of the governor general. Second, the existence of the royal prerogative of prorogation was reaffirmed because the opposition parties accepted the governor general's ruling with good grace and without demur. Finally, the vice-regal decision to allow prorogation provided a cooling-off period, which resulted in a compromise and avoided the dilemma between a premature election and the perilous adventure of a dubious coalition forming the government without one. Inevitably, this would have ensnared the vice-regal office in controversy. "The governor-general's decision took her out of the battle and tossed the government's fate back into the hands of the politicians, where it properly belonged," said C.E.S. Franks.[47] This mirrors the opinion of Patrick Monahan. While the governor general may legitimately exercise the reserve powers when it is unclear whether the prime minister has the confidence of the House, he says:

> … on balance, the governor general's decision to accept the prorogation request was the correct one. Although it involved a postponement of the confidence vote, the period of delay was limited and publicly known, and the fate of the government would be determined by the political actors rather than the governor general. The considerable risks and uncertainties associated with the alternative option, combined with the much more prominent political role it would have involved for the governor general, indicate that it would have been both unwise and imprudent for the governor general to have refused Mr. Harper's request.

Monahan added an important note: "The time-limited nature of the prorogation request was significant. Had the prime minister sought a longer prorogation, without adequate or proper explanation of the need for the additional grant of time, in my view the governor general would have been entitled to indicate that such a request would not be acceptable."[48]

On December 30, 2009, Prime Minister Harper again requested, and was granted, prorogation from Governor General Jean. This time the controversy was not over the legality of the process — the government had the confidence of the House — but rather over the circumstances. Harper was accused of trying to avoid parliamentary scrutiny over the treatment of Afghan detainees by the Canadian army.* The episode led to a resolution in Parliament in March 2010 that prorogation of more than seven days would require consent of the House of Commons, a measure of dubious legality and an example of the pressure to "codify" constitutional conventions.[49]

In sum, as Peter Neary points out, if a government has received the confidence of the House, "prime ministerial advice (other than advice which is illegal) must be accepted by the Governor General" with respect to dissolution (and presumably prorogation). Not to accept it "would be to venture onto the slippery ground of politics" and "risk a constitutional crisis. The vice-regal representative can never go wrong by putting the final decision about who should govern into the hands of the democratic electorate, which is where, by definition, dissolution puts it."[50]

With the benefit of over eight decades of hindsight, it seems that Governor General Byng would have been right to refuse dissolution to Mackenzie King shortly after the election of 1925, as he made clear to the prime minister at the time; eight months later, however, as the 1926 King-Byng Affair showed, the governor general would have been prudent to let the electorate decide the fate of the government.

THE RESERVE POWERS: APPOINTMENT AND DISMISSAL

Appointments of first ministers are normally routine, in that election results usually produce a potential prime minister or premier who can at least face the House with a minority government. If, however, a first minister resigns or dies, that person is no longer able to provide advice, and no one else can do so. Then the governor general or lieutenant governor must consult elsewhere. We have already noted how Lord Dufferin asked opposition leader Alexander Mackenzie to form a government after the resignation of Sir John A. Macdonald in 1873. In 1892,

---

* The prime minister was also criticized for discourtesy in telephoning the governor general to ask for prorogation instead of calling on her at Rideau Hall. However, most prorogation requests have been treated as routine and have not required a meeting with the governor general.

Governor General Lord Stanley named Sir John Abbott prime minister on Macdonald's death. When Abbott resigned the same year, the governor general appointed Sir John Thompson in his place. Thompson died in 1894 while visiting Queen Victoria at Windsor Castle, and Governor General Lord Aberdeen appointed Sir Mackenzie Bowell, a senator, to succeed him. In 1896, however, Bowell lost the confidence of this own cabinet. After momentarily considering inviting opposition leader Wilfrid Laurier to form a government, Aberdeen called on Sir Charles Tupper, then high commissioner to London (to whom he would refuse judicial and senatorial appointments after his electoral defeat). Both governors general consulted widely in making their choices. Since then, no prime minister has died in office and party conventions have produced leaders in the case of resignations.

Provincially, lieutenant governors of Quebec had to act three times in the case of a death of a premier — in 1959 (Maurice Duplessis), 1960 (Paul Sauvé), and 1968 (Daniel Johnson), in each case relying for the choice of a successor on the recommendations of the government caucus. Sudden resignations of premiers occurred in British Columbia in 1991 (William Vander Zalm) and 1999 (Glen Clark) and in New Brunswick in 1997 (Frank McKenna). The lieutenant governors accepted caucus recommendations in these cases too, although Ronald Cheffins observed that, while this is a practical reality, it is technically not "advice" and could presumably be declined by the lieutenant governor.[51]

The reserve power of the Crown for *dismissal* of the first minister and government is very rarely used. It could, however, be activated where democratic government was threatened. Suppose a government tried to hang on to power and not call an election after the five-year maximum life of a Parliament or Legislature? This would be manifestly illegal and, as guardian of the constitution, the governor general or lieutenant governor could proclaim dissolution and trigger an election. Giving another example, Eugene Forsey asserted that if "a Cabinet with a majority in both Houses tried to use that majority to prolong the life of Parliament indefinitely, a forced dissolution would be the only constitutional means of preserving the rights of the people."[52] If governors believe that there is a genuinely major emergency, they can dismiss the first minister and government. Frank MacKinnon called the emergency powers of the Crown "constitutional fire extinguishers."[53] The fact that they are very rarely used does not mean that they are not real. And politicians know that. Which is why, in our system, there have been so few attempts at constitutional illegality and very few cases of dismissal in both Canada and Australia.

The most notorious example was in Australia in 1975, when there was an impasse between the House of Representatives and the Senate, which refused to vote supply. The governor general, Sir John Kerr, refused the dissolution requested by Prime Minister Gough Whitlam, dismissed him, and asked the leader of the opposition, Malcolm Fraser, to form a government on condition that he would end the Senate blockade and then ask for dissolution. This was, of course, a highly controversial move.[54] In any event, Fraser resolved the supply impasse, was then granted dissolution, and won a majority government in the ensuing election, which would appear to have vindicated the governor general. Nevertheless, the negative repercussions of the episode were considerable, fuelling the republican movement in Australia and leaving a legacy of bitterness. Kerr became an unpopular figure and was forced into early retirement. One commentator drew the lesson that "the exercise of the prerogative powers of the Crown does not require gratuitous political bloodletting [...] It should at all times, if possible, be conducted gently and in a spirit of constitutional comity."[55]

Situations of this kind are, fortunately, extremely rare. The royal reserve powers help keep it that way. As Norman Ward put it, "the mere existence of the power will, in fact, tend to prevent the need for its exercise arising."[56] In a similar vein, challenging the pervasive view that in Canada the legislative branch no longer acts as a check on executive absolutism, a Canadian law professor writes that "social science models frequently miss (and misunderstand) the very real significance of rarely invoked or rarely infringed constitutional limits and powers. In particular, they tend to miss the fact that a formal power may be rarely exercised precisely because [...] it is sufficiently clear and powerful that those subject to its constraints generally prefer to avoid its actual implementation by *limiting themselves*."[57] David Lam, lieutenant governor of British Columbia, said "the lieutenant governor exists to deny the government absolute power."[58] Of course, the courts see to that. But so do the representatives of the Crown. Eugene Forsey said:

The danger of royal absolutism is past; but the danger of Cabinet absolutism, even of Prime Ministerial absolutism, is present and growing. Against that danger the reserve power of the Crown, and especially the power to force or refuse dissolution, is in some instances the only constitutional safeguard. The Crown is more than a quaint survival, a social ornament, a symbol, "an automaton, with no public will of its own." It is an absolutely essential part of the parliamentary system. In certain circumstances, the Crown alone can preserve the Constitution, or ensure that if it is to be changed it shall be only by the deliberate will of the people.[59]

THE QUESTION OF HONOURS[60]

The Crown enjoys another historic prerogative: that of presenting honours to deserving citizens. In a monarchy, the Sovereign is the "fount of honours," which means that in Canada, the Queen is the ultimate source of official recognition by the state. Drawing attention to meritorious service in this time-honoured way is an important role for the monarch and her representatives. Queen Elizabeth II herself has spoken in a practical way about honours: "I think people need pats on backs sometimes. It's a very dingy world otherwise."[61] Like most royal prerogatives, that of honours is now mainly exercised "on advice" by the government of the day, although there are some exceptions, such as honours in the "personal gift" of the Sovereign.*

There are three types of honours: orders (fellowships of honour — the senior category of recognition), decorations (awards for gallantry, bravery, and special contributions), and medals (long and exemplary service, anniversaries, military campaigns, and service). In the United Kingdom, peerages and the upper levels of some orders that confer knighthoods

---

* In the United Kingdom, the Order of the Garter, the Order of the Thistle, the Royal Victorian Order and Medal, the Royal Victorian Chain, and the Order of Merit are the personal honours of the Sovereign.

provide another prestigious form of recognition. Interestingly, as will be noted later, in Canada the creation of national honours and the approval of their insignia remain personal prerogatives of the Queen. While the prerogative of honours is not as momentous as the others discussed above, it has nonetheless been a source of controversy.

The history of honours in Canada has been erratic and ambivalent, reflecting the country's colonial origins. The kings of France conferred the *Ordre royal et militaire de Saint-Louis* on military officers associated with Canada, among them the well-known governors Frontenac and Vaudreuil. In 1700, King Louis XIV created the only Canadian title of nobility by making Charles LeMoyne, seigneur de Longueuil, the first Baron de Longueuil (the barony still exists, as the British government guaranteed it in the Treaty of Paris in 1763).[62] From 1763 until 1919, British or imperial honours were awarded to Canadians by the monarch, on the advice of Canadian and British prime ministers and sometimes governors general. Prior to Confederation, a number of non-hereditary knights bachelor were named and several hereditary baronetcies were also granted.[*] Lord Monck, last governor general of the united Province of Canada and the first governor general of Canada after Confederation, tried to start an indigenous Order of St. Lawrence in 1866, but was unsuccessful with British officialdom.

Honours after Confederation

After Confederation in 1867, honours were generally recommended by the Canadian prime minister to the Sovereign through the governor general, although governors general continued to make some recommendations of their own. A few hereditary peerages[**] were awarded to Canadians in

---

[*] Knights bachelor (Kt) are entitled to be called "Sir" but do not pass on the title to their heirs. Baronets (Bt) passed on their titles to their heirs but did not sit in the House of Lords. Technically they were not knighted, but were still called "sir."

[**] Hereditary peerages in the United Kingdom, providing at the time for membership in the House of Lords, were, in order of seniority: duke, marquess (marquis in Scotland), earl, viscount, and baron. Canadian peers were almost all barons.

the post-Confederation period, and non-hereditary knights bachelor were appointed. Also conferring non-hereditary knighthoods were the top two grades of the Order of the Bath and the Order of St. Michael and St. George.* The Royal Victorian Order, established by Queen Victoria in 1896 as a personal gift of the Sovereign for services to her and the Royal Family, included among its five grades Knight Grand Cross (GCVO) and Knight Commander (KCVO).[63] Created by King George V in 1917, the Order of the British Empire similarly conferred knighthoods in its top two grades — Knight Grand Cross (GBE) and Knight Commander (KBE). One GBE and eight KBEs were awarded to Canadian between 1917 and 1919. This order represented a major democratization of British honours. It was the first British order to include women, and its five grades and its medal recognized large numbers of citizens from all walks of life. The Order of the British Empire became the "workhorse" of the honours system, a role it fills to this day in the United Kingdom and in some of the smaller realms.

Peerages and knighthoods (titular honours, i.e., conferring titles) became discredited in Canada because of the partisan nature of some of the appointments; there were frequent complaints about the snobbery and inequality of titular honours in a democratic egalitarian society. The controversy came to a head during the First World War, when Sir Robert Borden was prime minister. In March 1918, his government passed an order-in-council requiring that in future honours only be given on the advice of the Canadian prime minister and that no further hereditary honours (peerages and baronetcies) be conferred. This still allowed, however, for non-hereditary knighthoods. Later the same year, a Conservative-Unionist MP, W.F. Nickle, introduced a resolution in the House of Commons asking the King to cease conferring hereditary honours on Canadians. Adopted by the House, this non-binding resolution was followed by another parliamentary resolution in 1919, instigated by a special committee chaired by Nickle, extending the ban to all titular honours, including non-hereditary knighthoods. The "Nickle resolution" of 1918 and the second resolution of 1919 were used as a rationale for avoiding honours for decades thereafter. The practical outcome was

---

* Persons appointed to these grades of orders are first dubbed as knights bachelor.

that, after the First World War, few honours were awarded to Canadians, apart from military decorations and those for civilian bravery. Even the non-titular levels of orders — commanders/companions, officers, and members — were excluded.[64]

The Bennett Revival of Honours

There was a brief revival of honours by Conservative Prime Minister R.B. Bennett between 1933 and 1935. Bennett adhered strictly to the 1918 Nickle resolution: no hereditary honours were included among the 17 knighthoods and 189 non-titular honours awarded in 1934 and 1935.[65] Other grades of orders — the commander/companion, officer, and member levels, and medals — were widely awarded in this brief interlude. What is striking is the diversity of the awards across fields of endeavour and social background, with strong representation of women. In 1935, the year of the Silver Jubilee of King George V, some 9,200 Canadians were awarded the Silver Jubilee Medal on the recommendation of the Bennett government. Again, there was much diversity among the nominees. While we find only the occasional Aboriginal name — a reflection of the times — francophones are well represented and so are women.

Indeed, of particular note is the number of women recognized during the Bennett revival of honours. Thirty-two women received honours in the first 1934 list, most of them for social work at the officer level of the Order of the British Empire (OBE). Of the twenty-six commanders of the Order (CBE) awarded in 1934 and 1935, half were to women. Bennett was proud of this. Responding to a critic of the first honours list, he said, "Why should not the services of women who have worked their hands off for many years in the interests of the needy be recognized by their sovereign?"[66] There was much favourable media comment. The *Vancouver Province*, for example, stated that, while pre-1919 honours "amounted nearly to a public scandal," in the 1933–35 revival Bennett "would appear to have achieved the impossible" in his nominations. According to the *Winnipeg Tribune*, Bennett had "scored heavily by the nature of his recommendations ... the awards are so precisely right."[67] The praise was amply justified: Bennett had shown that honours could recognize meritorious citizens with integrity. The awards were made to a wide range of deserving recipients and were resolutely non-partisan — unlike the patronage-ridden conferral of knighthoods prior to 1919. The 1933–1935 honours were a presage of the Canadian system, both federal and provincial, which would emerge much later. Christopher McCreery justifiably calls Bennett "the father of the modern Canadian honours system."[68]

Honours Disappear — and Re-emerge

With the return of William Lyon Mackenzie King and the Liberals to power in 1935, the door was again firmly shut on British honours for Canadians, despite the success of the two-year revival. Mackenzie King vigorously opposed the conferring of honours, although he himself was a Companion of the Order of St. Michael and St. George (CMG — awarded in 1906 when he was deputy minister of labour); after 1935 he refused to wear its insignia. R.B. Bennett, while prime minister, had declined the honour of Knight Grand Cross of the Order of St. Michael and St. George (GCMG) from King George V in 1935 and offered it to Mackenzie King, an offer which the latter turned down on principle.[69] When Bennett, by then retired to England, was made a viscount in 1941, King would not allow the House of Commons to send congratulations, although he did send personal good wishes.[70] The moratorium on honours continued for another three decades, except during the Second World War, when Canada reverted to British or imperial honours for both military personnel and civilians. A few awards were also made to service personnel during the 1950–1953 Korean War, but not to civilians. Military decorations, headed by the Victoria Cross, included those awarded for valour, as they had been in the First World War; those given for exemplary service or bravery, such as the Distinguished Service Order (DSO), Military Cross (MC), and Distinguished Flying Cross (DFC); and numerous campaign medals. The wartime non-military honours came to an end with the Dominion Day list in 1946 — the last civilian honours list until 1967.

The Move to National Honours

It was obvious from the 1933–1935 revival and the Second World War experience that Canadians needed and deserved both civilian and military honours. Actually, the first two indigenous Canadian honours — medals rather than higher profile orders or decorations — appeared in the 1930s and 1940s. The first was the RCMP Long Service Medal, recommended by Prime Minister R.B. Bennett and approved by King George V in 1934.[71] The second was the Canadian Forces' Decoration (CD), for twelve years' service in the regular and reserve components of the armed forces. This was approved in 1949 by King George VI on the advice of Prime Minister Louis St. Laurent.[72]

Vincent Massey, diplomat and future governor general, had tried in vain to revive the Order of St. Lawrence idea in 1935; Mackenzie King was adamantly opposed. On the initiative of a government Awards Coordination Committee, a Canada Medal was approved in 1943; a few medals were struck but never awarded.[73] The same committee recommended a five-level Order of Canada in 1944–45, but the idea went nowhere. After King's retirement in 1948, efforts resumed. Vincent Massey, now chair of the Royal Commission on National Development in the Arts, Letters and Sciences, made another proposal for a five-level Order of St. Lawrence in 1951. This time it was Prime Minister Louis St. Laurent who was not interested. A federal policy of 1956 did allow a limited number of bravery and gallantry awards.[74]

Finally in 1967, marking the centennial of Confederation, the Liberal government of Prime Minister Lester Pearson launched the Order of Canada.[75] Influenced by Vincent Massey, Pearson took advice from, among others, John Matheson, who had played a role in the design of the new Canadian flag of 1964, and Esmond Butler, secretary to the governor general. Conrad Swan, a Canadian who was a herald in the College of Arms in England, helped too; in particular, he advised Pearson not to place legislation creating honours before Parliament, which was bound to be controversial, but simply to use the royal prerogative of honours and establish them by order-in-council.[76] This was the route Pearson followed (he had originally preferred legislation, believing it would make the honour more secure). Bowing to pressure from anti-honours sentiment in his cabinet, however, Pearson decided the order would have only a single level, which restricted the variety of people recognized. The never-awarded Canada Medal was eliminated.

The Order of Canada was an immediate success. A prime reason for the effectiveness of the new honour was its non-political basis: the order's secretariat was the responsibility of the office of the governor general at Rideau Hall, and the selection of recipients was made by an independent advisory council from among nominations from the public, then ratified by the governor general. This was totally unlike the partisan political appointments of the pre-1919 honours (although, as we have seen, Bennett's 1933–1935 appointments had been non-partisan) and unlike the honours of Britain and France, which are largely recommended by government departments. It was a model for future honours in Canada, Australia, New Zealand, and elsewhere and was closely observed in the United Kingdom and France. In 1972, the Order of Canada was restruc-

The insignia of Companion of the Order of Canada. Established in 1967, the order is the centrepiece of the Canadian Honours System.

Corporal Roxanne Shewchuk, Rideau Hall. © Her Majesty The Queen in Right of Canada, represented by the Office of the Secretary to the Governor General (2013)

tured into its present three levels of Companion (CC), Officer (OC), and Member (CM), correcting the error made in 1966–1967. The Order of Military Merit, with three levels — Commander (CMM), Officer (OMM), and Member (MMM) — was added,[77] as were long-overdue civilian bravery decorations — the Cross of Valour (CV), Star of Courage (SC), and Medal of Bravery (MB).

Significantly, in 1972 Esmond Butler, secretary to governors general since 1959 and an architect of the honours system, was allowed to accept the Queen's offer of the rank of Commander of the Royal Victorian Order (CVO) — the first appointment of a Canadian to the order since 1946. Thus the Royal Victorian Order achieved status as one of Canada's national honours.[78] The Queen continued to award her personal honours to Canadians, mainly the Royal Victorian Order, but also the Order of Merit,* bestowed on neurosurgeon Wilder Penfield in 1953, former prime minister Lester Pearson in 1971, and, in 2009, former prime minister Jean Chrétien.[79] A British government honour, the Order of the Companions of Honour,** was conferred by the Queen on Dr. Charles Best, co-discoverer of insulin, in 1971, Commonwealth secretary-general Arnold Smith in 1975, former prime ministers John Diefenbaker in 1976 and Pierre Trudeau in 1984, and General John de Chastelain in 1998.

The Canadian honours program expanded into a comprehensive system of orders, decorations, and medals. These now include a three-level Order of Merit of the Police Forces established in 2001; three military valour decorations, headed by a Canadian Victoria Cross, in 1993; three Meritorious Service Decorations (both military and civilian) in 1984; exemplary service medals for police, corrections, fire services, coast guard, emergency medical services, and peace officers between 1982 and 1998; military service and campaign medals; and commemorative medals such as those for the Centennial and the 125th

---

* Established by King Edward VII in 1902, the Order of Merit is in the personal gift of the Sovereign and is considered the top honour in the UK.

** The Order of the Companions of Honour (CH) was founded by King George V in 1917 and is limited to sixty-five living members in the Commonwealth realms. It is not a personal honour of the Sovereign but is awarded "on advice" of the British government.

anniversary of Confederation and for the Queen's Silver, Golden, and Diamond Jubilees.

The Canadian provinces, however, were excluded from consultation and participation in the national honours program, apart from occasional presentations of medals by lieutenant governors. It was a weakness of the system which would have early consequences. We will examine this in Chapter V.

III

The Provincial Crown in Canada — From Subordinate to Coordinate

Adapting the Crown in 1867 to our unique federal constitution was for the authors of Confederation a bold and daring innovation. [...] Our Crown would be represented by a team of twelve: the Sovereign, the governor general and the ten lieutenant governors.[1]

— Jacques Monet

[F]rom being perceived as an institution amenable to enforcing Macdonald's highly centralized federal ambitions, the Crown became a constitutional foundation for active and independently minded provinces.[2]

— David E. Smith

THE BEGINNINGS

The first prime minister of Canada, Sir John A. Macdonald, and some of the other Fathers of Confederation, perhaps the majority, wanted a centralized state with most of the levers controlled by Ottawa. That was reflected in the text of the 1867 legislation adopted by the Parliament of the United Kingdom, the *British North America Act*. What was the place of the Crown in the new federal state?

The colonial governors had exercised most of the Sovereign's powers in the British North American colonies. But in the *British North America*

Act (now the *Constitution Act, 1867*), the new lieutenant governors lost some of those prerogatives. They were — and still are — appointed and removable by the governor general, not the Queen, on the advice of the federal prime minister and with no formal input from the provinces. They were and are paid by the federal government. True, they exercised some of the royal prerogatives in their provinces: reading the speech from the throne, granting royal assent to legislation in the name of the Queen (not of the governor general, although this had been the original intent), signing orders-in-council, formally appointing the premier, and swearing in the cabinet. They possessed a Great Seal and summoned their legislatures directly in the Queen's name. Yet they were not considered as directly representing the Queen but as subordinate to the governor general and intended to function as federal officers.

Section 12 of the *Act* was explicit about this subordination: "All Powers, Authorities, and Functions which […] are at the Union vested in or exerciseable by the respective Governors or Lieutenant Governors of those Provinces […] shall […] be vested in and exerciseable by the Governor General." Furthermore, one of the powers of the lieutenant governors was "reservation"[3]: they could "reserve" royal assent to provincial bills and refer it to the governor general for consideration, which meant in effect a veto for the governor general's advisers — the federal cabinet. There was also another form of federal veto called "disallowance": the federal cabinet could simply declare a provincial law to be invalid within a year of its adoption.[4] These measures remain in the *Constitution Acts* to this day. Indeed, a lieutenant governor is still expected to forward to the Minister of Canadian Heritage (formerly the Secretary of State for Canada) within six months of prorogation of the Legislature a copy of all legislation which has received royal assent (now this is usually sent by the legislative assembly). The legislation is reviewed by the federal Ministry of Justice, theoretically to consider if disallowance may be invoked within the one-year limit.

During the discussions in the 1860s leading to Confederation, much attention was paid to the office of lieutenant governor. At the Charlottetown Conference in September 1864, some of those asserting centralist views thought that no such office was required and that the speaker of the assembly could fulfil its functions; they grudgingly accepted that there should continue to be a lieutenant governor in each province,* provided that person was appointed by the governor general, thus ensuring subordination of the office to the central government. "If an officer filling the place of Governor is required (for which, however, under the supposed circumstances I can see no necessity)," said Lieutenant Governor Arthur H. Gordon of New Brunswick, "let him be named by the Governor General."[5] Gordon had first proposed the Charlottetown Conference to consider union of the three Maritime colonies. Having a low opinion of New Brunswick politics and politicians, he wanted a legislative union of Prince Edward Island, New Brunswick, and Nova Scotia, to be called Acadia — a strong, centralized union, because he disliked federalism — which could be precursor to a legislative union of British North America.[6] With an exalted idea of the governor's role even under responsible government, he resented the hijacking of his conference by the politicians and its expansion into consideration of a federation of all the British North American colonies. Historian Christopher Moore commented wittily, if unfairly, "we *have* come a long way, if an office now so wrapped and bound in absolute irrelevance could be the springboard of confederation."[7]

By the time of the Quebec Conference a month later, in October 1864, there was still debate over whether the lieutenant governors should be appointed by the federal government or directly by the Crown[8]; but, in the end, there was enough agreement for the following motion by John A. Macdonald to be approved: "That for each of the Provinces there shall be an executive officer, styled the Lieutenant-Governor, who shall be appointed by the Governor-General in Council under the Great Seal of the Federated Provinces during pleasure ..."[9]

In the discussion, Macdonald commented that "[t]he Lieutenant-Governor will be a very high officer. He should be independent of the Federal Government, except as to removal for cause, and it is necessary

---

* At this time Newfoundland had a "governor," whereas Nova Scotia, New Brunswick, and Prince Edward Island had "lieutenant governors." The united Province of Canada had a "governor general," who had the title of Governor General of British North America. The colonies of Vancouver Island and British Columbia (merged in 1866 as British Columbia) also had a "governor" but were not part of these discussions.

that he should not be removable by any new political party. It would destroy his independence."[10]

In the follow-up to the Quebec Conference, the debate between centralists and decentralists over the vice-regal office continued. Vigorously defending provincial autonomy, Leonard Tilley, premier of New Brunswick, emphasized in December 1864 that "[we] retain as now a Lieutenant Governor, the representative of the Crown, but who will be, — as now he is *not*, — appointed from ourselves [i.e., not sent from Britain]."[11] But the colonial secretary, Edward Cardwell, objected to granting the royal prerogative of pardon to the lieutenant governors. In a statement that would come back to haunt the provinces in the subsequent struggle to assert their vice-regal offices, he said, writing to Governor General Monck in December 1864, "with respect to the exercise of the Prerogative of pardon. It appears to Her Majesty's Government that this duty properly belongs to the representative of the Sovereign, — and could not with propriety be devolved upon the Lieutenant-Governors, who will, under the present scheme, be appointed not directly by the Crown, but by the Central Government of the United Provinces."[12]

Lord Monck even thought that "there should not be a separate Lieutenant-Governor for Upper Canada [to become Ontario], but the Governor-General should also be the local Administrator, with his seat in Ottawa."[13] The lieutenant governors of New Brunswick and Nova Scotia, respectively Arthur H. Gordon and Sir Richard MacDonnell, opposed having a provincial vice-regal position. Notes of their comments on the Quebec Resolutions record that "Sir R. Macdonnell [*sic*] and Mr. Gordon object to the continuance of Lieutenant-Governors. The former regards the proposal as a bribe, or as affording means to bribe."[14] Gordon and MacDonnell, in fact, opposed Confederation altogether. Both eventually had to be strong-armed into submission by the British government, which strongly favoured the plan. Gordon changed his tune under pressure from the colonial secretary, Edward Cardwell, and from 1865 actively promoted the pro-Confederation side in New Brunswick. MacDonnell gratefully accepted a transfer to Hong Kong and was replaced by Sir William Fenwick Williams, who had a mandate from the Colonial Office to push for Confederation in Nova Scotia. Governors George Dundas of

Prince Edward Island and Anthony Musgrave of Newfoundland tried, unsuccessfully, to convince their political leaders to join in the proposed federal union. Throughout the process, Lord Monck vigorously lobbied his colleagues in favour of Confederation. It was a time when governors had a great deal of influence — and used it.

In December 1866, the Fathers of Confederation met in London to frame the *British North America Act*. The status of the lieutenant governors was still in flux, judging from the resolutions and successive drafts of the legislation. The London Resolutions of December 28, 1866, changed John A. Macdonald's Quebec conference resolution of October 20, 1864, to read "For each of the Provinces there shall be an Executive Officer *styled the Governor* [our emphasis]."[15] An undated rough draft of the bill in January 1867 stated: "35. The Governor-General may appoint Governors for the respective Provinces ..."[16] and "38. For each of the Provinces there shall be an Executive Officer styled the Governor ..."[17] Referring thereafter to "the Governor," this draft went on to specify:

> 39. The Governor, subject to the provisions of this Act and any Act of Parliament, and of such instructions as he may from time to time receive from the Governor-General, shall administer the Government of the Province for which he is appointed upon the principles of the British Constitution. He shall have power from time to time to prorogue or dissolve the Legislature; he may reserve any Bill passed by the Legislature for the consideration of the Governor-General, and may from time to time, except in capital cases, reprieve or pardon prisoners convicted of crimes, and commute and remit such sentences in whole or in part, which belong of right to the Crown.[18]

The decentralists evidently had had an influence, replacing the title "lieutenant governor" with "governor"; and, while they conceded to the central government "reservation" of provincial legislation, they also asserted the royal prerogative of pardon for the provincial vice-regal office in the face of Edward Cardwell's objection two years earlier.

This assertion of provincial vice-regal status was short-lived; indeed, it seems to have provoked a sharp centralist reaction, for the next draft of the legislation, dated January 23, 1867, referred, in an ultimate slap in the face to provincial autonomy, to the "Superintendents of Provinces": "For each Province there shall be an Officer, styled the Superintendent, appointed by the Governor-General in Council, by an Instrument under the Great Seal of the United Colony."[19] The third draft, dated February 2, 1867, backtracked from this centralist position, reverting to the title of lieutenant governor: "For each Province of Upper Canada, Lower Canada, Nova Scotia and New Brunswick, there shall be an officer, styled the Lieutenant-Governor, to be appointed by the Governor-General in Council, under the great seal of Canada."[20] In an (undated) fourth draft, this was changed to read: "For each of the Provinces of Ontario, Quebec, Nova Scotia, and New Brunswick, there shall be an officer, styled the Lieutenant-Governor, to be appointed by the Governor-General in Council, under the Great Seal of Canada."[21] In the final draft, dated February 9, 1867, this became, "For each Province there shall be an Officer, styled the Lieutenant-Governor, appointed by the Governor-General in Council by Instrument under the Great Seal of Canada."[22]

Those defending provincial autonomy in Confederation through the vice-regal office had managed to fend off the proponents of a legislative union. But the office of lieutenant governor remained, at least on the books, an institution subordinate to federal power. Its ambivalent status was not helped by the sometimes dismissive attitude of federal prime ministers. Christopher McCreery points out that "scarcely a decade after their offices came into existence Prime Minister Alexander Mackenzie suggested that it was time to 'terminate the regal splendour, so entirely out of keeping with actual circumstances' of Lieutenant Governors. Mackenzie had little time for the role and aspired for the Lieutenant Governors to be little more than perfunctory judges minding affairs on behalf of Ottawa."[23]

A dozen years after Confederation, the Toronto-based intellectual Goldwin Smith, who did not believe Canada could survive as a nation and called for annexation to the United States, was caustic about the monarchical institution in the Dominion and particularly its provincial manifestation: "The king who reigns and does not govern is represented by a Governor-General who does the same, and the Governor-General solemnly delegates his impotence to a puppet Lieutenant-Governor in each province."[24] Echoing the views of the two Maritime lieutenant governors in 1865, he went on to say, "[t]he Lieutenant-Governorships are bestowed by the party leader invariably on his partisans and usually on worn-out politicians. That they form a decent retirement for those who have spent their energies in public life but on whom the public would not consent to bestow pensions, forms the best defence for their existence. Political value they have none."[25]

A century later, scholar J.R. Mallory, less bluntly, noted the original subservience of the lieutenant governors to Ottawa:

> The office [of lieutenant governor] was conceived by the federal government as an important element in preserving the dominant role of Ottawa over the provinces. Canadian federalism in the beginning was, in Sir Kenneth Wheare's phrase, "quasi-federal." It was clearly based on the old colonial model, with the government in Ottawa playing the role previously played by the British government, but playing it more obtrusively and more effectively ...[26]

This quasi-colonial provincial vice-regal status was reflected in symbols. Instead of the nineteen-gun salute to which the colonial governors and now the governor general were entitled on formal occasions (the governor general was to be upgraded to twenty-one guns in 1949), the lieutenant governors received a fifteen-gun salute — and this was only grudgingly conceded by the British Admiralty in 1905. Instead of the title "Excellency" enjoyed by their colonial predecessors and the governor general, the lieutenant governors had to be content with the half-baked "Your Honour," also used by magistrates. "Pour bien marquer la subordination des lieutenants-gouverneurs, le gouverneur général lord Dufferin (1872–1878) insiste pour que ceux-ci soient appelés non pas *Votre Excellence* comme lui, mais plutôt *Votre Honneur*."[27] It was not until the 1950s that Canadian lieutenant governors received the same right as their Australian counterparts to have an audience with the Sovereign during their term of office.

THE DIVISIBLE CROWN

Canada has certainly changed a great deal from the quasi-centralized state that was envisaged in 1867. David E. Smith makes an important historical point: "although Canada's federation was conceived as a highly centralized form of government, the provinces inherited cohesive societies that pre-dated Confederation and monarchical forms of government to give those societies institutional expression."[28] Indeed, he says, the provinces replacing the original colonies "were as legitimate products of English constitutional evolution as was the government at Ottawa, actually more so, because of their longer lineage."[29] To the "question of how to reconcile monarchy and federalism, a constitutional form pioneered by Canada in 1867," says Smith, "[t]he answer was to create a federation of *compound monarchies* [our emphasis], each province of which within its jurisdiction might claim the statutory and prerogative power necessary to realize its constitutional objectives."[30]

During the first decades of the twentieth century, the realization grew in the British Empire that the Crown, far from being rigid and monolithic, could be divisible. As we have seen, the Balfour Report of 1926 and the *Statute of Westminster* of 1931 provided the constitutional basis of separate Crowns for the same monarch in Canada, Australia, New Zealand, South Africa, and the United Kingdom. This was alluded to at the coronation of King George VI in 1937 and fully recognized on the accession of Queen Elizabeth II in 1952. Well before that, however, the divisibility of the Crown was evident in the Canadian compound monarchy. This most certainly influenced the Australian federation established in 1901 (it will be pointed out later that the Australians got the forms right where Canada did not). Noel Cox observes that "[t]he evolution of provincial autonomy was not caused by the existence of the Crown, but the Crown was the means through which it was obtained [...] the existence of the Crown meant that each provincial government could claim, and did so successfully, that it was imbued with some of the authority of the Crown."[31] Thus the lieutenant governor now plays the same role in provincial jurisdiction as the governor general does in federal jurisdiction: he or she formally heads the executive; represents legitimacy; holds emergency powers of the state; and is a symbol of unity. The courts were crucial in this evolution.

The issue of "judicial activism" is sometimes controversial today. However, this is nothing new. From the earliest days of Confederation, the courts had to rule on numerous federal-provincial disagreements over their respective powers. The *British North America Act* was not conclusive on this vexed subject. While the delineation of legislative powers between Parliament and the provinces was reasonably clear in the *Act* — although not clear enough to prevent frequent federal-provincial litigation — the delineation of prerogative and executive powers was uncertain. It was up to the courts to sort it out, and this they did, generally asserting the co-ordinate, not subordinate, status of the provinces in the federation. This was thanks in large part to the efforts of Ontario Premier Oliver Mowat, who, aided by Liberal MPs Edward Blake (briefly Ontario's premier) and David Mills, pursued legal action on behalf of the provincial autonomists in the 1880s and 1890s, especially through the Judicial Committee of the Privy Council in London. While judgments of the provincial superior courts and the Supreme Court of Canada tended in this direction, it was the Judicial Committee that most forcefully asserted provincial co-sovereignty.

Even though the Supreme Court of Canada was established in 1875, the Judicial Committee of the Privy Council (JCPC) was the final court of appeal for civil cases until 1949 (for criminal cases until 1885). Between the 1880s and the 1920s, especially under the leadership of Lord Watson, then of Viscount Haldane, the Judicial Committee interpreted the *British North America Act* in a way that tilted Canadian federalism from the centralizing model of Macdonald to a much more decentralized form where the provinces enjoyed genuine autonomy within Confederation. The legal cases referred to the Committee were intriguing, involving such matters as alcohol and saloons, rivers and streams, bankruptcy, escheats, and Queen's Counsel. John Saywell pointed out that by the end of the nineteenth century "the principle of coordinate federalism was generally accepted" by the courts and that the Judicial Committee had "authoritatively asserted the independent status of the lieutenant governor as the representative of the crown for all purposes of provincial government."[32] In short, provincial autonomy revolved around the office of lieutenant governor.

Legislative Sovereignty

The judicial path to coordinate federalism was not an easy one, however, and Oliver Mowat had a long fight on his hands. In 1880, in *Parsons v. Citizens Insurance Company of Canada*, the Supreme Court, citing Parliament's jurisdiction over trade and commerce, overturned 1879 rulings by the Ontario Court of Queen's Bench and Court of Appeal that Ontario's legislative powers included the right to regulate the terms of insurance policies. The same year, in a New Brunswick case, *Russell v. The Queen*, a William Russell appealed his conviction under the *Canada Temperance Act* of 1878. Upheld by the New Brunswick Supreme Court, the conviction was appealed to the Judicial Committee. In 1882, the JCPC also upheld the federal prohibition statute, on the grounds of Parliament's right to legislate for "peace, order and good government" (called by constitutional lawyers the "POGG clause"). This trumped provincial jurisdiction over property and civil rights.

"*Russell*, however, turned out to be the high-water mark of judicial centralism."[33] By 1881, the JCPC had reversed the Supreme Court's ruling on *Parsons*, reinstating the judgment of the Ontario courts. In 1883, in *Hodge v. The Queen*, the Committee, distancing itself from its own *Russell* decision of the previous year, upheld Premier Mowat's claim that Ontario had the right to administer its own liquor licensing system. A certain Archibald Hodge, "[c]onvicted of operating a billiard table in his tavern at times prohibited by the regulations of the Toronto Board of Liquor Commissioners,"[34] challenged the validity of the relevant Ontario act. Hodge won in the Ontario Court of Queen's Bench, but that decision was overturned by the Court of Appeal. As was his right at the time, Hodge appealed directly to the JCPC. He lost. The Judicial Committee agreed with the appeal court ruling. "Praising the judgments in the Ontario Court of Appeal, [Lord] Fitzgerald quickly disposed of the delegation argument with a ringing confirmation of the doctrine of coordinate federalism."[35]

Hodge v. The Queen had major implications: it established that provincial legislatures were co-sovereign and not delegates of Parliament and that provincial legislation was not subordinate to federal legislation. "Provincial legislative sovereignty within the boundaries of section

92 [of the *BNA Act*]," remarked John Saywell, "had been legally confirmed."[36] The next year, 1884, the JCPC gave an example of that confirmation by upholding in a private suit an Ontario law, the *Rivers and Streams Act*, which, since its first passing in 1881, had been disallowed no fewer than three times by Macdonald's federal government. In 1887, in *Bank of Montreal v. Lambe*, the JCPC upheld the right of provinces to legislate a tax on banks.

Executive Sovereignty and the Royal Prerogative

If the path to *legislative* autonomy of the provinces was arduous, the road to provincial *executive* sovereignty was positively tortuous. Initially, like the Supreme Court of Canada, the Judicial Committee and British officials were unwilling to recognize the status of the provincial executives. "They were very reluctant to accept that lieutenant-governors appointed by Ottawa could be representatives of the Crown in the same immediate fashion as lieutenant-governors appointed in London. They refused to admit that such officials could exercise the prerogative powers of the Crown — powers symbolic of sovereignty."[37] This, of course, revolved around the fact that lieutenant governors were appointed by the federal governor-in-council and not by the Queen, as had been the colonial governors (and as the Australian governors would continue to be from 1901). Therefore, the argument ran, the lieutenant governor, unlike the governor general, did not directly represent the Sovereign and could not exercise the royal prerogative in her name.

It was not a minor point — on the contrary — and provincial autonomists quickly grasped its importance. As Saywell put it, "[i]f the crown was represented directly within the provincial government, coordinate rather than subordinate status would be achieved in the executive branch as it was in the legislative."[38] Mowat, Blake, Mills, and their allies pointed out the anomaly that, if the lieutenant governor could not exercise the royal prerogative on the advice of the ministry, then the hard-won British institution of responsible government did not fully apply in the province. Under the British Empire, there had developed a tradition of minimal, indeed virtually nil, interference by the imperial authorities in the internal jurisdiction of the self-governing colonies. If the doctrine of the Crown propounded by the centralists were to carry the day, the provinces would enjoy less self-government than the colonies had.[39] At this point, other provincial premiers began to support Mowat's cause. In 1887, Honoré Mercier, *nationaliste* premier of Quebec, convened the first interprovincial conference. Four of the six other premiers joined him (the exceptions were Prince Edward Island and British Columbia). They "met in Quebec in October 1887, in evident parody of the conference of 1864, and there proceeded to discuss the fundamentals of Confederation. Their meeting and their public statements made it evident that in their eyes Confederation was a compact of the provinces which the provinces might modify or rescind."[40]

Queen's Counsel and Escheats

The protracted dispute over the right to confer the honour of Queen's Counsel on the legal profession illustrates, at one and the same time, the basic tension between the centralist and provincial perspectives on federalism, the key role in that dispute of the office of lieutenant governor, and the apparently trivial nature of issues leading to constitutional litigation.

At the time of Confederation, British officials maintained that, since the lieutenant governor did not represent the Queen directly, that officer could not exercise prerogative rights of the Crown such as pardon — a point made, as we have seen, to Governor General Lord Monck by the colonial secretary, Edward Cardwell, in 1864. As early as 1872, this assertion was put to the test. In that year, Nova Scotia and Ontario, through their lieutenant governors, conferred the title of Queen's Counsel (QC) on lawyers. Subsequently, both provinces passed legislation affirming their right to do so. However, in 1877, a federally appointed Queen's Counsel, J.N. Ritchie, successfully challenged the Nova Scotia legislation in that province's Supreme Court on the grounds that it denied him appropriate precedence over provincially appointed QCs.

The latter appealed to the Supreme Court of Canada in a case known as *Lenoir v. Ritchie*. In 1879, in a split 3–2 decision, the court not only upheld the Nova Scotia ruling about precedence but went much further in declaring that the provincial legislation of 1874 providing for the appointment of QCs was *ultra vires* (beyond legal power or authority) "because the lieutenant-governor had no right to exercise, and the Legislature had no right to confer, this prerogative power."[41] Justice John Wellington Gwynne argued that the lieutenant governor was a federal officer and not a personal representative of the Sovereign, that the Queen did not form part of the provincial legislatures, and that the provinces were subordinate to the Dominion. The Crown was not part of provincial governments. In the pithy words of Robert Vipond, the former colonies had "indeed been royally demoted."[42]

Justice Henri-Elzéar Taschereau, while accepting his colleague's view of the status of the lieutenant governors, did concede that provincial laws were enacted in the Queen's name. But he made a distinction between executive power and prerogative power: the former was shared with the Sovereign's council (i.e., the cabinet), but the latter belonged exclusively to the monarch and could not be shared in *provincial* jurisdiction. Prerogative power was shared *federally* because the governor general represented the Sovereign directly; this was not the case for the provinces and thus the lieutenant governors, unlike the governor general, could not exercise the royal prerogative in granting QCs. And yet, as we have seen, following centuries of evolution, the royal prerogative was almost entirely exercised "on advice" by the responsible ministers of the Crown, apart from the very rare exceptions of the reserve powers. For Oliver Mowat and his allies, Taschereau's distinction between executive and prerogative powers flew in the face of British constitutional evolution and denied full parliamentary sovereignty to the provincial legislatures. It was imperative to challenge the Supreme Court decision in *Lenoir v. Ritchie*.

Meanwhile, yet another legal battle over the royal prerogative had been brewing, this time over escheats — the prerogative of receiving estates left intestate. In Quebec in 1875, the same Justice Taschereau, at the time a member of the Quebec Superior Court, ruled in *Church v. Blake* that, like the appointment of Queen's Counsel, the prerogative of escheats belonged only to the federal Crown: "… ces droits appartiennent au souverain. Or, sous notre constitution, la souveraineté est à Ottawa. Il n'y a que là que Sa Majesté soit directement représentée."[43] However, this ruling was overturned by a unanimous decision of the Quebec Court of Queen's Bench in 1876 that escheats fell within provincial jurisdiction.[44]

In 1874, Premier Mowat's Ontario government had passed legislation declaring that the provincial attorney general had the right to receive escheats in the name of the Crown. This was in response to claims to the contrary over the estate of one Andrew Mercer, who died in 1871. The law was challenged by the Mercers; they eventually lost in the Ontario Supreme Court in 1880.[45] With both the federal government and Ontario agreeing that jurisdiction over escheats needed to be settled, the case was appealed to the Supreme Court of Canada. In 1881, in *Mercer v. A.G. Ontario*, Edward Blake and James Bethune argued the case for Ontario, affirming that "the executive authority of the Queen continues, and was to be carried out, in every part of Canada after Confederation, by the Governor-General in respect of Dominion matters and by the Lieutenant-Governors as her representatives in Provincial matters."[46] However, recalling their ruling two years earlier in *Lenoir v. Ritchie*, the majority of the Supreme Court ruled against Ontario: escheats, like the appointment of Queen's Counsel, were a royal prerogative that the lieutenant governor could not exercise. Justice Taschereau reaffirmed his views from *Church v. Blake* in 1875. Justice Gwynne stirred the pot by asserting that the *British North America Act* provided for "certain subordinate bodies called provinces having jurisdiction *exclusive* though not 'Sovereign' ... of whose legislatures Her Majesty does not, as she does of the Dominion, and as she did of the old provinces [the colonies], constitute a component part."[47] Everyone recognized that an issue of this importance would go eventually to the Judicial Committee of the Privy Council.

Resolving the Standoff: The Maritime Bank Case and Beyond

An opportunity arose with a New Brunswick case involving the failure of a bank indebted to the provincial government. In an 1885 ruling, *The Queen v. Bank of Nova Scotia*, the Supreme Court of Canada had determined that the Crown had preference over other creditors — but again, only the federal, not the provincial, Crown. In 1888, the premier and attorney general of New Brunswick, A.G. Blair, argued, in *The Provincial Government of New Brunswick v. The Liquidators of the Maritime Bank*, that the provincial Crown had the prerogative right of precedence over other creditors in the case of the failed Maritime Bank. The executive prerogative in the person of the lieutenant governor, Blair maintained, was co-extensive with the division of powers between federal and provincial jurisdictions: "Divest the crown in the province 'of its executive rights as represented by the lieutenant governor, and the whole machinery of Government would stop.' The lieutenant governor was appointed by the governor general in the name of the queen and thus 'the whole scheme of Union is made consistent and harmonious. The Sovereign is not only the chief, but the sole magistrate of the nation, and all others act through her.'"[48] The Supreme Court of New Brunswick agreed.

The case was appealed to the Supreme Court of Canada. Surprisingly, in view of that court's centralizing tendency, it upheld the New Brunswick ruling in 1889, but not without a vocal dissent from Justice Gwynne. The case then proceeded to the Judicial Committee of the Privy Council. The resulting judgment of the JCPC in 1892, in *Liquidators of the Maritime Bank v. Receiver General of New Brunswick*, was as much a landmark ruling as had been that of *Hodge v. The Queen* in 1883. Lord Watson dismissed the argument that "Confederation had severed the connection between the crown and the provinces" and ruled conclusively that "a Lieutenant-Governor, when appointed, is as much a representative of Her Majesty for all purposes of provincial government as the Governor General himself is for all purposes of Dominion government." He went on to say "[t]he object of the [BNA] Act was neither to weld the provinces into one, nor to subordinate provincial governments to a central authority, but to create a federal government in which they should all be represented, entrusted with the exclusive administration of affairs in which they had a common interest, each province *retaining* its independence and autonomy."[49]

Saywell wrote, "This decision had formally recognized what Mowat had been asserting for twenty years: that the imperial sovereign formed part of the provincial as well as the Dominion government and that the two orders of government were therefore essentially equal."[50] It was a crucial judgment for provincial interests, with far-reaching effects. In a somewhat anticlimactic JCPC decision in 1898, Lord Watson finally confirmed that the prerogatives of the provincial Crown did indeed include the right to appoint Queen's Counsel,[51] as had been asserted since 1872 by Ontario — which is ironic, given that Ontario ceased making appointments of QCs in 1985. Mowat had triumphed. It was appropriate that, five years after the *Maritime Bank* judgment, he was appointed lieutenant governor of Ontario, serving from 1897 to 1903 in the vice-regal office he had done so much to enhance. And he was knighted by Queen Victoria: KCMG in 1892 and GCMG in 1897.

Provincial prerogative powers were extended into commercial matters by the decision of the JCPC in *Bonanza Creek Mining Company v. The King* in 1916. This case was about the right of the provincial Crown to incorporate companies operating beyond the province. A gold mining company, incorporated under Ontario legislation by letters patent issued by the lieutenant-governor-in-council under the Great Seal of Ontario, took out leases in the Yukon. The federal government argued that the company did not have this right and the Supreme Court of Canada, in a 3–2 decision, agreed. But when the case was appealed to the Judicial Committee, Viscount Haldane, Lord Watson's successor, ruled that "the charter of incorporation was an executive act, a prerogative act of the crown"[52] and thus within the jurisdiction of the province. While the judgment was strongly criticized at the time, and has been since, as going too far in the direction of provincial autonomy, Saywell pointed out that "Haldane's decision confirmed the principle, long contended for

SIR OLIVER MOWAT K.C.M.G.

Ontario Premier Oliver Mowat led the successful campaign for provincial autonomy in Confederation.

Library & Archives Canada, R1300-256

and established by *Liquidators*, that the legislative and executive powers vested in the provinces were co-extensive."[53]

Viscount Haldane soon carved out a reputation as an advocate for provincial co-sovereignty. In a 1919 decision in a Manitoba case, *The Initiative and Referendum Act*, he referred to the position of the lieutenant governor "as directly representing the Sovereign in the province."[54] The act in question provided for legislation to be adopted by referendum as well as through the normal legislative process. It was held to be unconstitutional because it interfered with the lieutenant governor's right to grant royal assent and therefore amended the provincial vice-regal office enshrined in section 92(1) of the *British North America Act*. Once again, the office of lieutenant governor was the linchpin of the constitutional order.

While the next dispute did not involve the royal prerogative, it is nonetheless of considerable interest: a challenge to the validity of federal legislation in 1919 regulating price increases immediately after the First World War. This was, comments Saywell, "an unprecedented peacetime interference with property and civil rights,"[55] which, of course, were and are under provincial jurisdiction. The Supreme Court of Canada was divided on the matter, but eventually came down on the side of the legislation, basing its decision on the federal powers for trade and commerce and "peace, order and good government" (the POGG clause) in the *British North America Act*. Alberta, Ontario, and Quebec appealed the decision to the JCPC. In 1922, the Committee, again presided over by Haldane, reversed the Supreme Court ruling. In so doing, said Saywell, "he turned property and civil rights into a jurisdictional wall to protect the liberty of the people of the province against the menace of the federal government."[56] The issue of civil rights[57] is a key argument in the book by Robert Vipond on the role of the provincial autonomists in reshaping Confederation. He points out that the provincial rights movement emphasized community values and collective choice but without sacrificing the liberal commitment to individual liberties: "the early theorists of provincial rights [...] argued consistently that their defense of community was a means to protect liberty."[58]

Haldane's last major federal-provincial case was *Toronto Electric Commissioners v. Snider*, in 1925. This was a challenge to 1907 federal labour legislation, the *Industrial Disputes Investigation Act*, considered from the start to be of dubious validity. Upheld in a Quebec trial in 1913, the act was ruled *ultra vires* in Ontario in 1923. This decision was reversed by the Ontario Court of Appeal, based again on federal competence in trade and commerce and in peace, order, and good government. A JCPC panel presided over by Lord Haldane overruled the appeal court, declaring the federal legislation *ultra vires* because there was no evidence of a major emergency, which, according to their interpretation of *Russell v. The Queen*, could justify intrusion into provincial jurisdiction over property and civil rights.[59] The *Snider* case is of particular interest because, in his judgment, Lord Haldane went so far as to say that the provinces were "in a sense like independent kingdoms with very little Dominion control over them" and "should be autonomous places as if they were autonomous kingdoms."[60] This would be music to the ears of the Quebec nationalists today — if they supported the monarchy!

Snider was the low point for the federal government. After Viscount Haldane's death in 1928, the Judicial Committee evolved in a different direction and did not always side with the provinces. Under the chairmanship of Lord Sankey, it produced some landmark rulings. In 1930, in the famous "Persons" case (technically *Edwards v. AG Canada*), the committee overruled a unanimous 1928 decision of the Supreme Court that women were not "persons" for purposes of appointment to the Senate. In his judgment, Lord Sankey declared, in an oft-cited comment, that "[t]he British North America Act planted in Canada a living tree capable of growth and expansion within its natural limits."[61]

The JCPC overturned the Supreme Court in another federal-provincial clash, this time over the right to regulate aviation. In 1919 Canada had passed the *Aeronautics Act* to fulfil commitments made at the Paris Peace Conference. This was challenged by Quebec in 1927 and referred to the Supreme Court. In 1930, despite being presided over by a central-leaning chief justice, Francis Anglin, the Court unanimously ruled that aviation came within provincial jurisdiction under Section 92 of the *BNA Act*. The Judicial Committee, under Lord Sankey, came to the rescue. In 1932, in the *Aeronautics Reference*, it ruled that aviation fell within the federal treaty-making power of Section 132. Meanwhile, Quebec, backed by Ontario and other provinces, had also challenged the *Radiotelegraph Act*, adopted by Parliament in 1927 to regulate radio communication, in compliance with an international convention. This time, the Supreme Court, in a split 3–2 decision in 1931 (the *Radio Reference*), upheld the validity of the Act. On appeal, the JCPC, presided over by Viscount Dunedin, agreed. Its 1932 ruling cited both Section 91 (the POGG clause) and Section 132, the treaty-making power. There was unease among some observers that the federal government could appropriate powers beyond its normal jurisdiction by making international commitments.

However, even the pro-British, pro-Crown R.B. Bennett, who was to be prime minister from 1930 to 1935, was dismayed by a JCPC ruling in 1926, *Nadan v. The King*, which overturned a prohibition, dating back to 1885, on appeals to the JCPC in criminal cases, on the grounds that dominion legislation could not have extra-territorial effect. (The JCPC reversed itself on the issue in decisions in 1932 and 1935, recognizing the supremacy of Parliament in dominion matters with respect to the imperial Parliament, just as *Hodge v. The Queen* had recognized provincial authority with regard to the dominion Parliament.[62]) In 1927, the JCPC ruled against Canada in the Labrador boundary dispute between Quebec and Newfoundland, awarding a huge area of Labrador to the Dominion of Newfoundland. In the context of the 1926 Balfour Report, Bennett concluded that it was time to end appeals to the JCPC.[63]

When he was prime minister, Bennett faced judicial obstacles himself. Progressive social legislation in 1935 to combat the Depression — the Bennett "New Deal" — included such far-reaching measures as unemployment insurance. It was challenged by the provinces as *ultra vires* of the federal government and, after Bennett's government was defeated in the election of 1935, was referred by Mackenzie King's Liberal government to the courts. The federal stand was that the measures were justified by the federal treaty-making power (Section 132 of the *BNA Act*), in this case to implement international labour standards — the argument that had carried the day in the *Aeronautics* and *Radio* cases of 1930–1932. The Supreme Court was now led by Chief Justice Lyman Duff, known to be in favour of provincial autonomy and more respectful of JCPC jurisprudence. In 1936, the Supreme Court found most of the legislation invalid, deferring to *Snider* and provincial jurisdiction over property and civil rights (Section 92). Justice Lawrence Cannon said, "[w]e have not a single community in this country. We have nine commonwealths, several different communities. This is in fact embodied in the law."[64] Lords Watson and Haldane could not have said it better.

The Judicial Committee of the Privy Council, presided over by Lord Atkin, heard the inevitable appeal early in 1937. Lord Sankey did not take part. Atkin was far less inclined to give the benefit of the doubt to Ottawa and more attuned to the Watson-Haldane approach. He rejected Sankey's "living tree" metaphor and returned to the "water-tight compartment" view of federal and provincial jurisdictions. The committee ruled that most of the Bennett "New Deal" measures were indeed *ultra vires* and, as the Supreme Court had stated, fell under Section 92. Bennett and his colleague Charles Cahan were dismayed. The campaign to end appeals to the JCPC gained momentum. In the meantime, Mackenzie King's government obtained consent from all the provinces, fatigued by a decade of Depression, for a constitutional amendment giving Ottawa jurisdiction over unemployment insurance. This was passed by the British Parliament in 1940.

DID THE JUDICIAL COMMITTEE OF THE PRIVY COUNCIL SUBVERT THE FATHERS OF CONFEDERATION?

Although there is general agreement that the Judicial Committee of the Privy Council played a major role in moving Canada to a more decentralized federalism, there has been much debate as to the appropriateness of its rulings. For a long time, the trend was to decry them as distorting the system envisaged by the Fathers of Confederation, by giving too much power to the provinces and weakening the federal government. Gerald Baier remarked on the "vitriol felt by Canada's legal academics towards the interpretation of federalism by the JCPC in the 1930s and 1940s."[65] These academics included law professor and poet Frank R. Scott and Bora Laskin, later to be chief justice of Canada. In 1938, reacting to the rejection of the Bennett "New Deal" legislation, MP Charles Cahan called for an end to appeals to the JCPC, exclaiming that the Judicial Committee "had so amended and redrafted the original constitution and so clothed it in fantastic conceptions of their own, that it bears the grotesque features of a jack-o'-lantern."[66]

This anti-JCPC attitude was not surprising in the 1930s and 1940s, the era of the Depression and the Second World War. It has continued in more moderate form to this day.[67] Eugene Forsey considered that the Senate's role in representing the regions had been pre-empted by "big, powerful, pushing provinces, working through the frequent federal-provincial conferences." He and those thinking like him considered that the "the Law Lords' generous awards to the provinces subverted the founders' vision."[68] The great historian of Confederation, Donald Creighton, emphasized the apparent consensus among the Fathers of Confederation for a strongly centralized Canada; some of them, including Macdonald, would have preferred a legislative union to a federation. This, of course, was not possible, due principally to Quebec, but also to a substantial number of Maritime delegates, such as New Brunswick premier Leonard Tilley. Like Macdonald, Creighton viewed Ontario premier Oliver Mowat as a troublemaker, who reneged on his commitments at the Quebec Conference of 1864. After all, Mowat had drafted the disallowance and reservation provisions of the *BNA Act*; Creighton alleged that his views once he became premier of Ontario "differed from — and in fact contradicted — the original conception of confederation."[69]

On the other hand, there has been a reaction against the notion that JCPC upset the centralized structure supposedly intended in 1867, and later historians have questioned the apparently overwhelming centralist thrust of the Fathers of Confederation. Christopher Moore points out that the Quebec Resolutions gave substantial powers to the provinces, with the strong backing of George-Étienne Cartier of Canada East and Leonard Tilley of New Brunswick. He asserts that Oliver Mowat became "a political giant, the first great provincial premier of confederation."[70] A key concession granted to the provinces was that each was to enjoy full responsible government, a political catchword in nineteenth-century Canada if there ever was one. According to Janet Ajzenstat, too, it is "not correct to suppose that all the Conservatives who participated in the drafting of the British North America Act, 1867 were centralists. [...] The better view maintains that the Fathers intended the BNA Act to balance an effective general government with secure powers for the provinces. The Judicial Committee's interpretations are an attempt to respect that balance."[71] Peter Russell observes that the Judicial Committee's constitutional interpretation "coincided with powerful political forces in Canada [...] the tide was running in favour of provincial rights and a balanced view of Canadian federalism."[72]

In any event, the JCPC rulings were not the only reason Canada evolved away from centralism. A respected scholar of Canadian federalism, Thomas Courchene, has pointed out that a number of other factors "conspired to ensure that Canada would likely end up as a decentralized federation." Among these factors were the union of three English-speaking, common law colonies with one French-speaking colony, with its own culture and civil law (Canada has always been a cultural, as well as a territorial, federation), and the assigning in the *British North America Act* of property and civil rights (already mentioned in the *Quebec Act* of 1774) to provincial jurisdiction — "what we would now call the social envelope." Another factor was the listing of exclusive powers for provincial jurisdiction as well as federal, which is not the case in the United States or Australia.[73] Courchene also observes that one reason why the Canadian provinces have gained power and autonomy is that "in terms of our national governing institutions, Canada surely ranks as the world's most centralized federation"[74] — a statement that must come as a shock to the countless commentators who have called Canada the world's most decentralized federation. He makes the point that, unlike most federations (for example Australia, Germany, and the United States), Canada has no representation of its sub-national units in its central institutions, notably the Senate. Nor do the provinces have any say in appointments to such bodies as the Supreme Court — or, indeed, their own superior courts, national regulatory bodies, or, as has already been noted, their lieutenant governors. David E. Smith points out that "[t]he Crown underwrites the autonomy of the provinces," not the upper chamber in Parliament as in many other federations.[75]

As for the office of lieutenant governor, symbolic of that provincial autonomy, in 1948 the Supreme Court of Canada went even further than the JCPC in clarifying the lieutenant governor's relationship with the federal government. The court unanimously found that the office of the lieutenant governor was purely provincial in nature: "[T]he nature of the federal and provincial legislative and executive powers is clearly settled and the Lieutenant-Governor, who 'carries on the Government of the Province' manifestly does not act in respect of the Government of Canada. All the functions he performs are directed to the affairs of the Province and are in no way connected with the Government of Canada."[76]

Perhaps, then, the attacks on the Judicial Committee of the Privy Council were a case of shooting the messenger. The historic tendency of social democrats to support strong central government as a way to introduce progressive national social programs was evident in both Australia and Canada. Indeed, in Australia, "Labor's program historically even went so far as to include the explicit goal of dismantling federalism, despite the party occasionally holding power in the states" — a part of the Labor Party constitution claimed to have been removed by Gough Whitlam in 1969.[77] In Canada, inspired by J.S. Woodworth, Frank Scott was co-founder of the League for Social Reconstruction in 1931–1932 with historian Frank Underhill, another centralist who later became a Liberal. Scott was one of the founding members of the Co-operative Commonwealth Federation in 1932 and, with Underhill, helped draft its 1933 Regina Manifesto, which reflected the desire of social democrats for political centralization and their distrust for provincial governments. "What the Regina Manifesto socialists proposed [...] was a virtual return to Macdonald's conception of what the federal union should be."[78] Frank Scott had great influence on the young Pierre Trudeau. At the time, however, Trudeau did not accept Scott's centralism. In 1951, criticizing a federal bill on the grounds that it extended the "POGG" clause of the *British North America Act* "far beyond what its drafters intended," Trudeau wrote that some parts of the bill "appear to be based on a fantastic conception of federalism [...] It is preposterous [for the federal government] to claim jurisdiction over the provincial governments *themselves*."[79]

The irony, of course, is that it was federalism that made progressive social programs possible in Canada. The CCF in Saskatchewan introduced hospital insurance as early as 1947 and their comprehensive health care program of 1962 led to Canadian medicare in 1968. The Saskatchewan Bill of Rights of 1947 was the first of its kind, enacted a year before the United Nations General Assembly adopted the Universal Declaration of Human Rights. Other initiatives in Saskatchewan, and those of the Quiet Revolution in Quebec in the 1960s, further illustrate the counter-argument to Scott and other social-democratic centralists. The argument can be made — and not only in Canada — that sub-national jurisdictions are frequently ahead of their national governments on key social issues. This reflects the principle of "subsidiarity," devolving responsibility and accountability to governments closest to the people. A contemporary assessment is that "Canadian provinces have sometimes found ways to innovate at a more rapid pace than the federal government to adapt to changing economic, social, and institutional circumstances. [...] Contrary to the wishes of some of the key founders of Canada, the provinces have not withered away; indeed, they have proven to be capable and innovative policy and administrative actors."[80]

In terms of culture and the arts, a similar centralist argument has been made. Provincial governments seem to be "too exposed to the interest groups which drive [...] jingoistic, moralizing and utilitarian agendas," said John Ralston Saul, while pointing out the successes of national institutions such as the CBC, Radio-Canada, and the National Film Board.[81] Once again, experience suggests otherwise. In 1948, the CCF government in Saskatchewan was the first in Canada to create a public arts funding agency, the Saskatchewan Arts Board. It also established a precedent-setting Archives Board in 1945 to preserve public documents. In contemporary terms, provincial educational television channels such as TVOntario have helped fill the cultural gap left by national broadcasters. A plethora of examples could be drawn from other jurisdictions. One does not need to disparage the undoubted success of federal cultural agencies such as the Canada Council and the national museums to recognize that provincial initiatives have also borne fruit. John Ralston Saul was closer to the mark when he said, in a somewhat back-handed compliment, that in Canada "[i]t has always been the inefficiency and duplication of a system involving three levels of government which has permitted freedom of speech and remarkable creativity. [...] it is the multi-levelled complexity of the federal-provincial-municipal system which has given so much energy to our cultural activities."[82]

In 1939, Charles Cahan, the Member of Parliament who had accused the Judicial Committee of giving the constitution "the grotesque features of a jack-o'-lantern," introduced a bill to abolish appeals to it from the Canadian courts; the bill was referred to those very courts for a test of its constitutionality. In 1940, the Supreme Court ruled that the bill was constitutional. Irony of ironies, this ruling was appealed to the JCPC itself by Ontario, British Columbia, New Brunswick, and Quebec, on the grounds that abolition would be a violation of provincial jurisdiction. However, in 1947, the Judicial Committee accepted the federal argument that, among other things, the "peace, order and good government" clause of the *BNA Act* entitled Ottawa to abolish appeals, noting that this would be consistent with the spirit of the *Statute of Westminster*.[83] Yet the end of appeals to the Judicial Committee of the Privy Council in 1949 and the assumption of the role of final arbiter by the Supreme Court of Canada did not, as the anti-JCPC school had hoped, lead to a major centralizing thrust in constitutional jurisprudence. Commenting on the Supreme Court's decision in the *Anti-Inflation* reference of 1976, Gerald Baier says:

> It is plain that the court did not satisfy centralist hopefuls, although Laskin did try. What the court did do was begin a new tradition of essentially ambivalent federalism jurisprudence.[...] By taking the middle ground, the court had done nothing more than endorse the model of Canadian federalism already at work. Rather than direct the shape of Canadian federalism as the Privy Council's law lords had attempted, judicial review now seemed to mirror the federalism status quo. The [Anti-Inflation] decision [...] reflected the balance of power in the federation fairly accurately.[84]

The JCPC interpretations of the *British North America Act* continue to reverberate. In 2011, the Supreme Court ruled against the federal government's attempt to create a single securities regulator. The trade and commerce clause of the *Act*, said the court, did not, contrary to the federal argument, give Ottawa authority to regulate the securities market. It was an infringement of provincial jurisdiction over property and civil rights in Section 92. "That would have been just too big a change in the distribution of powers," commented Thomas Courchene. "It would have gone really, really far into areas that are clearly provincial jurisdiction."[85] The Supreme Court decision, said Professor Tom Flanagan, was a welcome return to classical federalism and classical liberalism and away from executive federalism, with its blurring of the lines between central and provincial governments.[86] Seven decades after Mackenzie King's unemployment insurance amendment of 1940, a newspaper columnist asserted that Lord Atkin had been right to reject Bennett's abortive New Deal of 1935 as an "'easy passage' to all provincial powers and prerogatives." Terming the employment insurance scheme "a vast social-welfare bureaucracy that now maintains a permanent underclass of federally dependent people," he said "[i]n retrospect, Lord Atkin proved more perceptive than this country's determined centralizers. He perceived that the BNA Act protected Canadians' human rights by protecting their property rights from excessive federal power."[87] Oliver Mowat and his allies would have applauded.

There has always been and always will be a tug of war in a federation like Canada between the central and sub-national governments.[88] Says David E. Smith:

> Two operating conceptions of federalism are embedded in Canada's terms of union and provide the source for two broad and conflicting streams of interpretation that flow through the decades into modern Canadian politics. The first might be called the federal paramountcy stream. This operating conception sees the federal government as the paramount power in Canada with the provinces occupying a second, inferior level of government. [...] the second, "confederal," stream assumes that both orders (not levels) of government are equal and sovereign in their own constitutional spheres.[89]

The "confederal" stream appears to have come into its own. Following the reforms in Saskatchewan after the election of the first CCF government in 1944, even more so in Quebec after the Quiet Revolution in

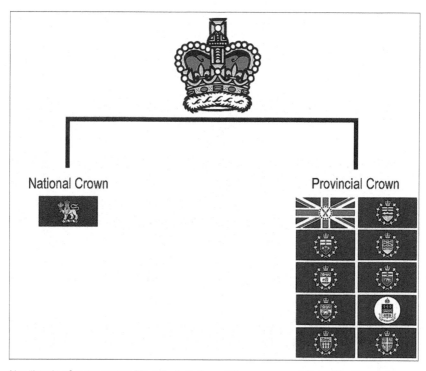

Not "levels of government," but "jurisdictions." The compound Canadian Crown is symbolized by the vice-regal flags of the governor general and the ten lieutenant governors.
Nathan Tidridge

the 1960s, and with the activist role of the central and western provinces reflecting the vastly increased importance of provincial jurisdiction over property, civil rights, education, and natural resources, there seems little chance of reverting to centralization, whether that of John A. Macdonald, Bora Laskin, William Lyon Mackenzie King, or Pierre Trudeau. The status quo inherited from the JCPC appears unlikely to be reversed by the courts. Arguably, then, the judgments of the Judicial Committee of the Privy Council, and notably those regarding the status of the provincial Crown and the lieutenant governors, helped Canada evolve into a true federation. No wonder that in 1947 four provinces, including Quebec, opposed the ending of appeals to the much-maligned JCPC. Five years later, in 1952, the lieutenant governor of Saskatchewan, "assisted by Her Majesty's Executive Council for Saskatchewan," issued a proclamation of the accession of Queen Elizabeth II. She was declared "Supreme Liege Lady in and over Saskatchewan." There was no mention in the proclamation of the governor general.[90] The provincial Crown had come into its own.

COMPARISON WITH AUSTRALIA

The Judicial Committee of the Privy Council made judgments similar to its Canadian rulings with respect to the Australian states, which, the Committee asserted, "possess legal and constitutional authority which is of precisely the same nature and quality as that of the central or Federal authority within its lawful sphere." This was echoed much later in a ruling by the High Court of Australia in 2000 that "sovereignty is shared between the Commonwealth and the member States of the federation."[91]

The arrangements for the federation of the Australian colonies in 1901 were influenced by the Canadian experience three decades prior. But they were affected in a contrary direction: Australians categorically rejected the Canadian model of provincial vice-regal representatives appointed by the federal government and nominally subordinate to it. "It would have been quite unthinkable for the Australian delegates to have contemplated giving the Australian government the power to disallow State legislation or to appoint State Governors."[92] Tasmanian Attorney General Andrew Inglis-Clark said, "I regard the Dominion of Canada as an instance of amalgamation rather than of federation, and I am convinced that the different Australian colonies do not want absolute amalgamation. What they want is federation in the true sense of the word."[93] Many Australians preferred the American constitutional model to that of the *British North America Act* because they believed that it better protected the autonomy of the states. They deliberately refused the Canadian term of "lieutenant governor," implying as it did a status subordinate to the governor general. Instead, they retained the title "governor" used in the pre-confederation colonies. To this day, the Australian states have jealously guarded the co-sovereign autonomy symbolized by their governors. State constitutions predate federation in 1901, and "the Australian state Crowns have always been recognised as indisputably separate from and largely independent of the Commonwealth [federal government]."[94]

Symbolically, the Australian state governors are entitled to a twenty-one-gun salute and the title "Excellency," unlike their Canadian counterparts. Their Government Houses, staff establishment, and general prestige are much superior to those of lieutenant governors in Canada. They were and are directly appointed by the Queen. From 1901 until the *Australia Acts* of 1986, these appointments were made on the advice of British ministers; since then, they have been made on the advice of the state premiers. In the 1980s, the issue of the appointment of the Australian governors required delicate negotiations between Canberra, the states, and Buckingham Palace. Finally, in 1986, it was agreed that the Queen could accept direct advice from her Australian premiers on the appointment of the governors.[95] This legislation "reinforced rather than diminished the claims of the six states to be considered at least quasi-sovereign monarchies in their own right."[96] Ironically, however, the Canadian provinces now appear to have more genuine autonomy than the Australian states, despite the superior status in theory of the latter's vice-regal representatives. The constitutional and political evolution in Canada brought its lieutenant governors *de facto,* if not fully *de jure,* to the status of their Australian counterparts. The evolution in Australia has been the opposite.

From the outset, Australians, unlike Canadians, did not have unlimited right of appeal to the Judicial Committee of the Privy Council; such appeals required a certificate by the High Court of Australia. For the first twenty years of federation, the High Court tended to give the benefit of the doubt to the states by limiting federal powers, for example, in the *Railway Servants* case decided soon after Confederation, in 1904. However, from 1920, rulings of the court steadily widened federal powers at the expense of the states, despite the status of the state Crowns and governors, who, unlike their Canadian counterparts, were prevented from appealing to the JCPC. Prime examples of federal intrusion were the *Engineers* case in 1920, *R. v. Burgess; Ex parte Henry* in 1936, *Koowarta v. Bjelke-Petersen* in 1982, *Tasmanian Dam* in 1983, *Ha v. New South Wales* in 1997, and *New South Wales and Others v. Commonwealth* in 2006. These centralist rulings often made use of the federal government's jurisdiction over foreign relations to reduce the powers of the states.[97] Canada, on the other hand, enhanced the status

of the provincial Crown and lieutenant governors through court decisions from the 1880s to the 1920s. The result was that both the Crown
and the vice-regal office became symbols and instruments of provincial
autonomy. Despite the theoretically superior status of the Australian
state Crowns and their governors, the centralizing trend has had the
upper hand in that country. Canadian lieutenant governors may not
match the prestige and protocol of their Australian counterparts, but
the autonomy of the provincial Crown in Canada appears to be more
effective. This is one among many paradoxes that characterize the institution of the Crown in the federal state.

IV

Lieutenant Governors —
Prestige, Obscurity, and Revival

It is ironic that, in the eighty or so years following the *Liquidators of the Maritime Bank* case, the prestige and profile of the lieutenant governors steadily declined despite their enhanced juridical status. There was even talk of abolishing the office as redundant and useless, although this was a constitutional non-starter.

VICE-REGAL POWERS:
REFUSAL AND RESERVATION OF ROYAL ASSENT

The normally routine prerogative power of royal assent to legislation provides an illustration of early provincial vice-regal intervention — and of its disappearance. Royal assent has not been refused by a British monarch since Queen Anne in 1707 and has never been refused by a Canadian governor general since Confederation. However, lieutenant governors cast their vice-regal veto no less than thirty-eight times between 1870 and 1945, almost always on the advice or with the concurrence of their cabinets as a handy tool to avoid awkward legislation. There was one exception, when the lieutenant governor of Prince Edward Island withheld royal assent from a bill on his own initiative in 1945. Interestingly, given the legislation referred to the Judicial Committee of the Privy Council in the 1880s, he did so on a liquor bill! It was the last time the power has been used.[1]

The *reservation* of royal assent by the lieutenant governor for the "Signification of the Governor-General's pleasure," i.e. the federal government, is another matter altogether. It is often confused with the federal power of disallowance of provincial legislation, but the only role of the lieutenant governor in disallowance was to announce the federal decision. Reservation was a clear centralizing device to permit the federal government to override provincial legislation. And it was by no means an idle threat. John Saywell records that 69 provincial bills were reserved (and 112 acts were disallowed) between 1867 and 1937, the *ultra vires* legislation of William Aberhart's Social Credit government in Alberta being the last target.[2] The policy clearly established by Prime Minister Sir John A. Macdonald in 1882 was that lieutenant governors should only reserve assent on direct instructions from Ottawa and "if the lieutenant-governor considered them to be *ultra vires* or in conflict with federal policies or interests."[3] In particular, Macdonald objected to provincial governments recommending reservation to their lieutenant governors. However, lieutenant governors reserved assent on their own initiative or that of their governments more frequently than on instructions from Ottawa, just as they did in refusing royal assent. Reservation thus became another form of vice-regal veto, often to the embarrassment of Ottawa. The power of reservation never really caught on as a normative constitutional practice and its use declined steadily after 1914.

The case of Alberta in the late 1930s was therefore unusual — but then, so were the times. The Great Depression led to the election of the maverick Social Credit government of William "Bible Bill" Aberhart in 1935. Aberhart's legislation on, among other things, credit and banking provoked clashes with the federal government of Mackenzie King and with the lieutenant governor. In Aberhart's first year in office, Lieutenant Governor William Walsh, a former chief justice of the province, wrote to the premier expressing concern about proposed legislation regarding settlement of debts, warning that it might be *ultra vires*, infringing on the federal power over banking, and hinted that he might reserve royal assent.[4] In the end, he did not. However, it was likely under his influence that the *Reduction and Settlement of Debts Act* was reviewed by the Supreme Court of Alberta, which ruled it unconstitutional the following year.

During 1937, Aberhart's government pushed through credit legislation of dubious legality. Walsh's successor, John Bowen, to be Alberta's longest-serving lieutenant governor, gave royal assent to three bills despite grave concerns expressed in Ottawa and his personal misgivings. Indeed, Aberhart's own attorney general, in a meeting with the lieutenant governor and the premier, advised against granting royal assent, whereupon Aberhart fired him! The federal government speedily disallowed the legislation. Later in the year, the Social Credit government reintroduced still more questionable legislation on credit. This time, Bowen was prepared to act. After warning Aberhart, the lieutenant governor reserved royal assent of three bills for the consideration of the governor general. The bills were referred to the Supreme Court of Canada, which ruled them *ultra vires* in 1938. Bowen was encouraged in his decision to reserve assent by federal justice minister Ernest Lapointe, but did not receive instructions to this effect from the federal government, as the wily Mackenzie King made clear.[5] The premier got his revenge by closing Alberta's Government House, residence of the lieutenant governor. He also challenged the powers of reservation and disallowance in the Supreme Court of Canada, which upheld both in another 1938 decision. The last exercise of the federal power of disallowance was in 1943, again for Alberta with its Social Credit government, when "An Act to Prohibit the Sale of Lands to any Enemy Aliens and Hutterites for the Duration of the War" was disallowed.

After that, both reservation and disallowance were considered obsolete. There was, however, a single revival of the power of reservation — in Saskatchewan in 1961, the only case in that province's history. Lieutenant Governor Frank Bastedo, a prominent Conservative lawyer who had been counsel for the oil industry and was an appointee of the Diefenbaker government, reserved royal assent on Bill 56, *The Alteration of Certain Mineral Contracts*, because he had doubts about its validity and whether it was in the public interest. The bill was intended by the CCF government of Premier T.C. Douglas as a last resort to rectify one-sided contracts between an oil company and farmers. Even the Liberal opposition conceded that the bill had some merit and some of its MLAs voted in favour. Bastedo's reserving of royal assent, recalled Allan Blakeney, a CCF minister at the time, caught both sides of the House by surprise. Liberal member Mary Batten exclaimed to Blakeney, "He can't do that!"[6]

The last reservation of royal assent was by Saskatchewan Lieutenant Governor Frank Bastedo in 1961; it cast a pall over the vice-regal office in the province for two decades.

Saskatchewan Archives Board, SAB R-B5532-2

In view of Sir John A. Macdonald's stricture that lieutenant governors should only reserve legislation on instructions from Ottawa, and of the understanding that the power was obsolete, Batten was right. Bastedo had not consulted the federal government, much less received instructions from Ottawa, as Prime Minister John Diefenbaker was quick to point out. But in the sense that early lieutenant governors had used reservation as a kind of veto in place of denying royal assent, Bastedo *was* following a precedent, albeit an outdated one. His previous connections with the oil industry rendered his motives suspect, to say the least. Sensitive to charges by the Saskatchewan CCF that the federal Conservatives were interfering in provincial jurisdiction, the Diefenbaker government hastened to conclude that the bill was *intra vires* and passed an order-in-council giving it royal assent. There were political reverberations: the national leader of the CCF, Hazen Argue, called for Bastedo's resignation, and his predecessor, M.J. Coldwell, "revived the CCF demand for abolition of the office." There were even rumours of possible dismissal of the lieutenant governor, which would have been the first since 1900, but this came to naught and Bastedo served out the minimum five years in the vice-regal position, until 1963, when the Diefenbaker government hastened to replace him.[7]

The Bastedo incident had two consequences. First, it confirmed that the power of reservation in Canada was obsolete and would not be used again. The remedy for constitutional challenges to legislation was the courts or the political process, not the personal intervention of the lieutenant governor. Second, the incident cast a chill on relations between the lieutenant governor and the CCF/NDP, which lasted two decades. Many social democrats were already skeptical about the office of lieutenant governor, considering it an elitist social institution, political anachronism, and symbol of federal power and patronage. The CCF, then NDP, administrations of Premiers T.C. Douglas, Woodrow Lloyd, and Allan Blakeney saw their worst fears realized in the Bastedo affair. According to Allan Blakeney, in 1961 the CCF cabinet was apprehensive that Bastedo, given his exaggerated opinion of his vice-regal powers, might go so far as to dismiss their administration.[8] During the crisis over medicare in 1962, Premier Woodrow Lloyd, on receiving a telephone inquiry at home about the situation from Bastedo, feared the worst.[9] Did he anticipate use or abuse of the power of the vice-regal reserve power of dismissal?

VICE-REGAL POWERS: APPOINTMENT AND DISMISSAL, PROROGATION AND DISSOLUTION

What, then, about those other, potent, reserve powers of refusing dissolution of the Legislature to a premier and appointing or dismissing a first minister and government? In the early days of Confederation, these powers were exercised. Lieutenant governors refused dissolution to premiers three times between 1879 and 1891, in Quebec, New Brunswick, and Prince Edward Island; they dismissed premiers and governments five times between 1867 and 1903, twice in Quebec and three times in British Columbia.

In 1878, just before the Macdonald Conservatives returned to power in Ottawa, Quebec's lieutenant governor, Luc de Letellier de Saint-Just, a former cabinet minister in Prime Minister Alexander Mackenzie's federal Liberal government, dismissed the Conservative government of Charles-Eugène Boucher de Boucherville, despite its holding a majority in both houses of the Legislature. This was on the grounds of financial mismanagement with respect to railways — a controversial issue in nineteenth-century Canada. Letellier called on the leader of the Liberal opposition, Henri-Gustave Joly de Lotbinière, to form a government. When this was defeated in the Legislature, the House was dissolved; in the ensuing election the Liberals squeaked in with a one-seat majority. The next year, Macdonald's federal Conservatives engineered the rare feat of the dismissal of the lieutenant governor.[10]

In 1879, Letellier's successor, Théodore Robitaille, a Conservative appointee, refused dissolution to Premier Joly de Lotbinière when the upper house, the Legislative Council, refused supply; upon the premier's resignation, he asked the leader of the opposition, Joseph-Adolphe Chapleau, to form a government.[11] Chapleau's government won the ensuing election in 1879.* Another spectacular dismissal of a Quebec administration occurred in 1891. This time, Lieutenant Governor A.R. Angers, also a Conservative appointee, dismissed the notoriously corrupt government of Liberal premier Honoré Mercier — the *nationaliste* leader who had allied with Ontario's Oliver Mowat to challenge Ottawa centralism. The issue was once again railway financing. Angers summoned opposition leader Boucher de Boucherville — who had himself been dismissed by Letellier in 1878 — to form a government. Dissolution was then granted and an election held; the Conservatives trounced the Liberals, and Mercier's political career was virtually over.[12]

No fewer than three dismissals took place in British Columbia between 1898 and 1903, one of them with an unusual Quebec connection. After the election of 1898 produced a tie in the Assembly, Lieutenant Governor Thomas Edgar McInnes refused to sign some orders-in-council and dismissed Premier John H. Turner, calling on the Conservative opposition leader in the former assembly, Charles Semlin, to form a government. But eighteen months later, in 1900, McInnes dismissed Semlin in his turn when he lost his working majority in the House. The lieutenant governor then called on Joseph Martin, a maverick Liberal distrusted by the federal Liberal government of Sir Wilfrid Laurier, to be premier. Martin's government was promptly repudiated by the Legislature. At

---

* Chapleau moved into federal politics from 1882 to 1892 and then served as lieutenant governor of Quebec from 1892 to 1898. Joly de Lotbinière also was in federal politics from 1896 until 1900, when he became lieutenant governor of British Columbia.

Martin's urging, McInnes delayed dissolution of the House until directed to by the federal government. In the election, Martin's government was reduced to minority status and he resigned, to be replaced by mining and railway magnate James Dunsmuir. Soon after, McInnes became the second lieutenant governor to be dismissed by the federal government.[13]

His successor, Sir Henri-Gustave Joly de Lotbinière, was none other than the premier who had taken office in Quebec after the dismissal of Boucher de Boucherville in 1878. In the fractious politics of British Columbia, party lines were fluid and governments unstable. Joly de Lotbinière refused the resignation of Premier Dunsmuir in 1901, but had to accept it the following year and, on his advice, invited E.G. Prior to succeed him. In 1903, Prior's administration, like that of Honoré Mercier in Quebec, became mired in scandals over railway construction. The lieutenant governor dismissed Prior and called on another Conservative, William McBride, to form a government. Unlike the other dismissals, this one provoked little controversy. Indeed, it may have contributed to much-needed stability in British Columbia politics, as McBride remained premier until 1915.[14]

Interestingly, British Columbia's peculiar brand of politics caused headaches for its lieutenant governors decades later. The 1941 election saw Duff Patullo's Liberals returned with a minority twenty-one seats in a forty-seven-seat Legislature, the opposition split between the CCF and the Conservatives. The latter offered the Liberals a coalition to "stem the CCF tide." Patullo refused and prepared to face the assembly, whereupon a number of his cabinet ministers resigned. Lieutenant Governor W.C. Woodward considered refusing dissolution if so requested and consulted Ottawa; Mackenzie King, as usual, counselled caution. The issue was resolved when the Liberals elected a new leader, pro-coalition John Hart. Patullo then advised the lieutenant governor to invite Hart to form a government. Another minority situation occurred in the 1952 election: this time, the new, but leaderless, Social Credit Party virtually tied for seats with the CCF, with the Liberals and Conservatives left far behind. Lieutenant Governor Clarence Wallace was faced with conflicting claims for the premier's chair by CCF leader Harold Winch and W.A.C. Bennett, a former Conservative just elected as Social Credit leader. In the end, Wallace invited Bennett, who could count on more support in the assembly, to form the government, and the Social Credit dynasty in British Columbia began.[15]

In New Brunswick in 1883, Lieutenant Governor R.D. Wilmot refused dissolution to Premier D.L. Hannington when his government, elected eight months earlier, met the House and lost a vote of confidence after the defection of three members. After several days, Hannington resigned.[16] Interestingly, the leader of the opposition, recommended by the outgoing premier and called upon by the lieutenant governor to form a new government, was none other than A.G. Blair, who went on to launch the court challenge which led to the famous *Liquidators of the Maritime Bank* decision by the Judicial Committee of the Privy Council in 1892. In 1891, a similar change happened in Prince Edward Island. Lieutenant Governor J.S. Carvell refused dissolution to Premier N. McLeod when his Conservative government lost its majority in the assembly and, when McLeod resigned, called on the Liberal leader to form a government.[17] In 1922 in Manitoba, the Liberal government, which had been in a minority status since 1920 in a four-party assembly, faced a non-confidence motion. The lieutenant governor, Sir James Aikins, refused to accept the resignation of Premier T.C. Norris and his recommendation for dissolution. Instead, Aikins advised the premier to continue in office until supply had been voted. Norris accepted the lieutenant governor's advice and secured agreement from the other parties. The lieutenant governor accepted dissolution only after the business of the legislative session had been completed.[18]

There was a convoluted case in Newfoundland in 1972, when Lieutenant Governor John Harnum granted dissolution in dubious circumstances to the newly elected government of Frank Moores. The election in October 1971 gave Joey Smallwood's incumbent Liberals and Moores's Conservatives twenty seats each, with one seat to a member of a small party who eventually decided to support the Conservatives, and another seat undecided. Moores claimed the right to form a government, but Smallwood clung to office. Moores appealed to Governor General Roland Michener to intervene, which the latter rightly refused to do. Early in 1972, the disputed seat went to the Conservatives and Smallwood resigned. However, in a veritable imbroglio, the single party member switched back to the Liberals, a Liberal member did not take his seat, and a Conservative decided to support the Liberals! New Liberal leader Edward Roberts, now holding a margin of twenty-one to twenty, urged the lieutenant governor to require Moores to face the assembly, which Harnum apparently did. On the first day of the session, with a Conservative elected as speaker and another Liberal not taking his seat, there was a deadlock. Moores immediately requested and was granted dissolution. This embroiled the lieutenant governor in controversy, as the Liberals credibly argued that "Moores's fate should have been decided by a vote in the Assembly, not in Government House."[19]

Saskatchewan's vice-regal history began in controversy. The last lieutenant governor of the Northwest Territories, Amédée Forget, was appointed first lieutenant governor of Saskatchewan when the province was formed on September 1, 1905. It was his formal task to select the first premier. The last territorial premier, Frederick Haultain, seemed a logical choice. However, although he was leader of a non-partisan administration, Haultain had shown definite Conservative leanings and opposed the agreements on the new provincial status. At the instigation of the federal Liberal government of Sir Wilfrid Laurier, Forget appointed Liberal Walter Scott instead, even though he had not been a member of the Territorial Assembly. Scott's government swept the province in the first elections in December of 1905, and the Liberals remained in power until 1929. Forget was criticized for his selection of Scott, especially by the Conservatives, but the choice was not really his. Furthermore, it was an understandable decision in the circumstances, and, not for the last time, illustrated the partisan realities affecting the office of lieutenant governor.[20]

Forget was criticized, again by the opposition Conservatives, when Scott called a snap election in 1908 after only three years in office; but it was manifestly unfair to blame the lieutenant governor for the premier's undoubted right to request dissolution. The next controversial occasion, in 1916, also involved Walter Scott. This time the tables were turned: a Conservative federal government had appointed one of its own, former MP Richard Lake, as Saskatchewan's lieutenant governor in 1915. The same year in Manitoba, the lieutenant governor, a Liberal appointee, responded to charges of corruption by the Liberal opposition by threatening to use the prerogative of dismissal and effectively forced the Conservative government to launch an investigation. The charges were proved and led to the demise of their administration. In 1916, the opposition Conservatives in Saskatchewan used the same tactic in retaliation for the fate of their Manitoba counterparts: they levelled charges of impropriety against the government and, through Lieutenant Governor Lake, tried to force the government to either establish a royal commission or face dismissal. But Scott held private discussions with Lake and the matter was resolved without the lieutenant governor intervening.

Alberta provides more controversial examples of vice-regal intervention. In 1910, the province's first lieutenant governor, George Bulyea, engineered the dismissal of the first premier, Alexander Rutherford, due to unproven allegations of corruption and ensured that the chief justice, Arthur Sifton, succeeded him. In 1934, when Premier John Brownlee was involved in a scandal, he resigned and recommended to Lieutenant Governor William Walsh that Gavin Reid, the choice of his caucus, become premier. The lieutenant governor refused the resignation. When Reid showed up to be sworn in, Walsh declined to do so until he presented a complete cabinet. When this was done five days later, Walsh finally swore in Reid and his ministers.[21] During the 1937 standoff between Premier William Aberhart and Lieutenant Governor John Bowen, the lieutenant governor first considered refusing dissolution should it be requested and inviting the Liberal opposition leader to form a government. Then, after reserving royal assent to legislation, he envisaged dismissing the premier. Both courses of action were strongly discouraged by Mackenzie King's federal government. In 1938, there was a major confrontation between lieutenant governor and premier when Aberhart closed Government House, leaving Bowen without residence or staff. The lieutenant governor once again seriously considered dismissing the premier and inviting the Liberal leader to form a government. He was dissuaded from this radical course of action by Mackenzie King, who feared that it "might bring on a sort of civil war in Alberta" and, worse still from his point of view, cause the Liberals to lose the pending general election in Saskatchewan.[22]

Dismissal of a state premier has occurred only once in Australian history, in 1932, when the governor of New South Wales, Sir Philip Game, dismissed Labor Premier Jack Lang because of his refusal to comply with a judgment of the High Court in a dispute with the federal government. There appears to have been little negative fallout from this vice-regal action. In fact, "the governor's actions received a species of political endorsement in the overwhelming defeat of the Labour Party and the return of a new, successor conservative government."[23] Refusal of dissolution, on the other hand, has been more frequent in Australia than in Canada, partly because all the states except Queensland are bicameral and the possibility is very real of the upper house, the legislative council, refusing supply. Peter Boyce records, for example, that in the State of Victoria governors refused dissolution in 1943, 1950, and 1952. Tasmania was the scene of a standoff between governor and premier in 1948 where the latter, accused of and tried for (but eventually acquitted of) corruption following a royal commission report, was pressured to resign by the governor, Sir Hugh Binney. When supply was denied by the legislative council, the governor dissolved the assembly. The government was re-elected and supply was subsequently granted. When a "hung parliament" was elected in 1989 in the same state of Tasmania, the governor, Sir Philip Bennett, refused the advice of the Liberal premier to continue in office and instead called on the leader of the Labor Party to form a government with the support of the Greens. In 1987, a governor of Queensland rejected the advice of scandal-ridden premier Sir Joh Bjelke-Petersen to dismiss five ministers and allow him to form a new cabinet. There have been other examples of unconventional behaviour by premiers in Western Australia and Victoria, as well as in Queensland and Tasmania. The result has been a more frequent use of discretionary powers in Australia by state governors than by the governor general.[24]

FEDERAL OFFICER?

The framers of the *British North America Act* expressly identified the lieutenant governor as a federal officer, a role in their view more significant than that of provincial representative of the Crown. For Ottawa, the federal relationship with the lieutenant governors was intended to replicate that between London and the governor general. The governor general had the dual role of representing the imperial government in London while representing the Queen for purposes of the federal government. This imperial function, however, gradually faded away, and disappeared altogether with the Balfour Report of 1926 and the *Statute of Westminster* in 1931.

In the early years of Confederation, the lieutenant governors frequently acted as the eyes, ears, and agents of the federal government. This went beyond the constitutional prerogatives of reservation of royal assent and notification of disallowance. It involved information gathering and intelligence for the prime minister and his cabinet and communication of and support for federal policies, and provided a buffer in the event of federal-provincial disagreements. For example, the first lieutenant governor of Nova Scotia, Sir Hastings Doyle, actively campaigned against the secessionist government of the province, which was trying to undo Confederation. The first lieutenant governor of Manitoba, Adams Archibald, was equally diligent in that province on behalf of Prime Minister Macdonald. This activist role on Ottawa's behalf declined and all but disappeared early in the twentieth century. Prime ministers were able to use their national parties and their own ministers, senators, and members of Parliament, as well as the media, to communicate their policies. Eventually, intergovernmental conferences and bureaucracies provided formal channels for federal-provincial relations. The role of the lieutenant governor as federal agent was eclipsed even more quickly than that of purveyor of discretionary constitutional powers. By the mid-twentieth century, the lieutenant governor reflected in fact and perception the legal definition in the 1892 court decision: the provincial representative of the Sovereign. John Saywell neatly summed it up:

> ... co-ordinate legislative and administrative authority has replaced the intended subordination of the provinces to the Dominion. The Lieutenant-Governor is no longer in practice "a mere instrument of the federal cabinet" nor is he even an "agent and spokesman" for the central government. Reservation was from the beginning a cracked if not broken reed; disallowance was a more satisfactory and acceptable instrument of federal control; but in time judicial review largely ousted them both.[25]

VICE-REGAL APPOINTMENTS AND TENURE

What did not disappear, however, was the federal government's *appointment* of the lieutenant governor (again, contrary to the Australian system, where the state premiers formally recommend the appointment of the governors to the Queen). It has always been a jealously guarded prerogative of the prime minister, who usually named supporters of his own party as a reward for past services or loyalty. In the early years of Confederation, when the office of lieutenant governor was relatively powerful, it was also more prestigious, sought after, and characterized by high-profile appointees. (John Saywell commented that "a list of the pre-1914 Lieutenant-Governors reads like a roll call of the near-great in Canadian political history."[26]) Macdonald used the position "both to compensate important political figures who had been denied an expected cabinet post and to create needed cabinet vacancies."[27] A century later, when the office had declined in both power and prestige, it was no longer seen as a desirable position by anyone with political ambition. The prime minister's office generally selected incumbents by canvassing opinions among the local establishment of the party in the province. Former politicians — senators, members of Parliament, provincial members of the Legislature — predominated among the nominees.

Under section 59 of the *Constitution Act, 1867*, lieutenant governors are not appointed for a fixed term. They hold office "during the Pleasure of the Governor General" (in other words, the federal cabinet), but they have virtually secure tenure: for five years after their appointment, they can only be removed by the governor general "for Cause assigned" and communicated to both Houses of Parliament. As we have noted above, only two lieutenant governors have ever been removed from office by this process (although some have resigned) — that of Quebec in 1879 by the Macdonald government and that of British Columbia in 1900 by the Laurier administration.

In 1878, Quebec's lieutenant governor, Luc de Letellier de Saint-Just, dismissed the Conservative government of Charles-Eugène Boucher de Boucherville and called on the leader of the Liberal opposition, Henri-Gustave Joly de Lotbinière, to form a government, which was returned with a one-seat majority (later increased to three by by-elections) in the election that quickly followed. The new leader of the Conservative opposition, Joseph-Adolphe Chapleau, vigorously challenged Letellier's controversial action. Opposition leader John A. Macdonald moved a motion of censure of Letellier in the House of Commons. It was defeated by Prime Minister Mackenzie's Liberal majority, although it passed in the Conservative-dominated Senate, and Letellier continued his partisan support of the Quebec Liberal administration.

After the Macdonald Conservatives returned to power in Ottawa, pressure resumed to dismiss the Quebec lieutenant governor. Premier Joly de Lotbinière defended Letellier, to the point of going to London to intervene with the British government. Letellier's fate, however, was out of their hands and in those of the governor general, the newly arrived Marquis of Lorne (married to Queen Victoria's daughter, Princess Louise). The Conservative majority in the Commons wanted Letellier dismissed and, "après de houleux débats, la Chambre des communes demande au gouverneur général, le marquis de Lorne, d'user de son pouvoir et de révoquer Letellier."[28] In the absence of any precedent, Lorne was reluctant to act in the minefield of federal-provincial relations. The matter was raised with the Colonial Secretary in Disraeli's government and, since it involved her son-in-law, with Queen Victoria herself. The outcome was that the governor general was told to act on the advice of his Canadian ministers. Pressed by both Ottawa and London, Lorne acceded to the request and Letellier was removed from office in 1879 — causing a controversy almost as great as that of his dismissal of the government the year before.[29]

The second dismissal of a lieutenant governor, Thomas Edgar McInnes of British Columbia in 1900, was much less controversial. Although a former Liberal senator, McInnes incurred the displeasure of Laurier's government in Ottawa because of his dubious dismissals of Premiers Turner in 1898 and Semlin in 1900. Even more annoying to the federal cabinet was McInnes's selection of Joseph Martin to replace Semlin and his reluctance to dissolve the Legislature when Martin lost a confidence vote. Unfortunately for McInnes, Martin failed to secure a majority in the election and resigned, thus depriving the lieutenant governor of any rationale for the dismissal of Semlin. (Anger's dismissal of Mercier in Quebec in 1891 succeeded because Boucher de Boucherville — himself a previous "dismissee" — won a crushing electoral majority.) Laurier's cabinet had had enough of McInnes's machinations and asked him to resign. When McInnes refused to do so, the cabinet passed an order-in-council dismissing him. "[F]from first to last," said the minister of justice, "he never rightly grasped either the spirit or the principles of our system of government, so far as it related to the functions of the representative of the sovereign in a province of this Dominion."[30] This was the last dismissal of a lieutenant governor in Canada.

The erroneous notion of a five-year "term" for lieutenant governors derives from the minimum tenure prescribed in section 59 of the *British North America Act*. In discussions prior to Confederation, there was an assumption that the term would normally be about five years (that of the colonial governor had been six). Early federal governments were criticized by the opposition if they left lieutenant governors in place much longer. Cases in point were John Beverley Robinson in Ontario (1880–1887), Sir Leonard Tilley in New Brunswick (1885–1893), and Sir John Schultz in Manitoba (1888–1895). Second terms, that is, renewals of a lieutenant governor's commissions, have been rare — eleven in all.[31]

Since 1900, federal governments have tended to replace lieutenant governors within about a year after their fifth anniversary, but this is not a hard and fast rule. In Manitoba, some lieutenant governors served a decade or more, with Robert Fairbairn McWilliams holding the record of thirteen years, from 1940 to 1953. Alberta had a similar experience: in its first seventy years as a province, five of nine lieutenant governors remained in office nine years or more, with John Bowen (1937–1950) — the lieutenant governor who clashed with Premier Aberhart — matching the Manitoba record of thirteen years. This record was also equalled by David MacLaren in New Brunswick (1945–1958). In Saskatchewan, Henry Newlands was reappointed in 1926 after five years, the only such case in the province's history, and served a further four years in the position. During the Second World War, Mackenzie King's government asked lieutenant governors to stay in office for the duration. Thus Archibald McNab was Saskatchewan's lieutenant governor for nine years, from 1936 to 1945; Ontario Lieutenant Governor A.E. Matthews stayed for nine years, 1937–1946; and in Quebec, Sir Eugène Fiset held office for eleven years (1939–1950). Hédard Robichaud was New Brunswick's vice-regal representative for ten years (1971–1981). George Pearkes served in British Columbia for eight years (1960–1968). In Quebec,

Hugues Lapointe served for twelve years (1966–1978) and Lise Thibault for ten years (1997–2007). In Saskatchewan, William Patterson served for nearly seven years (1951–1958), as did Robert Hanbidge (1963–1970), while Lynda Haverstock served six and a half years, from 2000 to 2006.

Not only is the office of lieutenant governor protected by sections 59 and 92(1) of the *Constitution Act, 1867*, but it is so essential that a provincial government cannot function without it. If a lieutenant governor should die in office, the government cannot pass orders-in-council or special warrants or recall the Legislature. While an "administrator," usually the chief justice, can fill in for the lieutenant governor in the event of absence or illness, this is not the case if a lieutenant governor dies in office. The Letters Patent of King George VI of 1947 provide for the chief justice of Canada to act in the event of the death of the governor general, but no such provision applies to the lieutenant governor. In Saskatchewan in 1978, when Lieutenant Governor George Porteous died in office two years after his appointment, Chief Justice E.M. Culliton informed the government that he could no longer function as administrator.[32] A similar situation had occurred in Quebec in 1929, when Sir Lomer Gouin died, literally, in his office, just before prorogation of the Legislature. Prorogation had to be postponed until a new lieutenant governor had been sworn in. In March 1937, Alberta Lieutenant Governor Philip Primrose — successor to William Walsh and predecessor of John Bowen — died after fewer than six months in office. This prevented the government from introducing money bills and authorizing spending for the coming fiscal year. In all three cases cited above, the federal government acted speedily in making vice-regal appointments, to enable the provincial governments to continue to operate.

DECLINE OF THE LIEUTENANT GOVERNOR

The partisan nature of the vice-regal appointments by the federal government, often of people of a different political stripe than the provincial government, led to distant, sometimes even hostile, relations between the lieutenant governor and his ministers. Understandably, premiers and their cabinets did not view such lieutenant governors as impartial confidants, especially if they had held seats on the opposing side of the House in their own legislatures. It did not help when some lieutenant governors continued to indulge in partisan activity. As John Saywell put it:

> The decline in the influence of the Lieutenant-Governor [...] need not have been so rapid and so complete if one elementary maxim had been learned and scrupulously followed: the monarch may be politically biased but must be politically neutral. [...] To confide in the Lieutenant-Governor was too often like giving secrets to the enemy. [...] he was never beyond suspicion. [...] while normal constitutional development reduced the Lieutenant-Governor's power political partiality destroyed his influence.[33]

Relations between lieutenant governors and premiers ranged from cordial and correct to distant, formal, and sometimes downright hostile. Few premiers instituted regular meetings with their lieutenant governors. While most were realistic enough to accept the constitutional right of Ottawa to appoint lieutenant governors, what rankled with them was the lack of consultation on the selection of their royal representative. The federal government *might* observe the courtesy of informal consultation with a premier of the same political stripe, but always denied any requirement or even convention to do so. Often provincial governments of a different party were simply informed of the appointment — if they were so fortunate, before the formal announcement was made. CCF and NDP governments, given that their party had not held power in Ottawa, never had the luxury of such informal consultation as might be conceded to their Liberal and Conservative counterparts.

The first CCF administration of Premier T.C. Douglas in Saskatchewan learned this to its chagrin in 1944 when it requested consultation on the next appointment from the federal Liberal government. This was soundly rebuffed by Prime Minister Mackenzie King. (A year later King behaved similarly with Quebec premier Maurice Duplessis.) To drive the point home, King then appointed Reginald Parker (1945–1948) and John Uhrich (1948–1951), both former Liberal

MLAs and cabinet ministers. The next Liberal appointee, by Prime Minister Louis St. Laurent, was none other than the premier defeated by Douglas in 1944, William Patterson (1951–1958). Understandably, the Saskatchewan CCF hardly viewed these lieutenant governors as impartial arbiters, much less as confidants. From its point of view, things went from bad to worse when the Progressive Conservatives were in power in Ottawa. To succeed Patterson in 1958, Prime Minister John Diefenbaker appointed Regina lawyer Frank Bastedo, who had at one point served as president of a federal Conservative constituency association. As already noted, in 1961 Bastedo stunned the nation by reserving royal assent to a bill for the consideration of the governor general. It was the first time this had happened since 1937, in Alberta. It was the only use of the power of reservation in Saskatchewan and the last in the country. Although the federal government hastened to overrule Bastedo and give royal assent to the bill, not surprisingly the incident infuriated the Saskatchewan CCF and embittered them towards an institution that they had tolerated but never embraced. Bastedo's successor, Robert "Dinny" Hanbidge (1963–1970), was, in marked contrast to his predecessor, informal, low-key, and non-controversial. Still, he had been a Conservative MLA and MP and resigned his seat in the House of Commons to take up the position. Relations between the CCF, later the New Democratic Party (NDP), and the lieutenant governor remained frigid. The Saskatchewan vice-regal office had reached its lowest ebb.

In several instances, the hostility of provincial governments to the lieutenant governor and resentment over the federal appointments became bitter and personal. As early as 1898, New Brunswick's historic Government House in Fredericton had been closed by the province as an economy measure. In 1925, a backbencher in Alberta's United Farmers government proposed closing Government House in Edmonton and eliminating the position of lieutenant governor. A motion to close Government House was adopted by the Legislature and the House was put on the market. However, after only one bid was received, the motion was rescinded and Government House had a reprieve — brief, as it turned out. In 1934, at the height of the Depression, a motion was moved in the Saskatchewan Legislative Assembly to suspend the office of lieutenant governor; it was defeated. During the 1920s, 1930s, and 1940s,

Progressive, Social Credit, and CCF elected members in western Canada periodically urged the abolition of the vice-regal office as an undemocratic institution and an inappropriate expense. They were joined by politicians in Ontario and Quebec. Liberal Premier Mitch Hepburn of Ontario, elected in 1934, resented the lieutenant governor as a functionary of Ottawa, threatened to starve out the incumbent, and closed Government House, Chorley Park, in Toronto in 1937.

It was noted earlier that Premier William Aberhart of Alberta sought revenge on Lieutenant Governor John Bowen for his 1937 reservation of royal assent, as well as on the federal government for its use of disallowance, by closing Government House in Edmonton in 1938. There was a public confrontation, with Bowen refusing to leave the House and Aberhart cutting off the utilities and firing the staff. Forced to sign an order-in-council closing Government House, besieged by protesters, Bowen gave in and moved to a suite in the Hotel Macdonald. The furnishings in Government House were auctioned off, and the lieutenant governor was denied a car, driver, secretary, and supplies, despite the pleadings of Prime Minister Mackenzie King.[34] The rift between premier and lieutenant governor became painfully obvious during the tour

Ontario's Government House, Chorley Park in Toronto, was closed in 1937 by Premier Mitch Hepburn, who viewed the lieutenant governor as an agent of Ottawa.

of King George VI and Queen Elizabeth in 1939. The King had heard about the controversial closure of Government House and on arrival in Edmonton asked Bowen if they could drive by it. Aberhart tried unsuccessfully to keep the lieutenant governor out of sight during the visit. Bowen retaliated, when the King and Queen came for tea in his Legislature building office, by shutting the door in the face of Aberhart and his wife! Mackenzie King came to the rescue, going into the corridor, retrieving the couple, and bringing them to the tea. At the provincial dinner for the King and Queen, Aberhart and his wife, contrary to protocol, arranged to be seated next to the royal couple and monopolized the conversation, relegating Bowen and his wife to places near the ends of the head table. The lieutenant governor threatened to leave the dinner early but was dissuaded by Mackenzie King. The prime minister came to the rescue again, this time for Bowen: discovering that the lieutenant governor had no vehicle, because the premier had cut off his allowance the previous year, Mackenzie King offered him a lift home in his own car.[35]

Five years later, in 1944, early in the mandate of the first social democratic government in North America, CCF Premier T.C. Douglas announced the closure of Saskatchewan's historic Government House in Regina. He also recommended to the federal government that the position of lieutenant governor be eliminated and the duties carried out by the chief justice. "[T]he duties of the lieutenant governor are not onerous," he said, "and can be easily discharged by Chief Justice W.M. Martin, or a person in a similar position, without burdening him too heavily."[36] While the position of lieutenant governor was beyond the control of the province, protected by the *Constitution Act, 1867,* Government House was not. In shades of the Alberta saga seven years earlier, Government House's furnishings were sold by auction and the lieutenant governor's office moved to the Hotel Saskatchewan. There it remained for nearly forty years. In the pungent words of one commentator, "[f]or much of the ensuing half-century, Saskatchewan political society treated the lieutenant governor's position as the governmental equivalent of an appendix — only noticed if and when it gives you trouble."[37]

By the 1970s, the office of the lieutenant governor had fallen into obscurity, and not just in Saskatchewan and Alberta. One factor was the increased profile, prestige, and power of the federal government during and following the Second World War. A series of events and initiatives focused attention on Ottawa: defence during the Cold War, the introduction of national social programs like Medicare and the Canada Pension Plan in the 1960s, symbolic acts such as the Canadian flag of 1965 and the centennial in 1967, and the crisis of the *Front de libération du Québec* in 1970. Provincial governments were in eclipse and their vice-regal representatives even more so. Furthermore, in the 1950s and 1960s the office of governor general benefited from the appointment of prestigious Canadians: Vincent Massey (1952–1959), Georges Vanier (1959–1967), and Roland Michener (1967–1974). The lieutenant governors paled in comparison and the appointments were often, although by no means always, pedestrian in nature and primarily of former politicians or party faithful. It was a reflection of the diminished status of the provinces.

VICE-REGAL REVIVAL IN CANADA'S PROVINCES

Yet the seeds of change were being sown. The Quiet Revolution of the 1960s in Quebec propelled that most distinct province from political torpor into an unprecedented activist economic and social role for the state. In all provinces, the dramatically increased importance of health and education redirected public attention to provincial jurisdiction. So did the growing economic clout of provincial natural resources, especially oil and gas in Alberta, potash and uranium in Saskatchewan, and mining and hydro-electric power in Manitoba, British Columbia, Ontario, and Quebec.

In the 1970s, whether by coincidence or in consequence, the lieutenant governors started to recover from obscurity. One key factor was the selection of the incumbents. These individuals came from more varied backgrounds and did not necessarily have ties to the governing party in Ottawa. Eminent educator and writer Grant MacEwan was named to the Alberta position in 1966, followed eight years later by the first Aboriginal lieutenant governor in Canada, Ralph Steinhauer. Historian George Stanley was appointed to the New Brunswick post in 1981. Lincoln Alexander became the first vice-regal African-Canadian as lieutenant governor of Ontario in 1985; David Lam the first of Chinese origin, in British Columbia in 1988; and Yvon Dumont the first Métis, in Manitoba in 1993. The first women were appointed: Pauline McGibbon in Ontario in 1974, Pearl McGonigal in Manitoba in 1981, Helen Hunley in Alberta in 1985, and Sylvia Fedoruk in Saskatchewan in 1988. By 2009, all provinces except Newfoundland and Labrador had had female appointees. There is no doubt that this had a major effect on the profile and popular appeal of the office. One observer was of the view that the appointment of women, starting in Canada two decades earlier than in Australia, "helped transform both the image and the priorities of a lieutenant-governor."[38]

While some of the appointees after the 1970s owed their positions to their political connections or service, most of them easily transcended their partisan past. All had solid credentials. Hilary Weston brought a high business and philanthropic profile to the job in Ontario (1997–2002); her successor, James Bartleman (2002–2007), was a distinguished former diplomat and First Nations member. Lois Hole in Alberta (2000–2005) was a well-known gardening expert and author, and her successor, Norman Kwong (2005–2010), a prominent former athlete and business-man. Lise Thibault in Quebec (1997–2007), in a wheelchair herself, had been chair of the provincial Office for Disabled Persons. Herménégilde Chiasson, appointed lieutenant governor of New Brunswick by Jean Chrétien in 2003, was a prominent Acadian poet, artist, and playwright.

His successor was the first Aboriginal lieutenant governor of the province, provincial court judge Graydon Nicholas from the Tobique First Nation, named by Stephen Harper in 2009. Indeed, Harper, on becoming prime minister in 2006, had resumed Jean Chrétien's practice of generally sound vice-regal appointments. The first one that year, Gordon Barnhart of Saskatchewan, was clearly non-partisan. Mayann Francis, named as the first African-Canadian lieutenant governor of Nova Scotia, had been provincial ombudsman and director of the human rights commission. Barbara Hagerman, appointed in the same year in Prince Edward Island, was the wife of major Conservative fundraiser but was herself a widely respected musical educator. Steven Point, named as British Columbia's lieutenant governor in 2007, had been a First Nations chief and a pro-vincial court judge. His successor, Judith Guichon, who took office in 2012, was a well-known figure in agriculture, from a family that had been ranchers since the 1870s. David Onley, appointed to the Ontario vice-regal office in 2007, wheelchair-bound like Lise Thibault, had been a broadcaster and advocate for the disabled. Philip Lee, Manitoba lieutenant governor from 2009, born in Hong Kong, was a leading light in Winnipeg's Chinese-Canadian community. Retired colonel Donald Ethell, appointed lieutenant governor of Alberta in 2010, had had a distinguished military and professional career. So had Brigadier-General John Grant, appointed to Nova Scotia in 2012. Frank Lewis, a broadcast executive and community volunteer, was named lieutenant governor of Prince Edward Island in 2011. Appointed to the Saskatchewan position in 2012, Regina businesswoman Vaughn Solomon Schofield was well known for her volunteer support for the Canadian Forces.

Even the most obviously partisan appointees — Iona Campagnolo of British Columbia, a former Liberal cabinet minister in Ottawa and former president of the federal Liberal Party, appointed by Jean Chrétien (2001–2007), and John Crosbie, a former Conservative minister appointed in 2008 by Stephen Harper in Newfoundland and Labrador — enjoyed considerable prestige well beyond their own parties. Crosbie's successor, Frank Fagan, appointed in 2013, was a respected business, leader, humanitarian, philanthropist, and volunteer; he was the first to be selected through a vice-regal appointments committee announced in 2012. Harper chose well in his vice-regal appointees: they were committed to the Crown and the monarchy; they were not tokens for some particular group; and, having had prominent careers, they were respected in the community.

A problem faced by prime ministers is finding qualified individuals who will accept vice-regal positions. The lieutenant governor's office is no sinecure. People with careers hesitate before accepting a position which will mean for many a drop in income and difficulty in finding employment after they leave office. Retirees must weigh the demands placed on their health by the relentless vice-regal schedule. Another factor is the implications for the spouses of the candidates; their attitude and support can have a major effect on the success of the vice-regal position, which is not always to the taste of the partner. It is no wonder that some candidates turn down the offer of an appointment as lieutenant governor.

Promoting the Crown

Another aspect of the revived provincial vice-regal offices from the 1970s was their active promotion of the Crown. This came at the very time the federal government and successive governors general were downplaying the institution, ostensibly to "Canadianize" it — an approach that continued into the first decade of the twenty-first century. Whereas the governors general from 1979 to 1999 were clearly political appointees, the lieutenant governors were much less so. And whereas Rideau Hall minimized the royal connection and the role of the Sovereign, lieutenant governors actively portrayed themselves as the Queen's representatives. Consciously or unconsciously, they were asserting provincial status in Confederation through the vice-regal office. Christopher McCreery, calling the post-1970 lieutenant governors "stalwart promoters of the Crown," notes that, unlike the governor general, they had to rely "heavily upon the reflective prestige of the Crown for their own authority and status." At the same time, he said, they reinforced the provincial dimension of the Crown by explaining "their role as constitutional heads and ceremonial promoters of their respective provinces; this has tended to dovetail nicely with the promotion of the Crown and the role it plays within our democratic system."[39]

A Case Study: Saskatchewan

Prime Minister Pierre Trudeau appointed Stephen Worobetz in 1970 as the first Saskatchewan lieutenant governor of Ukrainian origin. This was an early signal of the changing approach to the provincial vice-regal office in Canada. A Saskatoon surgeon, Dr. Worobetz was a supporter of the Liberal Party. But, in a distinct break with the usual practice of the last six decades in the province, he was not active politically and had not held political office, either elected or within the party. In another departure from previous practice, he was first approached by Premier Ross Thatcher to see if he would accept the post before Trudeau called to offer it. Thatcher made it clear to the federal Liberals that it was long overdue for a person of Ukrainian origin to be appointed to the vice-regal office in a province where this ethnic group played a key economic and social role; Stephen Worobetz was the ideal candidate. The appointment was well received partly for this reason, but was also because Worobetz himself was widely admired. He had been decorated with the Military Cross for courage under fire as a doctor with the Canadian Army in the Italian campaign in the Second World War. His modest and unassuming character won him general respect. Allan Blakeney, NDP premier from 1971 to 1982, encompassing four of Worobetz's five years in office, considered that his appointment marked a turning point in the fortunes of the vice-regal office in Saskatchewan. The lieutenant governor was no longer a blatantly partisan appointee but someone chosen and respected for his own merits.[40]

All of the lieutenant governors who followed were able to maintain the upward trajectory. To succeed Worobetz in 1976, the Trudeau government appointed another person with exemplary war service and without political baggage: seventy-two-year-old George Porteous of Saskatoon, who had worked for the YMCA. Attached to the Canadian Army in Hong Kong, he was a Japanese prisoner of war from 1941 to 1945 and was made a Member of the Order of the British Empire for service to his fellow prisoners. Allan Blakeney respected this lieutenant governor as he had Worobetz and endeavoured to persuade the frugal Porteous to accept more resources from the provincial government, such as travelling with a car and driver rather than taking the bus.[41] But since Porteous died in office in 1978, he made relatively little impact on the vice-regal position.

This was not the case for Porteous's replacement, hastily chosen only days after his death in office, again by Trudeau. C. Irwin McIntosh, a newspaper publisher in North Battleford, was from a prominent Liberal family. While his father had been a Liberal MP for fifteen years, McIntosh himself had not held elected or party office. He appeared at first too outspoken for the provincial government's taste, but he soon earned their approval for his rock-solid support for the national unity campaign following the election of the first Parti Québécois government in Quebec. He also worked tirelessly for the seventy-fifth anniversary of the Province of Saskatchewan in 1980. By the time Irwin McIntosh left office in 1983, the lieutenant governor's role in public life had stabilized and regained momentum.

Trudeau's fourth vice-regal appointee built on this improved stature. Frederick W. Johnson was the archetype of the respected citizen: teacher, war veteran, school trustee, superior court judge, and, at the time of his appointment, chief justice of the Court of Queen's Bench. His attempts to win election for the Liberals federally and provincially had receded into the past. Johnson's appointment emerged after internecine squabbling between factions of the Saskatchewan Liberal establishment over potential candidates. The rumours exasperated Johnson to the point where he considered turning down the position if it were offered.[42] Fortunately, it *was* offered and Johnson accepted. Under the Conservative government of Grant Devine, he was to inaugurate a veritable renaissance of vice-regal prestige in the province.

The only Saskatchewan vice-regal appointment by Progressive Conservative Prime Minister Brian Mulroney was that of Johnson's successor in 1988. The first female lieutenant governor was a non-partisan academic, Sylvia Fedoruk, who had just retired from a distinguished career in cancer research at the University of Saskatchewan. In making this appointment, Mulroney relied on the counsel of Ramon Hnatyshyn, later to become governor general. The Saskatoon cabinet minister admired his fellow Ukrainian Canadian, and Fedoruk became a popular lieutenant governor. While she had no political experience, she quickly learned the ropes and proved to be an asset to governance in the province.

The appointments of Jack Wiebe in 1994 and Lynda Haverstock in 1999, when Roy Romanow was NDP premier, were Prime Minister Jean Chrétien's choices — individuals who had his confidence and respect. He consulted Romanow to the extent of checking with him on their suitability before making his final decision. Although Wiebe had once been a Liberal MLA and continued to be active in the Liberal Party, he had been out of electoral politics for some time. A popular, down-to-earth farmer, Wiebe was well liked by people of all political persuasions. Lynda Haverstock, on the other hand, had more recent political baggage. She had become provincial Liberal leader in 1989, the first woman to head a political party in Saskatchewan. After her election to the Legislature in 1991, she led the party from one MLA to eleven in 1995, when the notoriously fractious Saskatchewan Liberals ousted her in a caucus revolt. She served as an independent member of the assembly until retiring in the 1999 election.

Chrétien and Romanow shared some concern about Haverstock's recent partisan past, but they agreed that she would overcome this. And they were proved right. A university teacher, clinical psychologist, and expert on farm stress, Lynda Haverstock was energetic, eloquent, and persuasive in her public role and resolutely non-partisan. She vigorously supported and promoted Saskatchewan's arts, culture, tourism, and economy, culminating in the province's centennial in 2005. One observer said that "she made Saskatchewan people rethink the role of the lieutenant governor," adding that she projected "an image of confidence and grace; many appreciated that their Saskatchewan had such a devoted ambassador."[43] It was fitting that Haverstock served as president and CEO of Tourism Saskatchewan from 2007 to 2012 and that she received the Order of Canada and an honorary doctorate from Queen's University.

As already noted, Conservative Prime Minister Stephen Harper's first vice-regal appointment, shortly after the election of his minority government in 2006, was for Saskatchewan. It was not a well-kept secret that names of prominent sports figures and a former minister in Brian Mulroney's government were being considered. To his credit, Harper first approached a well-respected First Nations businessman. The lack of experience in Harper's new office team showed when this person not only turned down the appointment but, embarrassingly, and contrary to protocol, shared the news with a number of others. Considerable effort was made to keep this situation "under the radar." Harper learned the hard way that he should only offer vice-regal appointments after his staff had first confirmed the willingness of the candidate to serve.

Following this faux pas, Gordon L. Barnhart was named Saskatchewan's twentieth lieutenant governor. This time, the prime minister arranged for the candidate to come to Ottawa for a personal interview, where Harper requested, and received, his assurance that he would accept. It was a solid appointment. Barnhart had been clerk of the Saskatchewan Legislature for twenty years, from 1969 to 1989. After five years as clerk of the Senate in Ottawa, he returned to his home province to teach history at the University of Saskatchewan and turned his Ph.D. thesis on Walter Scott into a definitive biography of Saskatchewan's first premier. Barnhart filled two criteria for Harper. First, having retired from the university, he was at the end of his career and thus avoided the difficulty faced by Lynda Haverstock, who needed to find other employment after leaving the vice-regal office. Second, Barnhart was rigorously non-partisan, to the point that, as clerk of the legislative assembly, he had refused to vote in elections. Gordon Barnhart was also an acknowledged authority on parliamentary government and had been an international consultant on democratic institutions, which proved to be an asset in his constitutional role. Making good use of his experience and knowledge, he served diligently and competently in the vice-regal position until 2012. He then demonstrated how retired lieutenant governors could continue to serve the public good by chairing an International Minerals Innovation Institute to recruit skilled workers for Saskatchewan's booming mining industry, and by planning to add to his publications on Saskatchewan governance.[44]

After rumours among local Conservatives that several people had been approached and at least one had turned down the offer, Prime Minister Harper appointed Vaughn Solomon Schofield to be Barnhart's successor, bringing her to Ottawa for the announcement. She was a member of prominent Saskatchewan family; her father, George Solomon, had been a leading businessman in the province and was one of the first recipients of the Saskatchewan Order of Merit in 1985. Solomon Schofield was known to be a supporter of the federal Conservatives and the provincial Saskatchewan Party. However, she had proven credentials in business and she was a strong advocate for the Canadian Forces, fundraising for veterans and their families and serving as honorary lieutenant-colonel of an army reserve unit. It was a sign of the now assured prestige of the Saskatchewan vice-regal office that approval for her appointment cut across party lines, and NDP opposition leader John Nilson was one of those publicly congratulating her. Solomon Schofield hit the ground running: mere weeks after her installation she received the Prince of Wales and Duchess of Cornwall for their brief Diamond Jubilee visit to Regina. Presiding over the jubilee celebrations in the province, she quickly adapted to the position and proved to be an able speaker and host.

VICE-REGAL UPS AND DOWNS: THE STORY OF SASKATCHEWAN'S GOVERNMENT HOUSE[45]

The most obvious physical presence of the Crown in Saskatchewan is Government House in Regina, built in 1891 as the official residence and office of the lieutenant governors of the Northwest Territories. This substantial mansion was designed by Thomas Fuller, architect of the Parliament Buildings in Ottawa, to be an imposing symbol of national and imperial rule over the vast Canadian western plains and northern territories. At the height of the territorial empire, two-thirds of Canada was administered from Government House in Regina — all of present-day Saskatchewan and Alberta, much of northern Manitoba, Ontario, and Quebec, the Northwest Territories, Nunavut, and, until 1898, the Yukon. Following the creation of Alberta and Saskatchewan from the Territories in 1905, the Province of Saskatchewan inherited the facility. The story of Government House then mirrored the fortunes of the vice-regal institution in the new province. Amédée Forget, last lieutenant governor of the Northwest Territories and first of the Province of Saskatchewan, continued in residence after the inauguration on September 4, 1905. For forty more years, Government House and its ample grounds served as a social hub for Regina society and the Saskatchewan political class.

When the palatial Legislative Building was opened in 1912 during the province's first boom years, an office was provided for the lieutenant governor, but there is no evidence that it was ever used as such, except occasionally for ceremonial purposes. This was in contrast to the practice in Alberta, Manitoba, and Ontario, where the vice-regal offices are located in their legislative buildings; Saskatchewan lieutenant governors, like those of the other provinces, and in keeping with the principle that the Crown should be removed from partisan politics, operated out of Government House. There was an abortive plan in 1913 to build a large and elegant Government House on the shores of Wascana Lake opposite the Legislative Building. The outbreak of the First World War in 1914 meant that such grandiose projects were permanently shelved.[46] Instead, the existing Government House was expanded with the addition of a ballroom in 1928. Vice-regal entertaining continued even during the Depression years of the 1930s, although on a smaller scale. In 1939, Lieutenant Governor Archibald McNab hosted a memorable banquet in the ballroom for King George VI and Queen Elizabeth during their historic cross-Canada tour.

The Decline and Near Fall of Government House

With the Second World War, 1939–1945, came major changes: social, economic, and political. The Co-operative Commonwealth Federation, born of the Depression, swept into office in 1944. Skeptical of the vice-regal office, the government of Premier T.C. Douglas decided to close Government House as an unwanted symbol and unnecessary expense.* The premier said, "[t]he upkeep of Government House is a frill which we cannot afford particularly when this province is struggling to provide social services. It is a relic of a bygone age."[47] Without opposition in the Legislature, Douglas closed Government House in 1945, incurring the protests of the Saskatchewan Historical Society, the Regina Board of Trade, the Canadian Legion, and a Regina *Leader-Post* editorial ("it eliminates an inward as well as an outward bond of neighbourly association between the people of the province and the representative of His Majesty").[48] Most of Government House's furnishings were sold by auction at bargain-basement prices. Eventually all but four acres of the fifty-three-acre grounds would also be sold. For the next four decades, the lieutenant governors functioned in a small suite in the Hotel Saskatchewan, the smallest, cheapest vice-regal operation in the country.

---

* As previously noted, Government Houses had been closed for similar reasons by New Brunswick in 1898, Ontario in 1937, and Alberta in 1938.

Meanwhile, Government House itself lurched through several crises. From 1946 to 1957, it was leased to the federal government as a veterans' rehabilitation centre. In 1958, the provincial government resumed operation of the facility under the name Saskatchewan House, as a centre for continuous learning. The grand old edifice, stripped of its elegant furnishings, the victim of ad-hoc renovations adapted to the requirements of its various tenants, was deteriorating inside and out. The CCF government had considered its demolition in 1958. The threat was more serious under Ross Thatcher's Liberal administration after 1964. This galvanized a dedicated group of citizens who formed the Saskatchewan House Committee in 1969 (renamed, after restoration, the Government House Historical Society). In the vanguard of the heritage movement, the committee vigorously lobbied the provincial government to preserve the House as a historic property. It presented a brief to the Thatcher government in 1970 and was successful in having Government House declared a national historic site in 1971.

Revival and Renewal

In 1974, the NDP government decided in principle to restore Government House. The multi-million-dollar restoration was undertaken between 1978 and 1980 as a project for the province's seventy-fifth anniversary. The facility was in Premier Allan Blakeney's constituency, and he took a personal interest and considerable pride in the project. The Saskatchewan resource economy was booming, government revenues were escalating, and no expense was spared to restore the property to its original grandeur. The irony did not escape observers that the direct successor of the CCF administration that had closed the House was now scouring the province for the antiques and artifacts which its predecessor had "sold for a song" in the 1945 auction. But times had changed. On September 4, 1980, the date of the seventy-fifth anniversary of the inauguration of the Province of Saskatchewan in 1905, Lieutenant Governor McIntosh and Premier Blakeney, arriving in the recently recuperated provincial horse-drawn landau, presided at the official opening of the resplendent Government House Historic Property.

The main portion of the restored Government House was a museum, depicting the turn-of-the-century residence of Lieutenant Governor Amédée Forget and Madame Forget. It became a magnet for school groups from across the province. The House was also a venue for concerts, plays, functions of non-profit organizations, and an entertainment facility for the government, including the lieutenant governor. But, by a cabinet decision in 1977, it was *not* to accommodate the vice-regal offices (and a residence was out of the question). Twenty years later, Allan Blakeney did not recall any conscious opposition to the idea and thought that it would have happened in due course.[49] Others attributed the decision to the lingering hostility to the office of the lieutenant governor in the ranks of NDP politicians and officials. A trial balloon floated in 1981 to install the lieutenant governor's office (but not residence) in Government House was quickly shot down at the officials' level, although Blakeney himself expressed mild interest.[50] It was left to Blakeney's Progressive Conservative successor, Grant Devine, to take the next, logical step four years later. Devine directed that the north wing of Government House be converted into a suite of offices for the lieutenant governor, and the new office was inaugurated on Canada Day, 1984. But in 1991, ironically marking the centennial of the historic property, Devine's administration, nearing the end of its mandate, proposed to "privatize" the House by transferring it to the Government House Historical Society, a task well beyond the capabilities of the volunteer group. Fortunately, the House was again rescued by a change of government.

Revival and Renewal Redux — and Expansion

Soon after assuming office late in 1991, Roy Romanow and his NDP government made it clear that Government House Heritage Property was a prized public asset and that they would not countenance its privatization. Responding to Romanow's call for a long-range vision, a study was commissioned on the future of Government House. It identified considerable potential for tourism, school programs, government functions, and vice-regal activities and recommended construction of

Built in 1891, Saskatchewan's historic Government House faced demolition in the 1960s. It was restored in 1980 and expanded in 2005 for the province's centennial.
Office of the Lieutenant Governor of Saskatchewan

new facilities. Part of the plan was the restoration of the grounds to the 1905 Edwardian gardens of landscape architect George Watt. The report also proposed creation of a Crown foundation to raise some of the funds from the non-governmental sector. In 2001, the government of Premier Lorne Calvert approved the proposal on the understanding that the cost would be shared three ways, between the province, the federal government, and the foundation. The Government House Foundation was established and an architectural competition held for an addition to the original building.

In 2004, the Princess Royal (the Queen's daughter, Princess Anne) dedicated the cornerstone for the new Queen Elizabeth II Wing of Government House. By the end of the year, the addition was complete, incorporating offices, an elegant hall named after Lieutenant Governor Sir Richard Lake, and a display area for the landau. The J.E.N. Wiebe Interpretive Centre on the Crown was installed above the 1928 ballroom; it was the only one of its kind in the country and named in tribute to the lieutenant governor who contributed the idea. The original building was designated the Queen Victoria Wing. Other facilities were named after former lieutenant governors, emphasizing the links to Saskatchewan's monarchical and vice-regal history. In 2005, during her visit for the provincial centennial, Queen Elizabeth II officially opened the wing named in her honour, as well as the interpretive centre. The monarch attended a reception in the ballroom where her parents, King George VI and Queen Elizabeth, had dined with Lieutenant Governor McNab in 1939.

Premier Brad Wall's Saskatchewan Party government, taking office late in 2007, continued the momentum. In 2005, a shortfall in federal funding had prevented restoration of the Edwardian gardens. The new provincial government leveraged federal funding by committing its own, and the gardens were completed in 2009. In 2010, the museum was converted into a state-of-the-art self-guided tour. Thus Government House — reborn and renewed — realized its potential. So had those for whom it was built in 1891: the lieutenant governors.

V

The Contemporary Provincial Crown

Garant de la loi et de son autorité, le lieutenant-gouverneur incarne les trois pouvoirs de l'État: le législatif, l'exécutif et le judiciaire [...] le lieutenant-gouverneur se situe donc à un point stratégique d'équilibre entre l'autorité légale et le pouvoir légitime.[1]
— Lemieux, Blais, Hamelin

THE CONSTITUTIONAL ROLE

Lord Haldane's statement in 1925 that the provinces "should be autonomous places as if they were autonomous kingdoms" could be deemed excessive. Lieutenant governors do not see themselves as heads of autonomous kingdoms. But they do see themselves as the Queen's direct representatives for co-sovereign jurisdictions within Canada. It has been said that in Canada "sovereignty is vested in one individual, the reigning monarch, acting in Parliament for some purposes and in the provincial Legislatures for others."[2] First and foremost, the lieutenant governor is at the constitutional apex of the province, holding royal prerogative powers in the name of the Queen. It is a crucial role. The lieutenant governor is the incarnation of provincial autonomy in Confederation and acts as a constitutional umpire and guarantor. The Quebec authors already cited, referring to "la couronne, gardien du droit," state that "[l]e lieutenant-gouverneur incarne la continuité des pouvoirs législatif et exécutif qu'il remet au chef du gouvernement élu. [...] Chef de l'État provincial, le lieutenant-gouverneur veille à son fonctionnement selon la volonté du peuple et *dans le respect de la Constitution* [our emphasis]."[3]

How does the lieutenant governor carry out this role today? First, by acting as a conduit for the ministers who are his/her advisers. The key role of the Crown is to validate the acts of the executive. It has contributed significantly to the strength of provincial jurisdiction through investing the provincial cabinets with the powers embedded in the royal prerogative. This is evident when lieutenant governors formally appoint premiers, give royal assent to bills or sign orders-in-council, prorogue or summon the assembly, read the speech from the throne, and grant dissolution of the House for an election. Lieutenant governors are very much conscious that they are sanctioning executive acts on behalf of Her Majesty in accordance with the principles of responsible government.

Appointment and Dissolution

In a minority situation in the Saskatchewan Legislature in 1929, the lieutenant governor invited the leader of another party to form a government rather than dissolving the House and calling a premature election. In the election that year, no party was returned with a majority. The Liberal government of James Gardiner had won the largest number of seats (twenty-eight of sixty-three) and share of the popular vote. However, the Conservatives had twenty-four seats and Progressives and Independents the remaining eleven; a few days after the election, the opposition members signed an agreement to support a government headed by the Conservative leader, Dr. J.T.M. Anderson. They then called on Gardiner to resign. The premier refused, arguing that he could not advise the lieutenant governor to call on an uncertain coalition to form a government, and announced his intention to meet the Legislature.[4] The opposition petitioned Lieutenant Governor Henry Newlands to dismiss the government. The lieutenant governor declined, "declaring that the Liberals, as the largest group in the Legislature, had a constitutional right to meet the Assembly, where the matter would be resolved."[5] The Legislature met in special session three months after the election. The opposition moved a motion of want of confidence in the throne speech, the government was defeated, and Gardiner resigned. Thereupon Lieutenant Governor Newlands called on Anderson to form a "Co-operative" administration of Conservatives, Progressives, and Independents — the only Saskatchewan coalition government until 1999. Newlands had followed the correct course, leaving it to the elected assembly to decide the fate of the government.

In the 1985 Ontario election, the governing Conservatives lost their majority. David Peterson, leader of the opposition Liberals, presented Lieutenant Governor John Black Aird with a signed agreement with the New Democratic Party, led by Bob Rae, to support them in the House for a two-year period. The incumbent Conservative government under Premier Frank Miller, like the Liberals in Saskatchewan in 1929, exercised its right to test the confidence of the new Legislature. When the government was defeated in the House on the address in reply to the speech from the throne, Miller resigned and the lieutenant governor invited the Liberal leader to form a government.[6]

Dissolution and Dismissal: A Case Study — British Columbia[7]

Vice-regal intervention is usually low key and confidential, and the Crown's representative must always remain scrupulously neutral. But a lieutenant governor of British Columbia, David Lam, did lift the veil, albeit inadvertently, when he wrote that he had been prepared to use the prerogative of dismissal if a disgraced and compromised premier did not resign.[8] This occurred in 1991. Premier William Vander Zalm, nearing the end of his government's constitutional five-year mandate, was under investigation by Justice Ted Hughes for allegedly having contravened his own conflict-of-interest guidelines. There was a concern that, if the Hughes Report found him guilty (which in the end it did), the premier might simply ignore the findings and ask the lieutenant governor for dissolution and a writ of election, given that there was dissension about his leadership in his own caucus. It was increasingly uncertain whether the premier could retain the confidence of the Legislature; several prominent members of his cabinet had resigned in a very public and politically embarrassing manner.

Lieutenant Governor Lam, having consulted constitutional advisers, concluded that an election in these circumstances would place the governing party at an unfair disadvantage and thus that it would be inappropriate to grant the premier's request, if made. The lieutenant governor's refusal to accept the "advice" of the first minister in this regard would leave the premier no option but to resign. Should he refuse to do so, the lieutenant governor would be obliged — and was prepared if necessary — to dismiss him. It did not come to this, because contacts between the offices of the lieutenant governor and the premier resulted in an agreement that the premier would resign if the Hughes Report concluded that he had contravened his own conflict-of-interest guidelines. Vander Zalm visited Lam to do just that shortly after the conclusions of the report were made public. The lieutenant governor then asked the chair of the government caucus for a recommendation on Vander Zalm's successor. Their nominee, Rita Johnson, was invited by the Queen's representative to become premier of British Columbia (her Social Credit party was soundly defeated in the ensuing election). It is a telling example of how the vice-regal office can play a discreet but effective role. As one observer put it, "the exercise was handled with constitutional elegance, as a low-key and graceful interposition of the reserve powers"[9] and "has come to be regarded as a paradigm model of economy in the use of power."[10]

Special Warrants: A Case Study — Saskatchewan

One of the statutory powers granted to the lieutenant governor is that of approving and signing special warrants at the request of cabinet, to approve government expenditures outside the normal legislative appropriation process.* Special warrants are normally "used towards the end of a fiscal year, when the Legislature is not sitting, to provide for any shortfall between the estimated amounts that were appropriated for the use of departments and the amount that is actually spent."[11] They are then

---

* The legislative provision in Saskatchewan is found in section 14 of *The Financial Administration Act, 1993*. Other provinces and the federal government have similar legislation.

retroactively approved by the Legislature in supplementary estimates. Merrilee Rasmussen gives the following explanation:

> A special warrant is a statutory exception to the basic rule of law that requires parliamentary consent to government expenditures. It is an exception that permits the Lieutenant Governor, at the request of Cabinet, to approve government expenditures in the Legislature's place under certain limited conditions [...] the power to authorize by special warrant is given to the Lieutenant Governor and not to the Cabinet directly. This suggests an intention that the Legislature has purposely provided to the Lieutenant Governor the legal ability to exercise independent action, recognizing that *the conventions of the constitution* [our emphasis] will constrain the Lieutenant Governor to exercising that legal power only in situations in which a "constitutional fire extinguisher" may be necessary.[12]

The lieutenant governor, while normally accepting advice from the government to sign special warrants, may thus, in an emergency, exercise a reserve power to refuse such a request.

Special warrants were put to frequent and questionable use from the late 1980s in Saskatchewan. In 1987, the Conservative government of Premier Grant Devine chose not to recall the Legislature and present its budget in the normal period of February–March or even after the beginning of the fiscal year on April 1. Instead, the government resorted to special warrants "to finance ordinary and predictable government expenditures at a time when the Legislature had had no opportunity to review and approve, or even to begin the process of review and approval of the budget and estimates on which these expenditures were based."[13] This was an infraction of the intent if not the letter of the legislation. Political science professor Howard Leeson wrote to Lieutenant Governor Frederick Johnson, urging him to recall the Legislature and require the government to present a budget. Johnson declined to do so, citing the governing legislation as justification for him not to refuse "advice," although he might balk at signing warrants if they were repeated indefinitely. For Leeson, the lieutenant governor's refusal to act called into question the very rationale for the existence of the Crown. But Johnson was clearly unwilling to test his reserve powers unless forced by a prolonged and serious political crisis. The former chief justice preferred to stand by the letter of the law.*

His successor, Sylvia Fedoruk, faced a more serious challenge in 1991. The Devine government was near the end of its constitutional five-year mandate. In June of that year, faced with the possibility of losing a vote of confidence, the government abruptly prorogued the Legislature without allowing the vote. An unhappy Sylvia Fedoruk, her face like a thundercloud, entered the legislative chamber to declare a prorogation which evidently went against her personal judgment. Since a budget had not been passed, the government again resorted to a series of special warrants to finance its expenditures. There was a political and public outcry. The lieutenant governor came under considerable pressure to refuse her signature to the warrants and even to dismiss the government. Fedoruk was placed in a dilemma: either sanction a use of the special warrant that was unconventional and possibly illegal, or resort to a perilous and unprecedented use of the reserve power. After consulting constitutional experts and Governor General Ramon Hnatyshyn, she made clear to the premier her disagreement with the government's actions but was not prepared to go beyond this. She concluded that it was up to the electorate, and not to the edict of an appointed official, to render final judgment.[14] In November of 1991, that electorate swept the Conservatives from office.

Johnson and Fedoruk, by their unwillingness to act in the highly questionable use of special warrants and, in Fedoruk's case, prorogation, undoubtedly circumscribed even further the already minimal exercise of the lieutenant governor's reserve powers. Unlike Frank Bastedo, with his reservation of royal assent in 1961, Johnson and Fedoruk took a restrictive view of their constitutional role. It has been argued that Fedoruk should have refused prorogation and that by not doing so, she missed a unique

---

* Frederick Johnson made his view clear in a conversation with the author at the time. Under threat of legal action by the NDP opposition, the government did recall the legislature in June 1987 and passed the budget.

Saskatchewan's first woman lieutenant governor, Sylvia Fedoruk, faced challenges over special warrants and prorogation, but was also the first to enjoy regular consultation with the premier.
Government of Saskatchewan

opportunity to restore constitutional credibility to the vice-regal office. According to this view, she and her predecessor would have enjoyed wide public support had they refused to sign the dubious series of special warrants. But exercising unprecedented reserve powers of prorogation and special warrants would have taken the vice-regal office into uncharted and dangerous waters. It is one of the many paradoxes of the office of the Saskatchewan lieutenant governor that New Democrats, who had decried Bastedo's use of reservation and had questioned the value of the vice-regal function at all, urged the lieutenant governor to exercise reserve powers when they were in opposition.[15] On balance, Johnson and Fedoruk were wise to act as they did. They realized that in the late twentieth century the public expected the media, the courts, public opinion, and ultimately the voters to deal with erring governments, not a federal appointee. Acting in the circumstances of 1987 and 1991, however great the provocation at the time, might have appeared to be yielding to partisan pressure and compromised the hard-won impartiality of the office of lieutenant governor.

Saskatchewan is not the only jurisdiction where special warrants have aroused controversy. In 1983, the leader of the opposition in British Columbia, David Barrett, asked Lieutenant Governor Henry Bell-Irving to intervene when Premier Bill Bennett requested a special warrant at the beginning of a new fiscal year. The lieutenant governor declined to do so; a week later, the premier requested and was granted dissolution (and the government was re-elected).[16] In 1991, the same year as the second Saskatchewan episode, Premier Vander Zalm of British Columbia tried a similar ploy to that of his Saskatchewan counterpart. He obtained prorogation and then sought a large special warrant for the second year in a row because the budget was not complete. This ended up in a caucus revolt, once conflict of interest allegations surfaced.

In the late 1980s, the use of governor general's warrants was challenged in Parliament by Liberal MP Peter Milliken — later to be speaker of the House of Commons. After its re-election late in 1989, the Mulroney Conservative government convened Parliament briefly in December to pass its free trade legislation, but did not then, nor when Parliament resumed in April, request supply. Having run out of funds, the government obtained three special warrants totalling near $7 billion between January and April 1989. Milliken and others questioned the legality and constitutional propriety of the special warrants as not being justified for "extraordinary or urgent" purposes. Senator Eugene Forsey stated that "never before has there been this recourse to the Governor General's Special Warrants and I think it is wholly improper."[17]

Vice-Regal Intervention: A Case Study — Alberta

Since the 1930s, Alberta has been characterized by strong majority governments from long-serving dominant parties, United Farmers, Social Credit, or Conservative (there has never been a minority government in Alberta). Legislatures have been overshadowed, and the vice-regal office has had a modest profile. Nonetheless, in the 1970s, three decades after the spectacular confrontation between Lieutenant Governor Bowen and Premier Aberhart, another lieutenant governor was embroiled in controversy. Ralph Steinhauer, Alberta's (and Canada's) first Aboriginal lieutenant governor, was outspoken in his public speeches about First Nations rights, often disagreeing with the Conservative government of Premier Peter Lougheed. In 1977, Steinhauer joined a delegation of First

Nations chiefs visiting Buckingham Palace for ceremonies marking the centennials of Treaties 6 and 7. Contrary to a commitment given to the premier, the lieutenant governor raised Aboriginal issues when he was presented to the Queen (as Chief David Ahenakew had done in Regina in 1973).[18] The same year, the Lougheed government introduced legislation preventing Aboriginal groups from filing caveats to stop development or sale of lands while their land claims were being addressed, the oil sands being the prime case in point. Pressured by Aboriginal and human rights groups, Lieutenant Governor Steinhauer spoke against the bill and considered withholding royal assent. There were allegations in the Legislature that Premier Lougheed pressured Prime Minister Trudeau to silence the lieutenant governor. Steinhauer himself admitted that he had "got into hot water" and been asked by Ottawa "to cool his mouth off."[19]

In the 1990s, Alberta lieutenant governors Gordon Towers and Bud Olsen expressed concern about the use of special warrants by Premier Ralph Klein's Conservative government. In 1993, Towers refused advice to sign an order-in-council which he deemed inappropriate.[20] In 2000, Lieutenant Governor Lois Hole unwisely made remarks about a bill of Premier Klein's government that would have permitted the privatization of some health care services. "This innocent comment soon became blown out of all proportion, with some mischievous individuals in the press suggesting that the Lieutenant-Governor was going to refuse assent if 'Bill 11' passed through the Legislative process."[21] Public opinion tended, however, to support Hole for simply drawing attention to the controversial nature of the bill. In 2003, Lieutenant Governor Hole again made headlines when she deplored those who did not support the arts, public education, and libraries, which was perceived as a criticism of Klein's government. The next year, she called on the government to "celebrate Alberta's centennial by helping the poor, spending more on art, schools, libraries and sharing some provincial wealth with poorer provinces" — hardly the sort of remark to endear her to Klein's right-wing administration.[22] However, Lois Hole emerged unscathed, buoyed by her personal popularity in the province.

In 2005, at his installation ceremony, Lieutenant Governor Norman Kwong publicly disagreed with Premier Ralph Klein over his efforts to block a ban on smoking in public places proposed by his own health minister, several government departments, and a chief medical health officer. Once again, a media controversy ensued. The lieutenant governor was criticized by some for an inappropriate intervention. However, the premier backed off and, in the end, the smoking ban was passed in the Legislature. Alfred Neitsch concluded that "if we view democracy as being the will of the people the Lieutenant Governor was not going against the democratic process. He was supporting it."[23] Yet considerable caution is in order for vice-regal utterances. As Robert E. Hawkins appositely points out, "it is exactly because remarks by a lieutenant governor, however well meaning and innocent, will be twisted by politicians and the press, that the lieutenant governor should not make any public comment. Any such comment, however innocuous, threatens to become an issue and thus to destroy the vice-regal neutrality."[24]

Issues in Ontario

Ontario had a brush with vice-regal controversy in 1997. Former lieutenant governor Hilary Weston recounts how controversial legislation by the Conservative government of Premier Mike Harris aroused major public protests and an Internet campaign for her to refuse royal assent. The lieutenant governor's office was swamped with telephone, calls, letters, faxes, and e-mails. Noting that she was "duty-bound to assent to the Legislature's final act," Weston said, however:

> Rather than being a nuisance [...] I felt that this protest was an important exercise in democracy, a way for individuals to communicate with the lieutenant governor directly and to feel that they had explored all possible outlets for the exercise of their rights. The responsibility for the legislation was taken by the government, rather than the Crown. This was an extremely important lesson in how a parliamentary democracy operates and how the Crown stays above the fray, even though it must accede to unpopular legislation from time to time.[25]

Lieutenant Governor Hilary Weston dealt
with controversy in the Ontario legislature.

Gary Beechey, BDS Studios Inc.

She revealed in her memoirs that she reviewed each throne speech
in advance and tried to "provide some comments to soften its overtly
partisan nature. Some of these changes were accepted, but most were
not." Hilary Weston was unimpressed by boorish jeers and heckling from
opposition members during the reading of her first throne speech in
1998. But that speech involved her in controversy again, for it revealed the
identity of a young offender, in contravention of the law. Obviously, this
was entirely the responsibility of the Harris government, but it placed the
lieutenant governor in an awkward position, to the extent that there was
a possibility of her being questioned in the ensuing police investigation.
While that did not occur, the solicitor general resigned and offered an
apology to the lieutenant governor in the assembly. Weston also recounts
how the Ontario government resorted to different tactics to announce
prorogation and dissolution so as to minimize public scrutiny.[26]

The Liberal government of Dalton McGuinty made questionable use
of prorogation in October 2012. Hilary Weston's successor once removed,
David Onley, granted prorogation to McGuinty when his minority government, beset by scandals, faced a standoff and possible defeat in the
Legislature. The premier announced his pending resignation and proro-

gation until his successor was chosen. This was decried by the opposition parties and other observers as a misuse of prorogation, especially as a date for recall of the House had not been announced, as had been done by Prime Minister Harper in 2008. However, unlike the federal rules, those in Ontario do not require that a fixed date be included in the order. In any event, the Premier stated publicly that the Legislature would be recalled shortly after a new leader was selected, in about five months. "In light of the fact that the Premier had demonstrated the confidence of the House," said Robert E. Hawkins, "the lieutenant governor not only acted properly but had no constitutional choice but to grant the request."[27]

TO BE CONSULTED, TO ENCOURAGE, AND TO WARN

Should first ministers meet regularly with their governors, their advice might be more effective. The nineteenth-century British expert on the constitution, Walter Bagehot, stated in a now-classic aphorism that the Sovereign retained three rights in a constitutional monarchy: "the right to be consulted, the right to encourage, the right to warn." In the United Kingdom, the Queen exercises these rights by meeting weekly and privately with the prime minister, an opportunity greatly valued by British first ministers.[28] The Queen herself has said that the prime ministers "unburden themselves ... I think it's rather nice to feel that one's sort of a sponge and everybody can come and tell one things."[29] The governor general of Australia meets approximately monthly with the prime minister, but this has not usually been the case with Canadian governors general. Practices in the Canadian provinces and the Australian states vary considerably. In Australia, the governor of Queensland and the administrator of the Northern Territory only meet with their premiers "as and when required." However, the governor of Western Australia meets with the premier every two months, and the governor of Tasmania has held regular monthly meetings with the premier since 1995. In South Australia, the governor and the premier speak informally prior to the weekly meeting of the executive council — a body which in Australia and its states formally approves cabinet decisions and is chaired by the governor.[30]

In Canada, British Columbia lieutenant governors meet regularly with their premiers. In Nova Scotia they meet monthly, and in Prince Edward Island the two meet quarterly. By contrast, the lieutenant governor and the premier of Manitoba have not had meetings since the 1960s. Nor do regular meetings take place in Ontario, Quebec, or Alberta.[31] While Alberta's former premier, Peter Lougheed, did praise Lieutenant Governor Grant MacEwan as being "a great mentor and counsellor to me as premier,"[32] his enthusiasm for vice-regal consultation cooled when Ralph Steinhauer succeeded MacEwan.

A Case Study: Saskatchewan Resuscitates Bagehot

A disconnect between premier and lieutenant governor prevailed in Saskatchewan until the 1980s. This was due, in large part, to the perceived partisan nature of the vice-regal appointments and the hostility of the CCF-NDP to the office following the reservation of royal assent in 1961. Even Allan Blakeney, premier from 1971 to 1982, favourable as he was to the institution, did not have meetings with his three lieutenant governors. While his Progressive Conservative successor, Grant Devine, did not schedule regular appointments, he met quite often with the three lieutenant governors under whom he served. He always found these meetings helpful. The lieutenant governor was, he said — picking up Queen Elizabeth's image — like a "travelling representative sponge," absorbing the nuances of public opinion. Devine recalled three critical moments when he especially valued his private discussions with the lieutenant governor — an interest rate crisis in 1982–1983 with Irwin McIntosh, a prairie drought in 1988 with Frederick Johnson, and the provincial deficit at the end of the decade with Sylvia Fedoruk. For Devine, all three served as a "great sounding board" for the premier. They were people of integrity, discreet, confidential, and comfortable in their position. Devine recommended that all premiers take advantage of the lieutenant governor's role. "There is," he said, "no downside."[33]

On taking office as Saskatchewan premier late in 1991, Roy Romanow assumed that regular meetings with the lieutenant governor were part of his obligations as premier, unaware that this had not been the previous practice. Then Lieutenant Governor Sylvia Fedoruk asked to see him to discuss special warrants. "It was an issue," said Romanow, "which propelled us together." The issue cemented the relationship between lieutenant governor and premier, and regular meetings became the norm. In making these meetings systematic from 1992, Roy Romanow was to find them even more helpful than he had expected. The period from 1992 to 1994 was challenging for the NDP government, as it pulled the province back from the verge of bankruptcy. Due to the severe fiscal measures that were taken, support for the government in the caucus and party was dropping, as was public confidence. In those critical days, said Romanow, Sylvia Fedoruk was "very insightful and wonderfully intelligent. I needed somebody completely removed from the situation and I could tell her point-blank in confidence what I felt."

Frustration within the NDP came to a head during the preparation of the 1994 budget. There was an impasse in caucus, and Romanow realized, to his consternation, that he did not have a consensus to present a budget to the Legislature. At this point, he told the caucus that the province deserved a government that could put together a responsible budget. Going from the caucus meeting to Government House to see Fedoruk, he explained his dilemma to the lieutenant governor and told her that he was considering advising her to call an election on the issue of putting the public finances in order. In their discussion, Fedoruk put a number of questions to him about the consequences of such a drastic action. For Roy Romanow, this was a "seminal moment" in his appreciation for the vice-regal office. "If there had not been a lieutenant governor," he said, "emotion might have got the better of my reason." In the end, he returned to his caucus and the issue was resolved.

Roy Romanow's relationship with Jack Wiebe, lieutenant governor from 1994 to 2000, was especially warm, going back many years to when Wiebe was a rural Liberal MLA. Wiebe had astute political insights and knew the municipal sphere, an important asset at a time when the NDP was reforming health care and wanted to reform rural government — always a controversial issue in Saskatchewan and, as it turned out, unattainable. Lynda Haverstock, installed early in 2000, was lieutenant governor for only a year of Romanow's time as premier. By then, Romanow had been on the job for eight years. Still, he greatly valued his monthly meetings with Haverstock, given her own political experience, which was to benefit Romanow's successor, Lorne Calvert.

All of the lieutenant governors, in Roy Romanow's view, gave solid, honest, helpful advice in the best interest of the province. They had "no axe to grind, no election to be concerned about, no hidden agenda." They filled the role of a "house of sober second thought" and served as a steadying hand for a person pulling together a cabinet. Romanow gave them the fullest picture possible of legislation, budgets, and major issues. He saw three consistent characteristics in his three lieutenant governors: they were committed to the province and the public good; they had external qualifications, including intellect; and they were keen on strengthening the vice-regal office through their relationship with the premier.[34] This last point bears reflection. After 1970, the Saskatchewan lieutenant governors were well aware of the negative perception of the vice-regal office that they had inherited. Discreetly on the part of Stephen Worobetz and George Porteous, more positively on the part of Irwin McIntosh, deliberately by Frederick Johnson and his successors, they all set out to improve the prestige and role of the Crown in the interest of good governance in the province. By the time Lorne Calvert became premier in 2001, this objective had been achieved.

Calvert came to treasure his meetings with Lieutenant Governor Lynda Haverstock, which took place approximately every six weeks. Her office was, he said, the one room in the province where a premier could speak freely, in absolute confidence. As Roy Romanow had found with Jack Wiebe, it was helpful that she had political experience, including being a party leader. "I would seek her counsel on public policy issues because she had that experience. I could even talk to her about the cabinet!" Given her contacts, Haverstock would bring "case work" to the meetings, matters she could not raise publicly but could mention to him in confidence. Calvert continued the practice of regular meetings with Haverstock's successor, Gordon Barnhart. Echoing Grant Devine, he said, "I would recommend this practice to all my colleagues." Calvert also saw the role of the lieutenant governor as helping reduce the "erosion of the parliamentary system" — an interesting comment on the place of the Crown as constitutional guarantor.[35]

When Brad Wall was first elected to the Legislature in 1999 for the fledgling Saskatchewan Party, he had been a skeptic about the Crown. However, when Lieutenant Governor Jack Wiebe spoke to the new MLAs about the role of the vice-regal office during their orientation, he changed Wall's view on the institution. By the time Wall took office as premier in 2007, he needed no further convincing. His first meeting with Lieutenant Governor Gordon Barnhart, when he was formally asked by the Queen's representative to form a government, was, he recalled, a "surreal event," which underscored for him the intrinsic value of constitutional monarchy. Premier Wall had no hesitation in continuing the practice of regular meetings with the lieutenant governor, usually every six to eight weeks. "I have found my meetings [with Dr. Barnhart] to be invaluable. In the greatest of confidence we can talk about anything and everything," Wall said. He learned much from Barnhart, given his experience as parliamentary clerk, historian, and author. The new premier took "solace and counsel" from the meetings. He considered that Bagehot's three "rights" were genuinely achieved by Gordon Barnhart, "without any pretence, in no way interfering with the democratic system, and by only doing what was proper."[36]

THE DECORATIVE FUNCTIONS OF THE CROWN

Walter Bagehot placed much emphasis on what he called the "dignified" aspect of the constitution, represented by the monarchy, as distinct from the "efficient" or practical side fulfilled by the elected government. The view of some Canadian scholars is similar. "The Crown," wrote Frank MacKinnon, "acts as the repository for the decorative and emotional functions which are inevitable in any state." He went on to say that "[t]he duties of the Queen, Governor General, and Lieutenant-Governors include the decorative functions to facilitate the conduct of public business."[37] However, David E. Smith cautions that there is a need to "reclaim the institution of the Crown from Bagehot's dignified limbo [...] the Crown and its prerogatives empower the political executive and make it efficient in the very sense Bagehot intended when he used that term to describe the non-dignified elements of the constitution: that is to produce an effect." He concludes, "The Crown is dignified *and* efficient."[38] With this caveat, that the dignified and efficient functions are two sides of the same monarchical coin, let us look at the decorative function of the Crown.

A National Role

As we have seen, the role of the lieutenant governor as federal agent has disappeared. Indeed, Peter Hogg notes that once "an appointment is made the Lieutenant Governor *is in no sense an agent of the federal government* [our emphasis]: he or she is obliged by the conventions of responsible government to act on the advice of the provincial cabinet."[39] But Christopher McCreery has drawn attention to a different national role for the lieutenant governor, which has contributed to the reinvigoration of the provincial vice-regal offices. This "dignified federal role" is one of "representing the provinces to themselves and Canada in the provinces. [The lieutenant governors] are symbolic agents for the promotion of province and nation — not nefarious federal constitutional interlopers."[40] We have seen in the previous chapter how Saskatchewan lieutenant governor Irwin McIntosh vigorously supported the national unity campaign after the election of the first Parti Québécois government in Quebec in 1976. Other lieutenant governors did the same. In a welcome rewrite of their original centralist function, lieutenant governors have successfully melded their symbolic roles of promoting both national values and provincial autonomy.

Examples of this dual role are the lieutenant governors' participation in the presentation of some national honours and awards, citizenship ceremonies, annual events like Canada Day and Remembrance Day, and anniversaries such as the Queen's Diamond Jubilee. We have already referred to the vice-regal affinity for Canada's First Nations and will see how this has become a feature of the provincial Crown, notably on treaty days. Lieutenant governors may have no direct constitutional connection with the Canadian Forces, but they are considered by them as royal representatives. Their status is recognized by the royal salute they receive on military occasions, the gun salute fired at the opening of the Legislature, and the uniformed aides-de-camp from the Canadian Forces (or the RCMP or municipal police) who accompany them on their official duties. Says McCreery, "the lieutenant governors promote provincial identity while also advancing national cohesion and membership in the broader Canadian family through the multifaceted nature of the Crown." He calls this dual mission a form of "seepage," or a "blurring of the federal and provincial aspects of the lieutenant governor's role in the broad sense."[41] In this uniquely Canadian federal blend, the dignified role of the vice-regal office appears to be as valuable as the efficient.

The ceremonial aspect of the Crown, the "pomp and circumstance" at which the British monarchy excels, has its Canadian counterpart not only in visits of the Royal Family but in the public profile of the governor general and lieutenant governors. Examples are the opening of Parliament or Legislature, provincial visits of the governor general, vice-regal installations, presentations of honours, and state funerals. Uniforms, music, guards of honour, gun salutes, parades, flags, and other decor form part of the ambience of what, using a religious analogy, can loosely be called civil liturgy.[42]

A Case Study: Saskatchewan

Throughout the 1960s and 1970s, civil liturgy was on the decline in Canada, as a more casual, egalitarian society emerged. Nowhere was this more evident than in Saskatchewan, where the trend was exacerbated by official coolness to the vice-regal office. Lieutenant Governor Frank Bastedo, he who revived the obsolete power of reservation of royal assent, attempted to restore the ceremonial formality of his office by, for example, riding in the historic horse-drawn landau to the opening of the Legislature. Any initiative by Bastedo, however, was discredited because of the 1961 controversy over the reservation of royal assent. After he left office, the decorative functions of the Crown dwindled. By the time Irwin McIntosh took office in 1978, the dignified role of the lieutenant governor was a shadow of its former self. Gone were the landau and military guard of honour at the opening of the Legislature — McIntosh arrived at the Legislative Building virtually unnoticed to deliver the speech from the throne. The swearing-in of new lieutenant governors took place with little publicity in a perfunctory ceremony in the legislative library. The NDP government grudgingly provided the ceremonial minimum for an institution with which it had to co-exist but barely tolerated.

With the province's seventy-fifth anniversary celebrations in 1980, however, came a shift in attitude towards the vice-regal office. That year, the landau and guard of honour were revived for the opening of the Legislature, and historic Government House, the former vice-regal residence, was restored as a museum. In 1981, Premier Blakeney presided at the inauguration of the lieutenant governor's flag; Saskatchewan had been the only Canadian jurisdiction without a vice-regal flag. In 1982, for the first time, Blakeney personally met with the lieutenant governor to request the writ for the election of that year. In 1983, Premier Grant Devine's Progressive Conservative government staged the first televised swearing-in of a lieutenant governor for Frederick Johnson in the legislative chamber, a practice followed for his successors. In 1984, Devine returned the vice-regal office to Government House. In 1985, Devine's government launched a provincial honours program in which the lieutenant governor played a key role. The province secured a full coat of arms from the Queen in 1986, replacing for formal purposes the bland wheat sheaf logo that Blakeney's government had introduced in 1977 to pre-empt the traditional shield of arms dating from 1906. At the installation of his NDP government in 1991, Roy Romanow inaugurated a new Great Seal bearing the coat of arms. Romanow began the practice of swearing in new cabinet ministers at Government House.

His NDP successor, Lorne Calvert, ensured that Saskatchewan was the first jurisdiction in Canada to plan celebrations for the Queen's Golden Jubilee in 2002 — the fiftieth anniversary of the reign of Queen Elizabeth II. Calvert's government co-sponsored a bronze equestrian statue of the Queen, which the Sovereign unveiled in front of the Legislative Building during her visit for the provincial centennial in 2005. In a sequel to 1980, the showcase "built legacy" of the centennial was a major addition to the Government House, also opened by the Queen in 2005. In 2007, Brad Wall's Saskatchewan Party government was sworn in by Lieutenant Governor Gordon Barnhart at Government House, the first time for a new administration. In 2008, Premier Wall made a small but symbolic change: henceforth the clerk of the executive council personally brought orders-in-council to Government House for signature instead of sending them by messenger. In addition, the lieutenant governor was briefed on their content. Wall's government also completed the Government House centennial project and took early steps to prepare for the Queen's Diamond Jubilee in 2012. Indeed, Wall obtained an unprecedented audience with the Queen in London in 2011 to discuss just that. This litany of changes may appear to be one of form rather than content, of detail rather than substantive policy. However, it represented a consistent approach to the Crown over thirty years by five successive premiers from three different political parties. In conjunction with six lieutenant governors, they cumulatively raised the Saskatchewan vice-regal office from the weakest in the country to one of the strongest.

"ROYAL SASKATCHEWAN":
A CASE STUDY OF ROYAL TOURS

Until the 1970s, visits to Saskatchewan by members of the Royal Family had been sporadic. The Duke and Duchess of Cornwall and York, the future King George V and Queen Mary, came in 1901. The Prince of Wales, to be King Edward VIII for less than a year in 1936, toured the province in 1919 and returned with his younger brother, the Duke of York — the future King George VI — in 1927. George VI's historic cross-Canada tour with Queen Elizabeth in 1939 provided a boost to morale at the end of the Depression and a call to patriotism on the eve of the Second World War. After the war and with the expansion of air travel, royal visits became more frequent. George VI's daughter, Princess Elizabeth, and her husband, Prince Philip, came to Saskatchewan during their 1951 Canadian tour and returned in 1959 as Queen Elizabeth II and the Duke of Edinburgh.

Royal activities increased considerably from the 1970s onwards. Federal authorities arranged a visit to Regina by the Queen and her husband for the RCMP centennial in 1973. This proved attractive enough to Allan Blakeney's NDP government that they invited the Royal Couple to return in 1978 on their way to the Commonwealth Games in Edmonton. Somewhat to their surprise, the invitation was accepted, and Saskatchewan found itself for the first time co-hosting and co-organizing a major royal visit with Ottawa. It was an eye-opener. Both its popular appeal and the complexity of the planning, not to mention the "one-upmanship" games of federal officials, were a revelation. Even though the federal government of the day was manifestly not keen on the monarchy, it maintained a tight grip on the programs of royal tours in the provinces. Prime Minister Trudeau's Liberal government was trying to assert Ottawa's primacy over the provinces in the lead-up to the patriation of the constitution in 1982. Shortly after the Queen's 1978 visit, the provincial premiers, holding their annual meeting in Regina under Blakeney's chairmanship, turned thumbs down on Trudeau's plan to make the governor general, a federal appointee, virtual head of state in place of the Queen.

The 1980s brought a series of royal tours. Saskatchewan refined its organizing techniques and asserted its equal partnership (and paymaster) role with the federal government. During the province's seventy-fifth anniversary year, 1980, Blakeney's government received the Queen's sister, Princess Margaret, as royal guest for the celebrations. The success of the visit led to an invitation to the Queen's daughter Princess Anne to come in 1982; Grant Devine's Conservative government acted as host. Devine was also host for Queen Elizabeth the Queen Mother on a brief stop in Regina in 1985 and for a major six-day tour by the Queen and the Duke of Edinburgh in 1987. Their second son, Prince Andrew, Duke of York, and Sarah, Duchess of York, came in 1989 for the final royal tour while Grant Devine was premier.

Governments, whatever their political stripe, found that members of the Royal Family were hard-working, consummate professionals. They willingly celebrated anniversaries such as the centennial of Saskatoon in 1982 and the seventy-fifth anniversary of the Legislative Building in 1987. They helped focus on the province's natural resources — the Duke of Edinburgh and Prince Edward in 1978 and Princess Anne in 1982 visited potash mines, the Queen visited a farm in 1987, and the Duke and Duchess of York toured a First Nations–run sawmill in Meadow Lake in 1989. In addition, "the royals" drew attention to worthy causes, as when the Queen opened a hospital wing and toured a home for the mentally disabled in Saskatoon in 1978. Multicultural communities enjoyed basking in the royal limelight — the Ukrainian towns of Canora and

Kamsack and the Doukhobour village of Veregin were on the Queen's itinerary in 1987. Above all, the First Nations welcomed the monarch and her family. Princess Margaret toured a reserve in 1980. In 1987, the Queen dedicated Wanuskewin Heritage Park near Saskatoon, one of the most important Aboriginal archaeological sites in Canada. The Duke and Duchess of York visited historic Stanley Mission in 1989. In response to popular demand, visits occurred nearly every two years. Then, in the 1990s, the bottom fell out of the royal tour market.

During that decade, when Roy Romanow's NDP government was in power, there was only one visit by a member of the Royal Family — a brief, low-key trip in 1994 by the Queen's youngest son, Prince Edward. Devine's government had invited the Prince and Princess of Wales (Charles and Diana) to come during their Canadian tour in 1991, but the invitation had to be withdrawn when it became evident that a provincial election would be called at the time of the visit (Bob Rae's Ontario NDP government gladly recuperated the days allocated to Saskatchewan). Why the dearth of royal visits during the 1990s? It cannot be attributed to Romanow, who was a staunch supporter of the monarchy and of the office of lieutenant governor. There are several answers. The Province of Saskatchewan was in dire financial straits for the first half of the decade. The government's attention was focused elsewhere than on symbolic events like royal visits. The costs of such undertakings, while modest in real terms, seemed inappropriate when citizens were being asked to tighten their belts. The 1990s were also a decade in which the Royal Family was experiencing difficult times, including the divorces of several members. The Queen herself referred to the "annus horribilis" of 1992, which culminated in a major fire at Windsor Castle. Understandably, there was less public appetite for inviting "the royals." Finally, there was the old story of hostile officialdom, which had so often plagued the vice-regal office and the Crown in Saskatchewan: senior officials in Romanow's government blocked a proposed visit of the Prince of Wales in 1996.

During Roy Romanow's tenure as premier, however, there was a major step forward through Prince Edward's informal 1994 tour. For the first time, the federal government was not directly involved. The Prince was touring Canada under the auspices of the Duke of Edinburgh's Awards for young achievers. The province found that it could not only organize a royal visit on its own without intrusion of "the feds," but do so harmoniously, effectively, and on a small budget. This "working visit" (as distinct from an "official visit" organized with Ottawa) proved to be instrumental in closer relationships with the Royal Family. It paved the way for a series of such tours in the following decade under Premier Lorne Calvert, another avowed monarchist.

The Prince of Wales had been cold-shouldered twice by Saskatchewan when the Romanow government finally invited him to come to Saskatchewan in 2001. It was Lorne Calvert, taking over as premier early that year, who hosted the first tour of the heir to the throne. Prince Charles came with some baggage. His disintegrating marriage to the glamorous Diana had culminated in divorce in 1996, followed by her tragic accidental death in 1997. Furthermore, the Prince's views on architecture, town planning, complementary medicine, and organic farming were viewed as unconventional in many quarters. All of this provided ample satirical fodder for the invasive tabloid press in Britain. It was therefore with much curiosity that the government and the public awaited the Prince of Wales. The visit turned out to be a *tour de force*. The Prince charmed everyone with his self-deprecating sense of humour and his empathy for civil society causes — disadvantaged youth, the inner city, the environment, health care, sustainable agriculture, and the heritage movement, themes that pleased the NDP government. In addition, the Prince paid much attention to the First Nations, visiting Wanuskewin Heritage Park, which the Queen had inaugurated in 1987, accepting an Indian name and meeting with chiefs of the Federation of Saskatchewan Indian Nations. He also became the first honorary member of the Saskatchewan Order of Merit.[43] After the visit, Premier Calvert quipped to hitherto skeptical members of his cabinet that if the media-savvy Prince of Wales were in politics, none of them would want to run against him.[44]

Provincially sponsored working tours followed in quick succession. Prince Edward, now Earl of Wessex, came back in 2003 to celebrate municipal centennials in Regina, Moose Jaw, Lloydminster, and Melfort, inaugurate an arts centre in Prince Albert, open the First Nations University of Canada in Regina, visit Regina's Globe Theatre (of which he had been patron since 1992), and become colonel-in-chief of the Saskatchewan Dragoons, an army reserve unit in Moose Jaw. In 2004,

Princess Anne, now the Princess Royal, marked the sixtieth anniversary of the 1944 D-Day landings in Normandy with the Royal Regina Rifles, the regiment of which she had become colonel-in-chief in 1982. She also received an honorary doctorate from the University of Regina. Both royals soon returned — Edward to visit his regiment in 2006 and be invested as the second honorary member of the provincial Order, and Anne to celebrate the centennial of the Royal Regina Rifles in 2007.

The tour of the Queen and the Duke of Edinburgh for the provincial centennial in 2005 drew together all the strands of "Royal Saskatchewan." The Royal Couple visited the First Nations University. Prince Philip named an environmental enclave in Regina. The Queen inaugurated an Aboriginal mural in the Legislative Building, as well as the equestrian statue of herself and the new addition to Government House. They attended a provincial luncheon at the curling rink in the town of Lumsden, where they were entertained by Métis artists. Undaunted by their schedule, they paid tribute to fallen RCMP members at "Depot" Division, the Force's training academy in Regina, and toured the Canadian Light Source Synchrotron at the University of Saskatchewan. They presided at the spectacular Centennial

Queen Elizabeth II visited Saskatchewan in 2005 for the province's centennial. Here she inspects RCMP members at "Depot" Division in Regina.

Government of Saskatchewan

Gala of the Arts in Saskatoon masterminded by Lieutenant Governor Lynda Haverstock. The tour was flawless. Elizabeth II appeared to relish the position of "Queen of Canada," which had been promoted since her 1952 accession to differentiate the Sovereign from her otherwise predominantly British role. It was essential if the monarchy was to survive in the bilingual, multicultural, multi-racial Canada of the second millennium.

In 2012, celebrating the Diamond Jubilee of Queen Elizabeth, the Prince of Wales and Duchess of Cornwall made a one-day visit to Regina — the first for the Prince since 2001 and the first ever for the Duchess. It made up for its brevity by an intense and varied schedule. The Prince presented Diamond Jubilee Medals at the Legislative Building, which was marking its centennial. Then the Royal Couple opened a Jubilee exhibit at Government House and met with Aboriginal groups at the First Nations University of Canada. The Prince toured a cutting-edge environmental firm. They ended the day by attending a special concert of the Regina Symphony Orchestra, of which the Prince of Wales had become patron in 2008. The success of the visit was an encouraging sign for the future of the monarchy.

MORE THAN ONE CROWN?
PROVINCIAL HONOURS IN CANADA

Inevitably, the Canadian conundrum of the federal and provincial Crowns arose with respect to official honours. Every province now has an order, and some have other honours as well. Like the appointment of Queen's Counsel in the late nineteenth century, the path to provincial honours was not an easy one.

Provincial Honours — the Beginnings

In *The Order of Canada*, Christopher McCreery observes that in 1966, during planning for the national honour, Michael Pitfield, then a senior adviser in the Privy Council Office, expressed concern about "the possibility that the provinces would begin to found their own orders, which might be 'detrimental to national unity.'" On the other hand, some federal cabinet ministers "were unhappy that the Advisory Council [of the Order of Canada] consisted solely of federal officials, with no provincial input or involvement from beyond the governmental sphere."[45] McCreery notes that, as early as 1938, Mackenzie King's deputy minister of justice had "warned him that the provinces were quite capable of creating their own awards and having their respective lieutenant governors sanction them. Although such awards would not be 'official,' there was a fear that, with time, they would become viewed as such."[46]

Quebec was the first Canadian province to establish an honour, the Order of Agricultural Merit, in 1925. The origins of this award, however, went back as early as 1869. The Order was based on *l'Ordre du Mérite agricole* of France. Quebec also had an Order of Scholastic Merit from 1928 to the 1960s. In the 1960s and 1970s, British Columbia introduced the Order of the Dogwood, Manitoba the Order of the Buffalo Hunt, and Nova Scotia the Order of Good Cheer; these were a form of tourist recognition and not intended as serious honours. In any event, none of the above provincial awards was recognized officially by the federal government. Yet given the dynamics of Canadian federalism, it was not surprising that, following the creation of the Order of Canada, all ten provinces eventually entered the field of honours despite the active opposition of the Chancellery of Honours at Rideau Hall. The argument against provincial honours was:

- Only sovereign states can issue honours, and provinces are not sovereign states.
- The Queen has not authorized provincial honours, and the federal government will not advise her to do so.
- If provinces do issue insignia in the form of medals, they have no national or international status and cannot be worn with official honours. Such medals should not display the crown or be presented by the lieutenant governor.
- Provincial honours risk diluting, duplicating, and diminishing the prestige of Canada's national honours.

None of the provinces accepted this rationale. Defying the strictures of Ottawa, Ontario established the first modern provincial honour in 1973 — the Ontario Medal for Good Citizenship. This was soon fol-

All ten provinces have orders. Shown are the insignia of the Order of British Columbia (1989) and the Order of Newfoundland and Labrador (2001).

Government of British Columbia, Government of Newfoundland and Labrador

lowed by the Ontario Police and Firefighters Bravery Medals in 1975 and 1976, all with medals bearing the crown and presented by the lieutenant governor. Quebec established the first provincial order, *l'Ordre national du Québec*, in 1984; the Saskatchewan Order of Merit followed in 1985, the Order of Ontario in 1986, and in 1989 the Order of British Columbia. There was a pause as the remaining provinces assessed the domestic demand for honours and the experience of other jurisdictions. In 1997, the Order of Prince Edward Island appeared. The following year Alberta "regularized" its quasi-honour, the Alberta Order of Excellence, which had started as early as 1979.* By 1999, the Order of Manitoba was established.

---

* Alberta created the Alberta Order of Excellence by legislation in 1979, but, yielding to pressure from Ottawa, made it a medallion not worn by the recipient. This only changed in 1998, when Alberta turned the Order into a normal honour to be worn by the recipient.

In 2000, the honours secretariats of Saskatchewan and Ontario convened a national conference on honours in Regina, seeking to fill the leadership vacuum caused by Rideau Hall's reluctance to parley with other jurisdictions.[47] The conference gave impetus to the remaining Atlantic provinces to establish their own orders: the Orders of New Brunswick, Nova Scotia, and Newfoundland and Labrador appeared in quick succession in 2001. Thus all ten provinces now bestow orders, and half of them — Ontario, Saskatchewan, Alberta, British Columbia, and Newfoundland and Labrador — have decorations and medals as well. Except in Quebec, where *l'Ordre national du Québec* is presented by the premier, provincial honours come under the aegis of the Crown and are presented by the lieutenant governor. All provinces except Ontario have established their honours through legislation, rather than exercising the royal prerogative through order-in-council as Prime Minister Lester Pearson's government did for the Order of Canada in 1967. This is partly due to the perception that legislation helps insulate honours from political interference (as Pearson had thought), but also because of the ambiguity surrounding the royal prerogative of honours in provincial jurisdiction.

A Case Study: Saskatchewan and Provincial Honours

In Saskatchewan, with the support of then intergovernmental affairs minister and future premier Roy Romanow, a study of honours and awards was undertaken by the author during the province's seventy-fifth anniversary year, 1980. Its conclusion was that Canadian provinces had the right to create honours and that Saskatchewan should do so. Significantly, the study recommended that these be honours of the provincial Crown, bestowed by the lieutenant governor. The report was adopted in principle by Allan Blakeney's NDP government in 1982 and implemented in 1985 by Grant Devine's Conservative government, with the creation of the Saskatchewan Order of Merit. In its first decade, the Order had indubitable success in recognizing outstanding people such as former premier T.C. Douglas, Aboriginal artist Allen Sapp, cancer researcher and later lieutenant governor Sylvia Fedoruk, historian Dr. John Archer, businessmen George Solomon and George Morris, poet Anne Szumigalski, former lieutenant governor Frederick Johnson, and medical researcher Dr. Ali Rajput. Building on this and extending it to the grassroots, Roy Romanow's NDP government added the Saskatchewan Volunteer Medal in 1995 as a decoration to recognize the province's crucial volunteer sector. In 2003, the NDP government of Lorne Calvert announced two further honours: the Saskatchewan Protective Services Medal, awarded for twenty-five years of exemplary service to police, firefighters, emergency medical personnel, corrections workers, customs officers, Canadian Forces members, and others; and the Saskatchewan Centennial Medal, presented in 2005–2006 to 4,200 recipients.[48]

Saskatchewan's position on honours since the 1980s can be summarized as follows:

- As co-sovereign jurisdictions in Confederation, with their own representatives of the Queen, the provinces have every right to issue official honours of the provincial Crown.
- By the same token, their honours insignia may bear the crown and be presented by the lieutenant governor.
- While the Queen has not specifically authorized provincial honours, legislation or orders-in-council in her name have had the same effect. As "fount of honours," the Sovereign functions vicariously through her surrogates.
- Far from diluting, duplicating, or diminishing the prestige of Canada's national honours, provincial honours complement and enhance them by making Canadians more aware of, interested in, and respectful of honours of the Crown.

Referring to the legal struggles over the royal prerogative a century earlier, notably over the appointment of Queen's Counsel, Saskatchewan argued that provinces could indeed create honours of the Crown. A 1990 study reviewing the first five years of the Saskatchewan Order of Merit buttressed this position by referring to judgments of the Judicial Committee of the Privy Council already noted:

The *Constitution Acts, 1867 to 1982*, do not expressly assign honours to either jurisdiction; the provinces nonetheless have a good legal case for the validity of legislation which provides for the issuing of their own honours. Their legislative authority extends over their own provincial constitutions, the establishment of provincial offices and matters of a local nature in the province.

The *Constitution Acts, 1867 to 1982*, thus contain ample legislative authority for provincial honours; furthermore, in accordance with [the 1916 decision of the JCPC in the *Bonanza Creek* case], the division of executive and prerogative powers mirrors the division of legislative power. There is no reason to believe that legislative authority over honours was withheld from the provinces by the Canadian Constitution. It has long been an accepted principle of Canadian constitutional law that all legislative and executive authority in Canada is divided between the two orders of government. Since jurisdiction over "honours" is not granted exclusively to the federal government, and the matter is not a new subject unknown at the time of Confederation, the argument that the provinces can authorize the conferral of honours with respect to matters within provincial jurisdiction is a strong one.[49]

The paper cited the 1892 *Liquidators of the Maritime Bank* case asserting the divisibility of the Crown and therefore of the royal prerogative, and the Queen's Counsel dispute finally resolved by the JCPC in 1898. The study noted that QCs are appointed "under authority of provincial legislation and without direct approval of the Queen [...] a clear example of the right to create provincial offices under the Crown. Queen's Counsel appointed by the provinces are recognized by the federal government — a precedent for the recognition of provincial honours. Indeed, one can say that the office of Queen's Counsel is the first nationally-recognized provincial honour." The study did, however, concede that:

... the prerogative of establishing honours is one which the Sovereign has not delegated to her vice-regal representatives, either national or provincial. While the Queen acts directly with respect to Canada only infrequently, one of the areas where she continues to do so is in approving honours. Provincial honours established by legislation could thus be considered legitimate and valid within the provinces concerned, but irregular in that they have not received the Sovereign's direct approval and incomplete in that they are therefore not recognized nationally and internationally.[50]

The solution, then, was to come to an agreement with the federal government whereby provincial honours could be regularized. There was no direct response by Ottawa to the Saskatchewan study. However, subsequent developments showed that it had some influence. Pressure from Lieutenant Governor Sylvia Fedoruk, one of the early members of the Saskatchewan Order of Merit, on Governor General Ramon Hnatyshyn, himself from Saskatchewan, played a role,[*] and it is believed that Lieutenant Governor Lincoln Alexander of Ontario also intervened. A key factor was customary federal sensitivity to Quebec, as that province had requested status for *l'Ordre national du Québec* as early as 1984.[51]

In 1991, a compromise was found. Without recognizing them as national honours, the federal Honours Policy Committee granted status to provincial orders in the national precedence of orders, decorations, and medals, and a federal order-in-council was passed to this effect. In 1998, this status was extended to some other honours such as the Saskatchewan Volunteer Medal. However, there remained inconsistency in the system. Rideau Hall recognized the commemorative medals for the centennials of Alberta and Saskatchewan in 2005, but not the Saskatchewan Protective

---

* Rideau Hall, promoting the new Canadian Heraldic Authority, asked Sylvia Fedoruk to adopt a personal coat of arms; she insisted that it display the insignia of her Saskatchewan Order of Merit. Rideau Hall balked at this on the grounds that it was not a nationally approved honour. Fedoruk refused to accept a coat of arms until the Saskatchewan order received federal approval.

Services Medal or the Alberta Law Enforcement Long Service Medal. The federal argument was that exemplary or long service medals, like bravery decorations, duplicated their national equivalents. Yet provincial orders — all nationally recognized — could also be labelled as duplication. Furthermore, the national Honours Policy Committee had already recognized bravery awards in Ontario and Newfoundland and Labrador and fire exemplary service and bravery medals in British Columbia. Clearly, more work was required to harmonize Canada's honours.

Provincial honours come of age: Lieutenant Governor Lynda Haverstock invests the Prince of Wales as the first honorary member of the Saskatchewan Order of Merit in 2001.

Government of Saskatchewan

The Contrast with Australia[52]

Why such a federal-provincial issue over honours in Canada, when nothing similar occurred in Australia, that other Commonwealth federal monarchy? There are two factors. Until 1990, the Australian states continued their long-standing practice of recommending people directly to the Sovereign for imperial honours such as the Order of the British Empire. Since the states had this outlet for recognizing their residents, it mitigated pressure for establishing their own honours. More significantly, the Australian states were directly involved in the Order of Australia from its creation in 1975. All eight states and territories have representatives on the council of the Order of Australia. Furthermore, the governor general has delegated to the state governors the authority to present all awards of the Order of Australia except those at the companion level.

Contrast this with Canada. The provinces were, from the outset, excluded by Ottawa from any direct part in the honours system, despite the concerns expressed by some federal cabinet ministers. Given Michael Pitfield's hope that the Order of Canada would pre-empt provincial honours, it is ironic that the exact opposite happened, at least in part because of the exclusion of the provinces from the creation and management of the national honours system. The very success of the Order of Canada and the other national honours — following the nearly fifty-year honours vacuum after 1919 — stimulated an interest in honours and a desire by the provinces to recognize deserving people in their own jurisdictions. Provincial honours have (with the single exception of Quebec) raised the profile of the lieutenant governors and increased the relevance of the Crown to the people.

PUBLIC INITIATIVES AND CIVIL SOCIETY: THE SASKATCHEWAN EXPERIENCE

By definition, constitutional monarchs and their representatives do not play a direct role in public policy. This is the purview of their "advisers," first ministers and cabinets. However, monarchs and governors can exercise influence well beyond their closed-door meetings with prime ministers and premiers. In Saskatchewan, as the vice-regal office recovered from its low point in the 1960s, so did its influence.

Public Initiatives

The recovery of vice-regal influence did not start happily. In 1978, newly appointed lieutenant governor Irwin McIntosh expressed support for capital punishment; Premier Allan Blakeney admonished the lieutenant governor for taking a public stand on a controversial issue. But McIntosh quickly redeemed himself through his firm support for the national unity initiative in which Blakeney was a leader, following the 1977 election victory of the separatist Parti Québécois government in Quebec. The lieutenant governor also worked tirelessly to promote the province's seventy-fifth anniversary celebrations in 1980, which were a successful public relations coup for the NDP government. McIntosh thus sketched out a more active role for the vice-regal office.

Frederick Johnson concentrated his efforts on returning the vice-regal office to Government House, launching the provincial honours system, and strengthening the prestige of the Crown in the province. His successor, Sylvia Fedoruk, began a practice of touring schools and First Nations communities in northern Saskatchewan. Supported by the provincial education department, the lieutenant governor presented awards to leading, mostly Aboriginal, high school students in a move to promote role models and reward academic success. It was entirely consonant with the government's emerging focus on Aboriginal social and economic development as the First Nations and Métis grew in population and profile. Like Johnson, Jack Wiebe focused on reinforcing the role of the lieutenant governor. He contributed to the renewal of the administration of Government House, supported the expansion of the provincial honours system, and persuaded Premier Romanow that the government should produce an educational video on the Crown.[53]

It was Lynda Haverstock who developed the lieutenant governor's influence into a fine art. Like her national counterpart, Governor General Adrienne Clarkson (1999–2005), she moved vice-regal speech-making from cautious, feel-good bromides into substantive commentaries on social, cultural, and economic issues of the day, while carefully avoiding any hint of partisan politics. Lynda Haverstock's impact was especially felt in the Saskatchewan centennial, celebrated in 2005 — an echo of Irwin McIntosh's support for the seventy-fifth anniversary a quarter-century before. She gave

In 2005 the Queen unveiled a statue of herself riding her Saskatchewan horse "Burmese." It is located in the Legislative gardens in Regina.

Government of Saskatchewan

of herself tirelessly to the centennial medal program, personally presenting the vast majority of the 4,200 medals at eighty events around the province. As patron of the Government House Foundation, she backed the fund-raising campaign that eventually raised more than $2 million, a third of the cost of the addition to the 1891 building. When provincial and federal heritage officials tried to block the design for the Queen Elizabeth II Wing of Government House, Haverstock convened a meeting of parties to the project and knocked heads together until a compromise was reached.

Haverstock closely followed the development of the Queen's Golden Jubilee statue, a bronze sculpture portraying Queen Elizabeth II on her favourite horse, Burmese, a mare born and raised in Saskatchewan for the RCMP Musical Ride and presented to the Queen in 1969. She initiated the process after receiving correspondence about this remarkable connection between her home province and the Queen, and received wholehearted support for the project from both Premier Lorne Calvert and the RCMP. The lieutenant governor played a key role with the committee that oversaw the initiative, including public fundraising. She also helped overcome the resistance of officials in Calvert's government who tried to backtrack on the original prominent location selected in the legislative grounds and announced by the premier in 2001 (they wanted the statue relegated to an obscure location in the shrubbery). In 2005, the Queen, with obvious delight, unveiled the statue of herself and Burmese in the Queen Elizabeth II Gardens directly in front of the Legislative Building. It immediately became an artistic and tourist attraction.

Lieutenant Governor Lynda Haverstock masterminded Saskatchewan's Centennial Gala of the Arts in 2005. Special guests were the Queen and the Duke of Edinburgh.
Government of Saskatchewan

Lynda Haverstock's influence on the centennial did not stop there. She organized a program for recognition of artists and volunteers in the arts. She personally conceived and, aided by a handful of volunteers, brought to fruition one of the most spectacular events of the year: a Centennial Gala of the Arts. The lieutenant governor convened a blue-ribbon committee to raise funds. By sheer persistence, they overcame the skepticism of officials in Calvert's government and were able to obtain a significant grant from provincial coffers. Televised live nationally by CBC from Saskatoon, the production brought together performers like Buffy Sainte-Marie, Joni Mitchell, Gordon Tootoosis, Brent Butt, and the Amati String Quartet. Leading the more than ten thousand spectators were none other than Queen Elizabeth and Prince Philip. The gala sent reverberations across a Canada accustomed to considering Saskatchewan a cultural backwater.

Community Leadership

Lynda Haverstock extended the lieutenant governor's reach into "civil society," the intricate web of non-governmental organizations and worthy causes. Traditionally, Saskatchewan lieutenant governors, like those of other provinces, had lent their names and the prestige of their office to charities and community organizations. Richard Lake, lieutenant governor from 1915 to 1921, was knighted by King George V for his services to the Red Cross. Henry Newlands (1921–1930) supported the Save the Children Fund. Archibald McNab (1936–1945) promoted wartime charities. George Porteous (1976–1978) was an advocate of physical fitness and seniors. Patronage of community and non-profit organizations and promotion of worthy causes have been long established. Today, this goes well beyond acting as patron and cheerleader. It extends to organization and, in some cases, fundraising. Contemporary questions like literacy, fitness, women's issues, Aboriginal issues, multiculturalism, youth, and voluntarism appear in vice-regal agendas.

Sylvia Fedoruk, lieutenant governor from 1988 to 1994, emphasized outreach to Aboriginal people and northern Saskatchewan. This was to become a major theme for lieutenant governors. The First Nations were undergoing rapid change as their population grew and they sought to overcome endemic poverty, discrimination, and lack of education. "Indians" had been traditionally regarded as wards of the federal government, which indeed they were as long as most resided on reserves. As more and more First Nations people moved off reserve, however, the balance shifted, provincial and municipal responsibilities increased, and the lieutenant governors devoted much attention to Indian and Métis communities. The vice-regal affinity for the First Nations derives in part from their traditionally close relationship with the Crown dating back to the nineteenth-century treaties with Queen Victoria. Although this relationship had been primarily with the monarch and with the federal Crown represented by the governor general, the lieutenant governors began playing a more prominent role. A prime example of this was an initiative of James Bartleman, lieutenant governor of Ontario from 2002 to 2007 and himself a First Nations person. Bartleman organized a highly successful campaign to promote literacy among Aboriginal youth in northern Ontario by collecting books for them from across the province. In Saskatchewan, Lynda Haverstock made it a priority to attend First Nations treaty days. Like her Ontario counterpart, she also focused on the north of the province. Noticing the large number of stray dogs in Aboriginal communities, she organized a spay-neuter program across the north, obtaining *pro bono* veterinary services. This also helped her goals of promoting education for First Nations youth. Literacy and citizen recognition were among Haverstock's constant themes.[54]

Her successor, Gordon Barnhart, also concentrated on civil society issues. Referring to "the importance of governance in our society," he called for citizens to "become engaged in this important form of public service" and launched a major initiative, the Lieutenant Governor's Leadership Forum for youth. Gathering promising young people from across the province, half of them from northern Saskatchewan, the Forum introduced them to major figures in the public and private sectors. It was Barnhart's way of helping prepare the leadership of tomorrow.

Vice-regal representatives thus use their prestigious offices for strengthening civil society. Governors help to raise funds, indirectly publicize their causes through the media, and lobby their governments for support. In so doing, they expose themselves and their offices to more public scrutiny and media attention, for they are not really acting on "advice" but on personal initiative. There is a risk of blurring that fine line where the ministry is required by convention to defend the actions and expenditures of the Crown's representatives. But, as will be discussed later, this convention is on the wane. While one should take care that first ministers are well informed and on-side, these initiatives represent a welcome development of the vice-regal function.

ENHANCING THE PROVINCIAL CROWN

In the light of the developments previously noted, could the provincial Crown and notably its principal embodiment — the vice-regal office — be further improved or reformed? The key players are the federal government and the provinces themselves.

National Changes

First and foremost is the method of selection and appointment of the lieutenant governor. This is entirely the prerogative of the federal prime minister. The provinces have no formal role to play in the choice of their own vice-regal representative; at the most, they may be informally consulted prior to the decision. While the Australian system of appointment of governors by the Queen on the advice of the premiers may seem appealing, no one has the appetite for seeking a constitutional amendment to make this happen, even if Buckingham Palace could be convinced to accept it. Instead, the federal and provincial governments should work out a genuine and mutually acceptable method of consultation on the appointment. A promising development occurred in 2009: Prime Minister Stephen Harper announced that, in appointing Philip Lee as lieutenant governor of Manitoba, he had directly consulted with the premier and leader of the opposition, both of whom expressed their support. The prime minister pursued this approach in appointing Graydon Nicholas as lieutenant governor of New Brunswick later the same year. Although subsequent consultations were not publicized, they appear to have taken place discreetly. Then, in 2012, Harper announced an unprecedented form of consultation on vice-regal appointments through an advisory committee, not only for provincial lieutenant governors but for territorial commissioners and the governor general:

> The Advisory Committee — with a diverse member-ship coming from a range of sectors — will also include two temporary members who will be chosen from the jurisdiction of appointment in the case of Lieutenant Governor and Territorial Commissioner vacan-cies. The Prime Minister will initiate the Advisory Committee process when a vacancy in the office of the Governor General, Lieutenant Governor or Territorial Commissioner is anticipated. The process will involve consultation with key stakeholders on prospective candidates and advice to the Prime Minister on the progress of committee deliberations. As a final step, the Advisory Committee will present a report to the Prime Minister with a shortlist of proposed candidates for consideration.[55]

The announcement specified that the advisory committee would be chaired by Kevin MacLeod, Canadian Secretary to the Queen; among its first members were the distinguished francophone historian Jacques Monet and Robert Watt, who had been the first Chief Herald of Canada. Both the nature of the initiative — historic and non-partisan — and the high calibre of the first appointees augured well for future vice-regal appointments in Canada.

Symbols matter, and those of the provincial vice-regal offices should reflect today's reality that the lieutenant governors are royal representatives in co-sovereign jurisdictions in Confederation. As such, they should be entitled to a twenty-one-gun salute. Furthermore, they should also receive the title "Excellency." Meeting in 2004, the ten lieutenant governors, on the initiative of Lieutenant Governor Lise Thibault of Quebec, where the title "*Excellence*" is already used infor-mally, asked the federal government to make this official.[56] Neither of these changes requires constitutional amendment. They would be administrative decisions, like the one made by the federal government in the 1980s to grant the title "Your Honour" to the spouse of the lieutenant governor.

Ideally, the provincial vice-regal representatives should not be called "lieutenant governors" at all, but "governors," like their Australian counterparts. Hilary Weston, lieutenant governor of Ontario, queried her colleagues at their 2000 conference, "Lieutenant to whom? [...] Canadian lieutenant governors, a kinder, gentler species than elected politicians as a rule, are not understudies for higher office — we hold the highest office in the province, as head of state on behalf of our Sovereign. Perhaps we would better be termed governors, as our role is similar to that of the governor general, albeit for a province."[57] Unlike the other proposed changes, this would require an amendment to the *Constitution Act, 1867*, which is highly unlikely. The best one can hope for is an informal agreement to use the term "governor" in common parlance when legal terminology is not required, as is often done already in Quebec and Nova Scotia.

Constitutional Amendment?

Amending the *Constitution Acts* with respect to the Crown is technically feasible, but only with the agreement of both houses of Parliament and all ten provincial legislatures. This is intended to be — rightly — a rare and difficult process. However, should agreement be reached at some point to review the constitution, there are changes which would better interpret the nature of modern Canadian federalism and in the process enhance the position of the provincial Crown which reflects and incarnates it.

Section 90 of the *British North America Act* applies to the provinces sections 53–57, which deal with royal assent in Parliament. It substitutes the lieutenant governor for the governor general and the governor general for the Queen. While this may seem innocuous, it includes two measures which are inimical to the autonomy of the provinces in Confederation: reservation of royal assent by the lieutenant governor for consideration of the governor general and disallowance of provincial legislation by the governor general on the advice of the federal cabinet. Section 55 provides that the governor general may give royal assent to bills, or withhold it, or reserve it "for the Signification of the Queen's pleasure" — i.e., at the time, that of the British government. Section 56 provides that the governor general must send a copy of each act to the Queen through a (British) secretary of state for possible disallowance. The last time a Canadian bill was reserved by a governor general was by Lord Lansdowne in 1886. Since the *Statute of Westminster* of 1931, these provisions have been obsolete for Canada, but the provinces have not benefited from a "provincial Statute of Westminster" to nullify the archaic provisions which continue to apply to them. Canadian provinces still have the residual obligation of sending their legislation to Ottawa for potential consideration of disallowance. Disallowance, last invoked in Alberta in 1943, and reservation, last used in Saskatchewan in 1961, are now both considered obsolete. Although Bill C-60 of 1978 did provide for their elimination, this was not included in the patriation package of 1981. Thus they remain "on the books," leading to concern that they could be resurrected again. If constitutional amendments occur, section 90 is a prime target for repeal. (Section 9 of the *Australia Acts* of 1986 terminated the power of reservation in the Australian states.)

The power of reservation of royal assent is prejudicial to the perception of the role of the lieutenant governor. Obsolete or not, reservation may still be seen as a tool for a centralizing federal government; if it were removed, the federal selection of the lieutenant governor might be less problematic. Regardless, the method of appointment should be part of a constitutional amendment. Section 58 of the *British North America Act* states that the lieutenant governor is appointed "by the Governor General in Council." Section 59 provides that the lieutenant governor "shall hold Office during the Pleasure of the Governor General" and specifies the way in which a lieutenant governor may be removed. Two options for provincial vice-regal appointments could be considered: the Australian system of appointment by the Queen on the advice of the premier (section 7(5) of the *Australia Acts*); or formalizing consultation with the province, so that the governor general acts on the advice of the premier to the prime minister. In either case, sections 58 and 59 would be amended accordingly. It would be desirable to maintain a five-year minimum term of office for the lieutenant governor. Throughout the *Constitution Acts*, the title "lieutenant governor" should be replaced by "governor" — just as proposed in the pre-Confederation London Resolutions of December 28, 1866. Finally, the *Commission* and *Instructions* issued by the federal government to each lieutenant governor at the time of his or her appointment are clearly archaic and should be replaced: they reflect the pre-*Maritime Bank* view of the office's federal role through reservation of royal assent and notification of disallowance.

There are also improvements which are in the purview of the provinces.

Vice-Regal Resources and Accountability

Lieutenant governors need resources — adequate budgets for staff, offices, travel, entertainment, and media relations. Securing resources from any government is a challenge. There is a built-in bias in the system that vice-regal activities, while pleasant enough, are frills which need not be taken seriously by the treasury board. Politicians and bureaucrats and the public need to be educated on the Crown and persuaded that such expenditures are worthwhile.

Australia's Peter Boyce points to the practical constraints on the Canadian vice-regal offices in terms of budget and staff. Lieutenant governors' private secretaries lack the bureaucratic status of the Australian official secretaries; those in some of the offices are essentially executive assistants. The smallest Australian vice-regal establishment has a bigger budget than the largest Canadian one. Although Saskatchewan and New Brunswick have made substantial progress in this regard, only British Columbia and Ontario can compare with the Australian states — and Ontario does without a Government House. This limited support means that Canadian lieutenant governors are restricted, says Boyce, in "the quality of available in-house advice on constitutional matters, as well as an understanding of important precedents in protocol."[58] J.R. Mallory, writing fifteen years earlier than Boyce, had already commented, "Lieutenant-Governors have been hampered by an absence of the usual infrastructure of informed advice which is normally found in Government House, and have felt uncertain where to turn for advice."[59]

The cost of the Crown is minuscule in the overall scale of government expenditures. A 2013 survey by the Monarchist League of Canada revealed that the Crown cost Canadians $1.63 a year each. The office of the governor general accounted for $1.31; the lieutenant governors cost Canadians on average $0.28 per person. The survey compares the cost of the Crown with that of the Senate ($2.57 per Canadian) and of the National Gallery of Canada ($1.46 per Canadian).[60] This is indeed small potatoes. But in this day of increased accountability and freedom of information requests, even small potatoes are subject to media and public scrutiny. And financial accountability and public scrutiny of vice-regal offices have been an issue from time to time. A well-known federal example is the controversy over Governor General Adrienne Clarkson's circumpolar trip in 2003. The trip, like all such initiatives, was done on government advice. The 2003 trip was "instigated and approved by the government of the day, which delegated two ministers (Stéphane Dion and David Anderson) to accompany Madame Clarkson. [...] However, when public criticism of the trip's cost erupted neither the Prime Minister nor any of his ministers (least of all the ones who had gone along on the trip) came to the governor general's defence. Only the leader of the New Democratic Party, Jack Layton, pointed out that the governor general was just doing her job as requested by the government."[61] The governor general was vilified in Parliament — a clear breach of the time-honoured convention that the first minister and the ministry always defend the actions and expenditures of the Crown's representative. As Clarkson said in her 2006 memoir, "no politicians of any parties, including the government, stood up in the House of Commons to say that the Governor General never travels except under advice from the government. It was hugely disappointing to me that they could not, or would not, do that."[62]

Similar controversies have occurred in Nova Scotia and Quebec. The Quebec cases are particularly troubling. Jean-Louis Roulx, a distinguished stage and television actor and director, and a senator from 1994 to 1996, was appointed lieutenant governor of Quebec in September 1996. An avowed federalist, he had campaigned for the "no" side in the 1995 Quebec referendum on sovereignty, and his vice-regal appointment by Prime Minister Jean Chrétien aroused the ire of the Parti Québécois government. Unfortunately, Roulx revealed in a media interview that, as a nineteen-year-old student in 1942, he had expressed sympathies for the fascist Pétain regime in France and that of Franco in Spain (as had much of the Quebec population at the time). The resulting outcry led to a demand by Lucien Bouchard's Parti Québécois government that Roulx resign. Furthermore, there was a call to abolish the position of the lieutenant governor: the Quebec National Assembly adopted a motion "déclarant que la fonction de lieutenant-gouverneur est 'essentiellement symbolique et héritée du passé colonial du Québec et du Canada' et exprime le souhait qu'elle soit abolie."[63] Less than two months after his installation, the seventy-three-year-old Roulx resigned as lieutenant governor. To add insult to injury, the Bouchard government closed Government House, *la Maison Dunn*, making Quebec the only province other than Ontario not to have one.[64]

Lise Thibault was appointed as Roulx's successor, taking office in January 1997. She fulfilled the most delicate vice-regal role in the country with the utmost dedication and at great personal sacrifice for ten years. For this, Thibault won plaudits from all sides of the political spectrum in Quebec. However, financial irregularities in her office damaged Thibault's reputation and regrettably led to criminal charges. Her successor, Pierre Duchesne, former clerk of the Quebec National Assembly, was low-key. But even he was criticized by nationalists for reviving the tradition of a lieutenant governor's medallion in 2010; in its critique, the Parti Québécois called the monarchy "a symbol of English Canada's domination over francophone Quebeckers." The same year, Duchesne — rightly — refused to appear before a legislative committee examining his office's expenditures (he sent his private secretary instead), and was criticized for this by none other than Premier Jean Charest.[65] From these and other examples, it appears that the tradition of unconditional ministerial support for the Crown's representative is a thing of the past. Vice-regal budgets, modest as they are, will receive the same public scrutiny and criticism as any others. It is therefore important for vice-regal offices to be transparent and publicly accountable.

Bureaucratic Support

Bureaucratic support for provincial vice-regal offices is crucial. The premier may agree with the lieutenant governor that certain things should be done. But if the officials do not follow up, or drag their feet, or throw up roadblocks, things will *not* get done despite the best intentions of the premier. Hostility to the Crown is nothing new in Canadian bureaucracies. It characterized official Ottawa for decades and has appeared in several provinces, not only Quebec but also Nova Scotia and, as has been noted, Saskatchewan. Often the Crown is a matter of indifference or ignorance in the public service. Some political staff consider the vice-regal office to be a rival to the premier for publicity and prestige. Former lieutenant governor Hilary Weston of Ontario alluded to this problem in her 2007 memoirs. Noting that "the regular consultation between the LG and the Premier and his ministers was a custom from a bygone age," she found "the Premier and cabinet ministers approachable and willing to meet, but their staffs were less so. Breaches of protocol on their part were caused more by lack of knowledge than spite."[66]

Lieutenant governors and their staff need, therefore, to cultivate supporters and advocates within the bureaucracy. Crucial are provincial offices of protocol. In Canadian provinces and territories, these are responsible for state ceremonial, visits of international dignitaries (ambassadors, foreign heads of state and government, delegations), and tours of members of the Royal Family and the governor general. In all provinces except Alberta, Ontario, and Quebec, they are also responsible for honours and awards. Consequently, protocol offices directly handle much of the policy and programming related to the Crown. They are natural associates for the vice-regal offices. The two should work closely together, while taking care that the respective interests of executive government and the Crown are differentiated and safeguarded. It is in the interest of both parties that the role and status of the lieutenant governor be respected in events such as the opening of the Legislature, investitures, key international visits, and royal tours. Strong protocol offices that enjoy the support of their government will make a substantial contribution to the well-being of the vice-regal office and, by extension, the entire institution of the provincial Crown. Weaker ones, by contrast, can hinder and even undermine that institution. There is an immense difference between protocol services that are policy-oriented and led accordingly and those that are relegated to fulfilling operational functions.

Key to the provincial Crown are senior officials such as deputy ministers to the premiers and those responsible for vice-regal budgets. Understanding, knowledgeable, and sympathetic senior officials can accomplish great things. Conversely, a clueless, even hostile deputy minister can wreak havoc. Any lieutenant governor's office can cite chapter and verse about both types. Since senior officials typically are unaware of the value or significance of the vice-regal office, it is a matter of forging a relationship with them and gradually educating them. If that does not work, and as a last resort, a governor may have to ask the first minister to intervene. This, of course, is contingent upon a supportive and informed premier.

The relationship of vice-regal representatives with their first ministers is, or should be, a vital one. In Saskatchewan, as previously discussed, Lieutenant Governor Sylvia Fedoruk proposed to Premier Roy Romanow in 1991 that they meet monthly in private to discuss issues of the day. The premier agreed with alacrity. Regular meetings have continued since between five lieutenant governors and three premiers, and the practice has been of immense value to both parties. It is a genuine application of the principle enunciated by Walter Bagehot, that the Sovereign or her representative has three rights: to be consulted, to encourage, and to warn. If governors and first ministers develop this kind of relationship, it will not only help defuse controversy but also enhance and solidify the role of the Crown. Ultimately, the citizens are the beneficiaries. Each position ensures that "the people" are the recipients of distinctly different contributions. Premiers oversee public policy and financial governance. The Crown represents every individual regardless of political persuasion, socio-economic status, age, location, gender, or religious affiliation. The premier's strength is, appropriately, politically and ideologically based. The Crown's strength is derived from its non-partisanship.

Commenting on the monthly meetings between the governors and premiers of Tasmania in Australia, the vice-regal official secretary in the state said that recent governors "have each been eminently qualified to provide reasoned, impartial advice."[67] It is unfortunate that not all provincial governments have followed the examples of Tasmania and Saskatchewan. It would greatly enhance not only the vice-regal office but also the entire political process if they did so.

VI

Canada: Federal Monarchy — or Federal Republic?

No part of this country has ever been a republic or part of a republic and to become one would be an abrupt break with our history. Our monarchy, our British monarchy, our Anglo-French monarchy, our historic monarchy, is part of the Canadian tradition. It is not something alien. It is bone of our bone and flesh of our flesh.[1]

— Eugene Forsey

Even if, unlike Australia, there has been little organized republican movement in Canada,[2] the relevance and desirability of the constitutional monarchy have been questioned. Given the evolution of Canadian society into a multicultural mosaic, and the substantial economic and political changes in the country, institutions such as parliamentary democracy, the electoral system, and the monarchy are constantly under scrutiny. With its British origins and continuing connection with the Sovereign of the United Kingdom, the monarchy is an easy target for skeptics labelling it as archaic and foreign. It is true that the "head of state," if this term must be used, is non-resident, drawn from the British royal family and, therefore, one particular ethnic and religious strand. There may seem to be disadvantages to this in a modern multicultural society. The coolness of Quebec towards the monarchy since the 1960s has been a major consideration in Canadian attitudes towards the Crown.

DOWNPLAYING THE MONARCHY

Starting as early as the 1950s and accelerating during the 1960s and 1970s, there was a clear trend in official Ottawa to downplay and downgrade the monarchy and related symbols. The historic term "dominion" was jettisoned. Historian Donald Creighton commented acerbically that the word "seemed to have aroused in [prime ministers] King and St. Laurent a curious, almost pathological resentment; and ever since 1936 they had been systematically removing it from public documents and replacing it simply with the word 'Canada' or the phrase 'government of Canada.'"[3] "Royal Mail" yielded to "Canada Post," and Canada's royal coat of arms of 1921 disappeared from mailboxes and postal vans. In 1955, when the Canadian Pacific Railway proposed to name its new streamlined transcontinental passenger train The Royal Canadian, the federal government reportedly pressured the company into deleting the word "royal." The national maple leaf flag, inaugurated in 1965, replaced the too-British Red Ensign.[4] The coat of arms gave way, in most instances, to the maple leaf logo. The unification of the Canadian Forces in the late 1960s was an opportunity to abolish the *Royal* Canadian Navy and the *Royal* Canadian Air Force and the traditional army, navy, and air force uniforms. The monarchical side of Canada's system of government was minimized in official documents, especially for immigrants and citizenship.

In 1971, there was an abortive attempt by the Trudeau government to change the name of the Royal Canadian Mounted Police to "Canada Police." There was a public outcry, and the idea was hastily dropped. In a travesty of parliamentary procedure in 1980, the national anthem was declared in a hurried House of Commons vote to be "O Canada" — which was fair enough, as the federal government had given notice as early as 1964, during the flag debate, that it intended to do so. However, according to the same notice, "God Save the Queen" was to be the official royal anthem, and this was omitted in 1980. Through another parliamentary subterfuge, the name of the national holiday was changed from Dominion Day to Canada Day by a quick voice vote in the House of Commons, with few members present, on a Friday afternoon in July 1982.

While many of the "Canadianization" measures, like the flag and national honours, were timely, the unilateral federal approach provoked some negative and lasting reactions. Even the motivation for the selection of the maple leaf flag in 1964 has been challenged by some scholars.[5] In reaction, the Conservative-governed provinces of Ontario and Manitoba adopted versions of the Red Ensign as their provincial flags in 1965 and 1966, respectively. "God Save the Queen" continued to be played or sung as the Canadian royal anthem in many events sponsored by provinces, municipalities, and non-governmental organizations, despite its lack of official status (the Department of Canadian Heritage issued a directive that the anthem was only to be used in the presence of members of the Royal Family and on other, unspecified occasions). Army reserve units, the repository of locally based military tradition, fought to keep dress uniforms at their own expense and to maintain or even acquire royal colonels-in-chief.* A decades-long campaign to reverse the symbolic aspects of unification, although not the actual administrative merger, bore its first fruit in 1985, when Brian Mulroney's Progressive Conservative government restored distinctive uniforms to the three services. Finally, in 2011, Stephen Harper's Conservative government brought back the names Royal Canadian Navy, Royal Canadian Air Force, and Canadian Army. Evidently, there had been deep-seated and enduring unease about the efforts to dismantle Canada's monarchical traditions. From 2006, the Conservative government capitalized on this discomfort.

However, for five decades, to all intents and purposes, the Canadian Crown, despite its historical and constitutional originality, was conflated with the British Empire and things British. Both were considered passé and undesirable after the Second World War, as Canada embraced the new imperialism of the United States. True, the monarchy retained too much of its British aura in Canada. The Royal Family and their staff had not yet fully grasped the implications of the 1952 title "Queen of Canada," as they would increasingly do from the 1970s. Yet for much of Canada's history "British" and "Canadian" had been considered complementary, not contradictory, even, as we have seen, paradoxically in Quebec. "Simply put, the British tradition is not something foreign: it is a constitutive part of Canadian identity," said

---

* The Royal Regina Rifles, for example, acquired their royal title and Princess Anne as colonel-in-chief in 1982.

one writer, adding, "[i]ndignant publicists, steeped in neo-nationalist doctrine, will continue the Quixotic fight to be free of our 'colonial' past, tilting at imperial windmills."[6] It is only recently that Canadian historiography has looked more kindly on the British connection. "Britishness," says Jonathan Vance, "was not an unthinking attachment to anything and everything emanating from the British Isles [...] On the contrary, it represented an affection for British liberal ideals [...] Britishness as it evolved in Canada was uniquely Canadian ..."[7]

Indeed, governors general from the United Kingdom had been staunch proponents of Canadianism and were especially partial to francophone Canada. This has already been noted with respect to the post-conquest and pre-Confederation governors, such as Amherst, Murray, Carleton, and Elgin. Viscount Monck, the first governor general after Confederation, had proposed a Canadian honours system as early as 1866. Lord Lisgar (1868–1872) worked assiduously to ensure that Manitoba and British Columbia joined Confederation. His successor, the Earl of Dufferin (1872–1878), established the vice-regal residence at *La Citadelle* in Quebec and led a campaign to preserve the historic city from wanton redevelopment. Dufferin was keen to promote the arts in Canada and became patron of the Ontario Society of Artists. "I believe the cultivation of art to be a most essential element of our national life," he said.[8]

The Marquis of Lorne (1878–1883), married to a daughter of Queen Victoria, Princess Louise, did much to cement British Columbia's attachment to Canada. Termed by a biographer "the enthusiastic Canadian," Lorne founded the Royal Canadian Academy of Arts, the National Gallery of Canada, and the Royal Society of Canada, and was the first to suggest a federal ministry of culture.[9] Lord Stanley (1888–1893) promoted hockey and donated the famous Stanley Cup; he also defended Canada's interests to the British government in disputes with the United States.[10] Lady Aberdeen, wife of the Earl of Aberdeen (1893–1898), was an advocate of social reform. She was appalled by the living and working conditions of poor women and children, such as baby-farming in Quebec and sweatshops in Toronto. "Against tremendous odds," said Sandra Gwyn, "she established almost single-handedly first, in 1894, the National Council of Women and, in 1897, to celebrate the Diamond Jubilee, the Victorian Order of Nurses."[11] Both institutions have endured. The Earl of Minto (1898–1904) was an avid fan of the Canadian outdoors, hunting, fishing, skiing, hiking, canoeing, and mountain-climbing. He appreciated First Nations culture when this was not fashionable. Like other governors general, he was partial to Quebec and worked to improve French-English relations.[12] Earl Grey (1904–1911) masterminded the three hundredth anniversary celebrations of Quebec City in 1908 and donated the Grey Cup for football. Lord Byng (1921–1926) was thoroughly indentified with Canada through his successful command of Canadian troops in the First World War. The Earl of Bessborough (1931–1935), fearing for the survival of theatre in Canada, established the Dominion Drama Festival in 1933.[13] Lord Tweedsmuir (1935–1940), the novelist John Buchan,[14] instituted the Governor General's Literary Awards in 1937. It was indicative of the "Canadianization" of the British governors general that Lord Tweedsmuir — first governor general appointed after the *Statute of Westminster* — said in 1937, the year of the coronation of King George VI, "Canada is a sovereign nation and cannot take her attitude to the world docilely from Britain or from the United States or from anybody else. A Canadian's first loyalty is not to the British Commonwealth of Nations but to Canada and Canada's King."[15]

"Canadianization" of the monarchy was already in the air. King George VI's private secretary, Sir Alan "Tommy" Lascelles, recorded in his diaries a meeting in 1945 in London with Sir Shuldham Redfern, secretary to the governor general of Canada, where Redfern "propounded a scheme for the closer association of the Sovereign with Canada by making periodic flights to Ottawa, opening Parliament and conducting other governmental and social business." The idea was prescient but ahead of its time, and Lascelles discounted it in practical terms.[16] Later the same year, Viscount Alexander, just named governor general of Canada on the recommendation of Mackenzie King, met with Lascelles. He announced his intention to appoint a Canadian secretary at Rideau Hall, which Lascelles applauded. Alexander was to be the last "British" governor general, but the vice-regal office and the monarchy were already viewed very much in Canadian terms, not least at Buckingham Palace.

Lord Tweedsmuir, the novelist John Buchan, was the first governor general appointed after the 1931 *Statute of Westminster*. Shown here in 1936, he advocated Canadian nationalism.

Kaiden-Kazanian Studios Inc., Library & Archives Canada

From 1952 to 1974, the first three "Canadian" governors general — Vincent Massey (1952–1959), Georges Vanier (1959–1967), and Roland Michener (1967–1974) — ably carried forward the indigenous traditions of the Crown. Yet it was during this period that federal governments began dismantling them. Prime Minister Lester Pearson is said to have wanted to phase out the monarchy had he ever secured a majority government.[17] Early in Pierre Trudeau's time as prime minister, a number of his cabinet colleagues, notably Mitchell Sharp, minister of external affairs, were keen on eliminating the monarchy.[18] By the time Jules Léger (1974–1979) became governor general, the de-monarchizing campaign was in full swing under the Trudeau government. It would accelerate in the following three decades with Léger's successors. Significantly, the titles of two vice-regal biographies were *The Imperial Canadian* for Massey[19] and *The Last Viceroy* for Michener.[20] Roland Michener was the last governor general to wear the British "civil uniform."[21]

His austere successor, Jules Léger, in sharp contrast, had little use for monarchical pomp and circumstance. Stories abounded of his objections to uniforms, aides-de-camp, and the normal trappings of the vice-regal office, although he eventually developed a good relationship with Queen Elizabeth and enjoyed corresponding with the monarch. Léger's incumbency pro-

The Queen opens Parliament in Ottawa in 1977, her Silver Jubilee year. The Trudeau government was reluctant to invite the monarch.

CP Images

vided suitable terrain for Trudeau's 1978 "governor general as head of state" initiative. The Queen and members of the Royal Family did make a number of tours in Canada during the 1970s and 1980s, but these were increasingly at the request of provinces, municipalities, and non-governmental organizations. Trudeau's administration was reluctant to feature Queen Elizabeth II's Silver Jubilee in 1977. Grudgingly, it arranged a short visit to Ottawa for the monarch, during which she opened Parliament, for the second and only time since 1957. The Queen had come with her entire family the year prior for the summer Olympics in Montreal and would return a year later with her youngest son, Prince Edward, for the Commonwealth Games in Edmonton, when she also visited Saskatchewan. The brief 1976 Silver Jubilee visit and a short tour in British Columbia in 1983 (following a visit by Queen to California) were said to have been masterminded by Esmond Butler, secretary to the governor general, with his colleagues at Buckingham Palace, despite the distinct lack of enthusiasm of the Trudeau government.[22]

Liberals were not the only ones to minimize the monarchy, even though the prime movers were unquestionably the governments of St. Laurent (1948–1957), Pearson (1963–1968), and Trudeau (1968–1979, 1980–1984). Diefenbaker's Conservative government of 1957–1963 did resist the trend, inviting the Queen to open Parliament in 1957 and to undertake a lengthy country-wide tour — the last of its kind — in 1959, but appeared out of sync with the times. Joe Clark's brief Conservative minority government of 1979 was not in office long enough to demonstrate a propensity one way or the other (although it did secure the title "royal" for the Royal Newfoundland Constabulary). Brian Mulroney's Progressive Conservative government (1984–1993) did little to promote the Crown. It included a Canadian version of the Victoria Cross (VC) among the military valour decorations established in 1993, but this came only after the federal honours policy committee, ignoring calls from the Royal Canadian Legion and others for a VC, proposed instead a "Cross of Military Valour." A media leak and intense lobbying persuaded the government to change its mind.[23] Federal governments, whatever their stripe, under the baleful influence of Rideau Hall, minimized the monarch's involvement in the national honours system. The last time the Queen personally conferred Canadian honours (other than the Royal Victorian Order) was in 1973, despite ample opportunities to do so.[24]

In any event, for decades the mindset of the senior federal bureaucracy was anti-monarchical and even republican in tone. This was, in part, but certainly not entirely, a reflection of the strong francophone presence in the Ottawa public service since the bilingualism campaign which followed passage of the *Official Languages Act* in 1969. The office of the governor general, Rideau Hall, became one of the principal foyers of anti-monarchical sentiment following the appointment of Jeanne Sauvé as governor general (1984–1990). In her first year in office, Sauvé dismissed the highly respected Esmond Butler as secretary to the governor general. He had been in the position for twenty-five years, serving governors general since the iconic Georges Vanier and carefully shepherding the "Canadianization" of the Crown by preserving some traditions while introducing new ones, such as the honours system begun in 1967. Those cool on the monarchy, however, resented Butler's robust defence of the institution and his initiatives to obtain royal tours. Butler's departure left the "de-monarchizers" in control of Rideau Hall, to the extent that, by the 1990s, some wags were calling it "Republican Hall."

Governor General Jeanne Sauvé was not enthusiastic about royalty. In 1988, she received Letters Patent from Prince Edward, transferring the royal prerogative of heraldry to the governor general.

The guiding principles of the new regime appeared to be that the monarchy was un-Canadian and that the Queen and Royal Family detracted from or rivalled the governor general, who truly incarnated Canada. Jeanne Sauvé was heard to make caustic comments about Prince Edward when he represented the monarch at the transfer of the royal prerogative of heraldry to the Canadian Heraldic Authority in 1988.[25] During her tenure, the crown disappeared as a Rideau Hall emblem. Similar trends appeared in the Department of Canadian Heritage, responsible for symbols, state ceremonies, and royal tours. This would continue through the tenures of governors general Roméo LeBlanc, Adrienne Clarkson, and Michaëlle Jean. An indication of the deeply rooted attitude and pervasive influence of the federal bureaucracy was its success in stalling publication of an educational booklet on the monarchy, *A Crown of Maples / La Couronne canadienne*, for no fewer than fifteen years. (It finally came to fruition in 2008 — two years after the pro-monarchy Conservative government of Stephen Harper had taken office.[26])

GOVERNOR GENERAL AND PRIME MINISTER

In the early years of Confederation, Canadian governors general presided over formal meetings of the Queen's Privy Council for Canada, to swear in new members or put into effect decisions of the cabinet, technically "the Committee of the Privy Council" (governors general still preside over meetings of the equivalent Executive Council in Australia). The practice lapsed after the 1890s.[27] Thereafter, while some prime ministers met regularly with their governors general, others did not. Prime Minister Mackenzie King deliberately did *not* keep his governors general informed.[28] Jacques Monet, studying their daily agendas, discovered that Governors General Alexander (1946–1952) and Massey (1952–1959) had only rare meetings with prime ministers Louis St. Laurent and John Diefenbaker. In 1960, not a single visit was recorded from Diefenbaker to Governor General Georges Vanier.[29]

Then, from the 1960s, Governors General Vanier, Michener, and Léger met regularly, even weekly, with prime ministers Lester Pearson and Pierre Trudeau.[30] Roland Michener later commented on his very positive weekly meetings with Pearson and Trudeau.[31] Yet Trudeau did not meet regularly with Governor General Edward Schreyer (1979–1984), and, while he apparently did so briefly with Jeanne Sauvé (1984–1990), the pattern unravelled further when Brian Mulroney, a Progressive Conservative, became prime minister shortly after Sauvé took office. The relationship between a governor general appointed by a previous prime minister and that person's successor is often not an easy one, especially when the governor general is a former politician and the new head of government is from a different party. Thus, Mulroney's rapport with Sauvé could not be considered warm, nor was the relationship between Ramon Hnatyshyn (1990–1995), who had been selected by Mulroney after serving in his cabinet, and Liberal Prime Minister Jean Chrétien. It is not clear whether Chrétien met frequently with his own appointee, the low-key, nearly invisible Roméo LeBlanc (1995–1999).

After the illustrious Massey-Vanier-Michener era, prime ministers used their right to "advise" the Sovereign on the appointment of her governor general in a way calculated to minimize the import of the position. Jules Léger was due to be replaced in 1979, after five years in office overshadowed by a stroke he had suffered early in his tenure. Another distinguished diplomat — and this time a definite monarchist — George Ignatieff (father of a future leader of the federal Liberal Party, Michael Ignatieff) was in the running. Ignatieff seemed the ideal candidate. Of Russian émigré origin, he had served as Canada's ambassador to NATO, ambassador to the United Nations, and permanent representative to the Geneva Disarmament Commission. In 1972, he retired from the Department of External Affairs to become provost of Trinity College in the University of Toronto (where he had earned a Rhodes Scholarship in 1936*). His wife, Alison Grant, from another distinguished Canadian family, was the Queen's Canadian lady-in-waiting during her 1978 tour. However, Prime Minister Pierre Trudeau, in a fit of pique, it was rumoured, because George (or Alison) had talked about the potential appointment, in an abrupt *volte-face* appointed Edward Schreyer, the recently defeated NDP premier of Manitoba, as the next

---

* Another eminent graduate of Trinity College, Adrienne Clarkson, became governor general twenty years later, in 1999.

governor general. Schreyer's unusual nomination reportedly took both him and the Queen by surprise. Schreyer even said the telephone call asking him to accept the vice-regal appointment was "such a strange call I couldn't take it seriously."[32]

The decidedly uncharismatic Schreyer was unskilled in the small talk essential for vice-regal positions (his extrovert wife, Lily, compensated somewhat for his lack in this regard). He was evidently bored with his duties and was said to have spent his spare time reading encyclopaedias. His brief forays into constitutional issues were widely criticized — public speculation in 1979 about the reserve power of dismissal, hesitation that year about granting defeated Prime Minister Joe Clark's request for dissolution, and, in 1982, further speculation about forced dissolution over the controversial patriation of the constitution. Only forty-three at the time of his appointment, Schreyer was forty-nine when he left office. After a term as high commissioner to Australia, "his subsequent searches for other suitable employment, culminating in an unsuccessful bid to return to politics, somehow detracted from the dignity of the high office he once held."[33] (Michaëlle Jean, leaving office at age fifty-three, faced a similar challenge in 2010.)

Trudeau's 1979 appointment of Schreyer began a twenty-year period of political appointees to the national vice-regal office. In 1984, Trudeau named former Liberal cabinet minister Jeanne Sauvé, first female speaker of the House of Commons, to be the first woman governor general (Sauvé's anti-monarchical views have already been noted). Conservative Prime Minister Brian Mulroney maintained the pattern set by Trudeau when he appointed former cabinet minister Ramon Hnatyshyn to the vice-regal position in 1990. Although he was, unlike his immediate predecessors, sympathetic to the monarchy, Hnatyshyn proved unable or unwilling to counter the now-entrenched republican sentiment at Rideau Hall. Jean Chrétien, in his first vice-regal appointment as prime minister, appeared to seal the fate of the governor general in 1995 by naming an old-style Liberal politician from New Brunswick, Roméo LeBlanc, at the time speaker of the Senate. LeBlanc reversed what Hnatyshyn had been able to accomplish for the Crown, and the prestige of the governor general reached its lowest ebb ever. Perhaps it is no coincidence that the profile of the lieutenant governors rose during the period that the public image of the governors general declined. For appointees to the provincial vice-regal offices became, on the whole, less overtly political just as those to the national office became much more so. Whatever their individual merits and accomplishments, former politicians appointed governor general were handicapped by their partisan past, especially when the opposing party won the election during their tenure (as happened to Sauvé and Hnatyshyn). Just when the federal government tried to popularize the notion of the governor general as head of state in lieu of the Queen, the prestige of the national vice-regal office steadily declined, due largely to the same government's dismissive attitude to it. In 1999, David E. Smith declared "[n]otwithstanding the personal qualities of the appointees, which have often been extraordinary, the Canadian governor general has become a hermetic head of state — ignored by press, politicians and public."[34]

Jean Chrétien, however, redeemed himself when he appointed Adrienne Clarkson as governor general in 1999. The only point Clarkson held in common with LeBlanc was that, prior to entering Rideau Hall, she hastened to marry her long-time partner, philosopher and writer John Ralston Saul, just as LeBlanc had done with Diana Fowler. The fact that Clarkson was widely rumoured to be in the running for the position did not appear to bother Chrétien, as similar rumblings twenty years earlier about George Ignatieff had upset Trudeau. Adrienne Clarkson proved to be a superb choice. Her memoir makes clear that she enjoyed an excellent relationship with her first "first minister," who turned out to have a genuine understanding of and appreciation for the Crown. Clarkson recounts how Chrétien revived the tradition of regular consultation between governor general and prime minister, sometimes calling her before question period in the House of Commons. In 2003, for example, he told her about the decision not to send troops to Iraq before announcing it in the House.[35] (Deservedly, Jean Chrétien was recognized by the Queen in 2009 with a rare royal honour in her personal gift, the Order of Merit.)

The same cannot be said for Chrétien's Liberal successor, Paul Martin, who appeared not to appreciate or respect the vice-regal office. This was evident when he tried to have his government sworn in on Parliament Hill rather than at Rideau Hall — a change which Governor

General Clarkson rightly refused.[36] It culminated in Martin's dismal failure to defend the governor general's expenditures in Parliament in 2003 during the controversy over her international tours. Martin's dismissive attitude to the Crown was apparent in forthright comments, reported in various conversations, about the opportunity to move beyond the monarchy after the present Queen's reign.[37] However, through her energy, intellect, and artistic and literary talent, Adrienne Clarkson transformed the role of the governor general. Skilled in writing, public speaking, and media relations, she travelled tirelessly throughout Canada, giving thoughtful, substantive speeches where she drew attention to key current issues facing Canadians and vigorously promoted national identity. The same was true for her international voyages, when she led Canadian economic and cultural delegations with her husband, John Ralston Saul, even if their circumpolar tours came to grief due to lack of ministerial support. Clarkson and Saul made Rideau Hall a showcase for Canadian literature, art, cuisine, wines, and gardening.[38] (This followed similar efforts a decade earlier by Governor General Ramon Hnatyshyn and his wife, Gerda.[39])

In her nearly six years on the job, Adrienne Clarkson rescued and revived the national vice-regal office from the obscurity in which it had languished through twenty years of politicians in the position, culminating in Roméo LeBlanc's colourless tenure. It was unfortunate, therefore, that the very capable Clarkson and Saul chose to exalt the position of governor general at the expense of those of the Queen and the lieutenant governors and to promote the national vice-regal position as Canadian "head of state." Lieutenant governors resented what they saw as a condescending attitude towards the provincial vice-regal offices. Nonetheless, on leaving office in 2005, Adrienne Clarkson was widely regarded as the most effective and influential governor general since Roland Michener.

Late in 2005, Paul Martin made the unusual, even bizarre, appointment of Quebec television journalist and Haitian immigrant Michaëlle Jean to succeed Clarkson. As was the case with Jeanne Sauvé in 1984 and Ramon Hnatyshyn in 1990, the appointment was soon followed by an election where a new prime minister from another party took office. From early 2006, Conservative Stephen Harper headed the government, and an uneasy relationship ensued between first minister and governor general. This was echoed by a chilly rapport between Rideau Hall and the prime minister's office, exacerbated by ill-advised moves on the part of Jean and her staff. These included public comments on matters of public policy. In 2008, for example, Jean's office leaked her advice to Prime Minister Harper to repatriate a Canadian from U.S. detention in Guantanamo Bay, prompting the *Globe and Mail* to question "Ms. Jean's impartiality, and hence her ability to exercise her constitutional responsibilities." The governor general, said the newspaper, had the "right to warn, but not to leak."[40] In the same year, her opinion on the Afghanistan war was made public. In the field of national honours, Rideau Hall was embroiled in public controversy over the awarding of a bravery decoration. In at least one case, the process of appointment to the Order of Canada was expedited, said honours expert Christopher McCreery, "to allow the governor general a photo opportunity, a step that only serves to trivialize the honours system." He reported that there had been "muted complaints by former members of the advisory council that Madame Jean became overly involved in promoting particular nominations for membership in the Order of Canada. This is something that previous governors general assiduously avoided. As chancellor of the Order of Canada, the governor general is supposed to serve as a neutral arbiter, not a promoter of nominations."[41]

Consequently, it was no surprise that there were not regular meetings between Prime Minister Harper and Governor General Jean, and the exercise of Bagehot's rights became a dead letter in Ottawa. The situation was unfortunate. Despite her inexperience and *faux pas*, Michaëlle Jean had considerable personal charisma and media skills. Relying on wise counsel from advisers, she deftly handled the prorogation issue in 2008. She built on Adrienne Clarkson's foundation to popularize the institution of governor general even more in her travels across Canada and abroad. In the latter, she was particularly welcomed as a symbol of Canada's openness to immigrants and its empathy and aid for third world countries. On the other hand, there was concern in official Ottawa over Jean's apparent eagerness to compete for publicity with the prime minister and government. Governors general need to strike a delicate balance in the rapport with their first ministers; Michaëlle Jean did not.

The appointment of the next governor general by Stephen Harper in 2010 represented a welcome change from the practice of prime ministerial whims. Harper commissioned a group of expert, independent advisors to recommend candidates for the vice-regal position. The result of this consultation was the naming of David Johnston, president of the University of Waterloo.

A REPUBLICAN OPTION FOR CANADA?

Commenting on David E. Smith's *The Invisible Crown*, the editor of a book of essays in his honour observed that "[t]he significance of its subject matter was not evident to every political scientist, since many consider the Crown an almost exotic, mostly irrelevant artifact of Canada's historical ties with Britain, and thus an institution of doubtful importance as well as considerable nuisance value given its controversial nature to many Canadians."[42] Yet the history and practice of Canadian government and federalism, so well documented in *The Invisible Crown*, demonstrate that the Crown is far from being an exotic and irrelevant artifact. What, then, is the appeal of a republican option for Canada?

Apart from the British dimension of the monarchy, proponents of republicanism argue that the latter is inherently more democratic, based on popular sovereignty and therefore more conducive to citizen engagement. Glenn Patmore and John Whyte, in their call for an Australian republic, refer to "the invocation of a republican philosophy of thought as a value system or a paradigm":

> Republicanism is a rich political philosophy which does not merely entail the replacement of the monarch with a popularly chosen President. This philosophy rests on the idea that the highest collective human endeavour is the joining of citizens, who are approximately equal, in the ongoing political project of self-government. [...] Republicanism is, of course, profoundly anti-monarchical because it is about the rule by all citizens. [...] It is a constitutive principle requiring that both citizens and politi-

cal figures act in the public interest as opposed to, say, the mere satisfaction of wants or vindication of interests.[43]

This argument substitutes a totally different basis of political legitimacy for the concepts that have been traced in this book — a constitutional *tabula rasa* as against the historic evolution which has vested democratic ideals in the monarch and vice-regal representatives and entrusted their theoretical powers to the sovereign's ministers through the mechanism of responsible government. Those proposing a republic see the citizenry rallying around a popularly elected president as an effective symbol of the national identity.

However, despite its appealing theoretical basis, the argument would be more persuasive if it were empirically verified that, in fact, citizen engagement, equality, and the public interest are better served in republics than in monarchies. Examining monarchies such as the United Kingdom, Spain, the Scandinavian nations, and the Benelux countries, compared to republics such as the United States, France, Germany, Ireland, Italy, or Greece, one must seriously question this assertion. It has often been noted that constitutional monarchies are among the world's most prosperous, free, and stable countries. According to the 2011 United Nations Human Development Index, which rated living standards in 170 countries, seven of the top ten were monarchies, with Norway in first place, Australia in second, New Zealand in third, and Canada in eighth.[44]

Regardless of the formal vesting of power in the monarch, constitutional monarchies most assuredly depend on a variant of popular sovereignty mediated through responsible government. In a democracy, no form of government can survive without popular support, which is why unsuccessful monarchies have crumbled in countries as varied as Portugal, Italy, Greece, and Nepal (the monarchies in Albania, Bulgaria, Romania, and Yugoslavia owed their demise mainly to postwar Soviet influence and communism). Popular sovereignty is a fact of life in Australia, given the entrenched practice of referenda, to the point that the country has been called a "crowned republic." Similarly, governing by and through the popular will is a reality of political life in Canada and may well be expressed more frequently through referenda. New Zealand scholar Noel Cox has said:

... the British Crown has often been thought of, and described, as being republican. This is the sense that all power ultimately derives from the people. [...] Since modern constitutional monarchy vests political power in politically-responsible governments, it is potentially misleading to focus upon the notion of government by monarchy versus government by the people, wherever constitutional sovereignty may be vested [...] All modern liberal western states are democratic, which means that politically the people are the primary source of legitimacy, regardless of from wherever the highest office may derive its authority [...] In the Westminster system sovereignty is constitutionally based in the Sovereign-in-Parliament, and political legitimacy is derived from the understanding that ultimate political sovereignty lies with the people.[45]

This popular dimension of constitutional monarchy has a long history. Janet Ajzenstat traces it back to seventeenth-century England, when popular sovereignty was "invented" by the House of Commons: "popular sovereignty is a seventeenth century concept, and the British Constitution as much as the American rests on it. [...] Kings *may* rule but only with the sovereign people's consent [...] The doctrine of popular sovereignty lies at the heart of all free governments; it underpins all codes and bills of rights; it virtually defines the modern idea of political justice; [...] it grounds parliamentary government."[46] Ajzenstat emphasizes that the Fathers of Confederation and colonial legislators (committed, as we have seen, to the monarchical principle), "without exception [...] subscribed to the doctrine of popular sovereignty. The issue [...] was not *whether* to consult the people but *how* to consult them."[47] Should this be through referendum or through Parliament? The debate continues to this day. By the late nineteenth century, Walter Bagehot called the United Kingdom a "disguised republic,"[48] in the sense that, behind the dignified façade of the monarchy, power was in the hands of the representatives of the people. On the occasion of the Queen's Silver Jubilee in 1977, Ralph Heintzman, editor of the *Journal of Canadian Studies*, offered a thoughtful observation on the concept of sovereignty in a monarchy:

The idea of the Crown [...] is that the ultimate source of authority is not to be located in the people but in something higher, something that is above the people and to which they owe allegiance. [...] In a constitutional monarchy [...] the sovereign power may have its source above the people, but the power is exercised by the people and can do only what they themselves have decided upon. A country like Canada where the source of authority is held to be outside the people is no less free than a country like the United States where the people itself is declared to be the source of sovereignty. [...] The symbolic assertion that sovereign authority proceeds from a source above us reminds us that, while we are indeed free to act as we wish, we *ought* nevertheless to act in certain ways rather than in others.[49]

Head of State

The notion of "head of state" is of much concern to the proponents of republican government. The applicability of the term to constitutional monarchies poses a conundrum, especially in the Commonwealth realms and even more so when these are federal states. David Butler, in a book dealing with the delegated monarchies, *Sovereigns and Surrogates*, addressed it as follows: "The term 'Head of State' presents some difficulty. In most of the Commonwealth realms [...] the Queen remains in a formal sense Head of State. But, for almost all practical purposes, the Governor-General acts as Head of State in just the same way as the President of an independent state." To capture the essence of his position, Butler coined the term "Constitutional Head of State" to describe the vice-regal representatives.[50]

In his 2005 book *Head of State: The Governor-General, the Monarchy, the Republic and the Dismissal*, Sir David Smith, a former official secretary to the governor general of Australia, responded to republican arguments against a "foreign" head of state by asserting that the governor general was already head of state in that country. Sir David based his case on the text of the constitution and on accumulated precedents since 1901. It is worth quoting the relevant sections of *The Commonwealth of Australia Constitution Act, 1900.*

> *Section 2*
> A Governor-General appointed by the Queen shall be Her Majesty's representative in the Commonwealth, and shall have and may exercise in the Commonwealth during the Queen's pleasure, but subject to this Constitution, such powers and functions of the Queen as Her Majesty may be pleased to assign to him.

> *Section 61*
> The executive power of the Commonwealth is vested in the Queen and is exercisable by the Governor-General as the Queen's representative, and extends to the execution and maintenance of this Constitution, and of the laws of the Commonwealth.

For Sir David, Section 61 is the crucial text that empowers the governor general, while representing the Queen, to be Australia's head of state. To buttress his case, he cites numerous scholars, politicians (including, ironically, Gough Whitlam), and media articles attesting that the governor general is indeed head of state. His frustration is evident that it took Aussies so long — until the 1980s and the republican debate — to realize this.

Of particular interest are the parallels and contrasts Sir David draws with the constitutional situation in Canada and New Zealand. In those two countries, he asserts, the Queen is head of state and there is no equivalent of Section 61 to confer "head of state" powers on the governor general. He pointed out that Australia's "founding fathers had the *British North America Act* to guide them, and the distinctions they made in the Australian Constitution were quite deliberate" (this has already been noted with respect to the status of the state governors). The reason the term "head of state" does not appear in the *Constitution Act* of 1900 is that "[n]o-one would ever have dreamt of describing Queen Victoria as 'head of state.'" The term was not in use in the British Empire at the time.[51] It is certainly not found in the *British North America Act*. Section 9 of that Act states, "The Executive Government and Authority of and over Canada is hereby declared to continue and be vested in the Queen." Both this section and Section 12 (powers vested in the governor general) appear very similar to Sections 2 and 61 of the Australian constitution. The governors general of Australia and Canada (and presumably New Zealand) are in virtually the same position constitutionally.

Peter Boyce contends that asserting that the governor general is already head of state is constitutionally dubious and certainly unconvincing to republicans. "Recent occupants of Yarralumla [the Australian Rideau Hall] have consistently denied that they assumed the formal status (as distinct from the powers) of head of state." Boyce noted that Section 61 of the Australian constitution "explicitly states that the executive power of the Commonwealth is vested in the Queen and that the Governor-General exercises it on her behalf" (as in Canada). The governor general is appointed by the monarch and is therefore "not the most senior person in the structure of national authority." The governor general, in exercising powers such as royal assent, "acts specifically in the name of the Queen."[52] Smith's argument also has a major flaw in that it does not address the federal nature of the Crown. Promoting the notion of governor general as "head of state" not only marginalizes the Queen but the sub-national governors as well. The Crown reflects and embodies and guarantees the autonomy of the states and provinces, even more explicitly in Australia than in Canada. The "headship of state" is threefold: the Queen, the governor general, and the governors or lieutenant governors. Boyce sees the head of state debate as a matter of semantics: "it probably makes good sense," he says, "to describe the office of head of state in all three former dominions [Australia, Canada, New Zealand] as 'bipartite.'"[53] This statement is only appropriate, however, if the term "tripartite" is applied to the two federations.[54]

There may be a solution to this confusion: bypass the term "head of state" altogether. This is the view of David E. Smith, who notes that the term "head of state" was an invention of the continental European countries that ceased being monarchies. It was not originally used in the British Empire and the nations that emerged from it, or in other monarchies. In response to the 2009 "head of state" episode at Rideau Hall, a comment was made:

"'Head of State' was originally a very republican term, coined to define the significance of new offices like 'president' in nineteenth century Europe. Ancient republics tended not to define any one of their senior magistrates as head of state, even for formal purposes, but modern ones needed to emphasize that their highest official was the diplomatic equal of a king."[55]

The "head of state" issue is misleading, obscuring the subtle realities of Canada's constitutional monarchy. We have a sovereign, a governor general, and lieutenant governors at the head of our constitutional order; republican terminology is simply not relevant. The Buckingham Palace website does say, "The Queen is Head of State of the UK and 15 other Commonwealth realms." But it goes on to affirm: "As Head of State, The Monarch undertakes constitutional and representational duties which have developed over one thousand years of history. In addition to these State duties, *The Monarch has a less formal role as 'Head of Nation'* [our emphasis]. The Sovereign acts as a focus for national identity, unity and pride; gives a sense of stability and continuity; officially recognises success and excellence; and supports the ideal of voluntary service."[56]

In a revealing and timely book, published for the Diamond Jubilee in 2012, *Her Majesty: Queen Elizabeth II and Her Court*, veteran royal commentator Robert Hardman (author of the 2007 book and television documentary *A Year with The Queen*) tells the story of how this second role of the monarch was identified. It was the idea of Sir Anthony Jay, co-creator of the smash-hit television comedy series *Yes, Minister* and *Yes, Prime Minister* and writer of the landmark film documentaries *Royal Family* (1967) and *Elizabeth R* (1992). A student of Bagehot, Jay considers the "Head of Nation" role equally as important as the "Head of State" role, "but one with a much more personal dimension… [the duties] concerned with behaviour, values and standards; the ones which earn the respect, loyalty and pride of the people." Coming in the mid-nineties, a period of stress for the monarchy, says Hardman, "[t]his new job description struck an instant chord at the Palace." It has had a major, lasting, and positive effect on how the monarchy operates and is perceived. "It is the 'head of nation' role which requires the hard work and delicate judgement."[57] As noted in Chapter I, the "Crown" is not the same as the "State" — it has another dimension and a wider reach. This is why the term "head of state" is inadequate in a monarchy.

Presidential Powers and Status

The proven merits of the existing tripartite system of Sovereign, governor general, and governors in their symbolic and constitutional roles should be measured against the hypothetical advantages of a presidential or quasi-presidential system. The crux of the matter is first, how the president or presidential governor general would be chosen, and second, what this person's powers would be. An appointed governor/president might lead to further concentration of power with the first minister. An elected head of state would have even wider implications for the parliamentary system and risk being divisive as well: inevitably, there would be tension between the elected head of state and the head of the elected government in the Westminster model. Would the constitutional powers remain as they are now, with the head of state normally accepting the "advice" of the elected government but retaining the reserve powers? No one appears to have come up with a satisfactory, broadly acceptable alternative that would improve life for the citizenry. Advocates of the republican model have rarely addressed the crucial federal dimension of the Crown; indeed, in both Canada and Australia they have avoided doing so.

Although in favour of a republican polity, the commentators on the Australian and Canadian constitutions already quoted do not underestimate its difficulties and risks: "... the proposed change to our form of government may well open up new possibilities for the abuse of power in office and for the kind of misbehaviour that can lead to constitutional crises." Under the present system, the prime minister "has a popular constituency (based on election) while the Head of State [the governor general] carries an ancient and, in a sense, patriarchal responsibility for public peace and orderly public authority." If the head of state were chosen through some form of election, however, that person and the prime minister "could become entangled in a competition with each claiming to be the superior manifestation of the citizens' will and the superior interpreter of the citizens' wishes."

Another risk is that the president might be "tempted to become the actual governor" and "abandon any deference to the advice of the elected ministry" in those cases (such as the dissolution of Parliament) where a governor general normally plays only a formal role. In other words, the president "may be tempted to aggrandise his or her power."

Still another risk is the collusion between the two to "perpetuate the government's term of office."[58] The present system places constraints both on the governor general and the prime minister, in that the former has a historical legitimacy vis-à-vis the prime minister but at the same time is appointed and subject to removal by the Queen on the advice of the latter.[59] Abandon the monarchical tradition and both of these constraints would be lost. "There would be no historically-based responsibility for guaranteeing the propriety of political power" and no "historically-based constraint on the power of the Head of State to intervene in the parliamentary domain."[60] Or, as David E. Smith puts it:

> ... under the system of constitutional monarchy operating in Australia (and Canada), [the powers of the Crown] are exercised on political advice, while the reserve powers, exercised independently of ministerial advice, are seldom invoked [...] the "double" head of state that constitutional monarchy in Australia presents does have the advantage of sheltering the governor general under the Crown. In a republic, there will be no Crown; whence then will come the protection as well as the security that republicans promise?[61]

Smith also comments:

> ... monarchical parliamentary (federal) government in Canada has evolved into a highly complex arrangement of understandings and influences that are neither easily articulated nor altered without compensatory adjustment. This was the same reason that Australians, who by a wide margin favoured making their country a republic, rejected that proposal in a constitutional referendum in 1999. They could not agree on an alternative republican arrangement of power in place of the existing monarchical arrangement [and] they could not agree on how to disperse (or limit) the crown's prerogative and statutory powers exercisable on advice.[62]

In 1994, there was a surprise call in New Zealand by National Party (conservative) Prime Minister James Bolger for his country to become a republic by the millennium. However, not only was there little public support, but the move also caused dissension in Bolger's own party, with several ministers publicly repudiating him.[63] Nor did the opposition Labour Party show much evidence of support, although its leader, Helen Clark, when she later became prime minister, did state that she was personally in favour of a republic. The question became moot, because in 2008 Labour was defeated by the National Party led by John Key (re-elected in 2011). Prime Minister Key promptly restored the knighthoods in the New Zealand honours system, which had been discontinued by Clark. Quite apart from the Treaty of Waitangi and the Maori people, Noel Cox points out the suspicion in New Zealand, as in Australia, of a partisan political presidency:

> The inherent disadvantage of a republic, whether in Australia or New Zealand, would be that the highest office becomes a matter of partisan contest, or of factional division. This seems to be generally understood in New Zealand. A monarchical system of government removes the office of head of state from the realm of party politics. Any republican system risks the politicization of the highest office, whether the president is elected or appointed.[64]

Codification of the Reserve Powers?

Another issue that inevitably arises with respect to the powers of a president or governor general is the codification of the reserve powers of the head of state: that is, placing them in written form by statute or constitutional definition. In the existing constitutional monarchy, these powers are exercised — in the rare instances that they are exercised at all — according to convention, not written statute. The vagueness and ambiguity of this tradition vex those who prefer a more clear-cut, visible, and therefore codified repertoire of the reserve powers. An implication of codifying the royal prerogative powers is that it could lead in the long term to the replacement of the Crown by a presidential system; indeed, this may well be the aim of some of its proponents. The risk of codification, of course, is to render rigid and legalistic what is now flexible and pragmatic. One should take to heart the classic aphorism of Eugene Forsey about the reserve powers: to "embody them in an ordinary law is to ossify them. To embody them in a written Constitution is to petrify them."[65]

Australia's Peter Boyce has concluded that, in the interest of clarity, "surrogate's powers and rights" should be "accorded definition, preferably in statutory form," rather than resorting to "heavy reliance on constitutional conventions that are ambiguous, misunderstood or open to abuse."[66] Other scholars are more cautious. Eminent political scientist Peter Russell advises codification only for the maximum length of time between an election and the summoning of Parliament — he suggests a month — as is done according to the constitution in Australia (a month) and New Zealand (six weeks), and by well-established convention in the United Kingdom (three weeks). Otherwise, he prefers use of a cabinet manual.[67] But Robert E. Hawkins warns against "the politicization and judicialization of the reserve powers" and casts "doubt on the utility of reasons and codes in this context."[68] Requiring the governor general to give reasons for a use of the reserve power would give rise to a political debate and render them justiciable, subjecting the governor general to court challenges. Agreeing with Hawkins, Peter Neary has noted how, when the governing Conservatives in Ontario were defeated in the House shortly after the 1985 election, Lieutenant Governor Aird called upon the Liberals to form a government with New Democratic support. Although he made a careful statement about his decision, Aird declined media interviews about his reasons, preserving the discretion and confidentiality that are essential if the conventions of responsible government are to be protected.[69]

The only cases where governors have given reasons for using the reserve power have been in Australia. The first was when Governor General Sir John Kerr dismissed Prime Minister Gough Whitlam in 1975. The second was in the State of Tasmania in 2010, where an election produced a deadlock between the two major parties, Labor and Liberal, each holding ten seats in the twenty-five-seat House of Assembly, while the Greens held five seats. The opposition Liberal Party had more of the popular vote and claimed the right to form the government; indeed, their leader, Will Hodgman, wrote to the governor to say so. The Greens, however, indicated they would support a Labor government. The governor, Peter Underwood, declined the informal advice of the incumbent Labor premier, David Bartlett, to invite the leader of the opposition to form a government and asked the premier instead to meet Parliament and seek its confidence. Immediately afterwards, he published his reasons. He asserted that in a parliamentary system the governor should take into account only the number of seats in the House, not the popular vote, and that the incumbent first minister should try to obtain the confidence of the House. "I told Mr Bartlett," said the governor, that as "Premier of the State he had the constitutional obligation to form a government so that the Parliament could be called together and the strength of that government tested on the floor of the House of Assembly."[70] Bartlett did meet the House and a Liberal motion of non-confidence failed, because the Labor government reached an agreement with the Greens for their support by giving them two cabinet positions. The governor's decision was thus vindicated.[71] In both the 1975 and the 2010 cases, however, there was criticism of the governors, not for giving written reasons, but for the substance of the decisions themselves. Thus written reasons may well provoke political debate.

The election of 2010 in the United Kingdom resulted in a "hung parliament," where the incumbent Labour government was placed in a minority situation. Hoping for support from the Liberal Democrats, Prime Minister Gordon Brown hesitated about resigning, while negotiations took place between the three major parties, facilitated by senior public servants. The result was an agreement between the Conservatives under David Cameron and the Liberal Democrats, led by Nick Clegg, to form a coalition government — the first of the present Queen's reign. Brown then resigned, and Cameron was invited by the Queen to form a government. This avoided an intervention by the Queen in choosing a first minister or calling another election, both highly undesirable decisions for the monarch. Instead, "[t]he Queen gave legitimacy to what the politicians had worked out among themselves and her action was unchallenged."[72]

At the time of the 2010 British election, senior public servants, led by the cabinet secretary, Sir Gus O'Donnell, and including constitutional expert Vernon Bogdanor, drafted a cabinet manual outlining conventions along the lines of the New Zealand manual from the 1990s. The new prime minister, David Cameron, was skeptical about the need for such a document, preferring to rely on "the incredible flexibility and dignity" of the constitutional monarchy, which had just proved itself in the election. He mused that anxious civil servants were trying to codify conventions "by writing down what they think ought to have happened."[73] On the other hand, Patrick Monahan, like Peter Russell, suggests that the best solution to expressing vice-regal powers may indeed be a cabinet manual like that of New Zealand, which "would not be legally binding, but would merely restate the existing constitutional rules and principles."[74] The 1968 Canadian *Manual of Official Government Procedure* did not purport to codify constitutional conventions. "[I]nstead, it amounts to an official interpretation of convention" and "combines the characteristics of the practitioner's handbook and the cabinet manual [...] it describes and outlines potential courses of action rather than *prescribing* them, as a codified text would do."[75] However, other scholars shy away even from a cabinet manual. Expressing his agreement with British Prime Minister David Cameron, Robert E. Hawkins says that "even those [manuals] intended only as collections or precedents for guidance may be seen, in the future, as Gospels, that are binding. The more 'official' a manual's author, the greater the danger that the work will not be used as a matter of 'informed opinion' but will be treated as a part of the constitution."[76]

As a sidebar, excessive codification of the reserve powers caused a constitutional and political crisis in Papua New Guinea. With seven million people, it is the fourth most populous of the Queen's non-British realms. The former Australian territory gained independence in 1975 with the presumption of having a republican constitution. But the new country's leaders preferred that it be a monarchy and invited Queen Elizabeth II to be Sovereign. Under this realm's constitution, the governor general and prime minister are selected by the single-chamber Parliament. In 2011–2012, a prime minister, absent for surgery, was deemed unwell by Parliament, which selected another whom the governor general was required to swear in. When this appointment was overturned by the Supreme Court, the governor general brought back the ousted prime minister, whereupon Parliament appointed a new governor general — its own speaker. At one point there were two rival governors general and two prime ministers vying for support, and there was talk of appealing to the Queen. In the end, the governor general backed down and reappointed the prime minister elected by Parliament. The crisis passed, and an election in 2012 produced a kind of coalition. However, David Flint, of Australians for a Constitutional Monarchy, asserted that the imbroglio had occurred because Australian Prime Minister Gough Whitlam, pushing Papua New Guinea into "premature independence," had removed the vice-regal reserve powers and tried to codify conventions. This meant that problems would not be "solved informally and pragmatically." While Papua New Guinea remained a constitutional monarchy, it was one "without any of the safeguards the system normally provides."[77]

THE GOVERNOR GENERAL AS CANADIAN "HEAD OF STATE"

In *The Secret of the Crown*, an eloquent tribute to the monarchy in Canada, John Fraser places the "Canadian" governors general in two categories. The first are the "Right Royal" governors general, who revere the Sovereign, see themselves as her representatives, and never forget where the "fount of honour" rests. In this group are Vincent Massey, Georges Vanier, Roland Michener, Jules Léger, and Ramon Hnatyshyn; the most outstanding was Vanier. The second category is that of the "Crown Legatees," for whom the governor general is the "functioning" head of state. In this category are Edward Schreyer, Jeanne Sauvé, Roméo LeBlanc, Adrienne Clarkson, and Michaëlle Jean, with Clarkson considered the most successful.[78] While Fraser did not "rate" Governor General David Johnston, one can now place him in the "Right Royal" category. What was the view of the "Crown Legatees" of the governor general as head of state?

Trudeau's Bill C-60

The "head of state" issue has bedevilled the national vice-regal office in Canada for decades. In 1978, the Trudeau Liberal government tabled Bill

C-60, which would effectively have made the governor general head of state in lieu of the Queen. The Queen was to be styled "the sovereign head of Canada," which, in itself, was inoffensive. However, other sections of the bill were clearly controversial. One would have replaced the Queen with the governor general as one of the three component parts of Parliament. Another stated that "the executive government of and over Canada shall be vested in the Governor-General of Canada, on behalf and in the name of the Queen." Still another clause asserted that the *Act* should not be construed as "precluding the Queen [...] from exercising while in Canada any of the powers, authorities or functions of the Governor-General under this Act." Thus the Queen would derive her authority from the governor general and not vice versa. Another troubling implication was that the governor general's role would become a statutory, not a prerogative, office. Conventions such as the royal reserve powers might also become statutory and, therefore, justiciable.[79]

Bill C-60 met with opposition from those who saw in it what Eugene Forsey called "crypto-republicanism."[80] But it was also unanimously and vigorously opposed by the provincial premiers. They objected to a federal appointee as Canadian head of state, questioned the putative status of the lieutenant governors under the proposed arrangement, and saw the bill as another centralizing device. Meeting in Regina at their annual conference in 1978, chaired by Saskatchewan premier Allan Blakeney, the premiers voiced their disagreement. None was more vocal than René Lévesque, the Parti Québécois premier of Quebec, who exposed Bill C-60 for what it was: an assertion of federal power over the provinces. The federal government of the 1970s, and indeed its successors for the next thirty years, in David E. Smith's words, "misperceived the complexity of the Crown [and] failed [...] to recognize its federalist dimension. In this conceit they proved themselves true descendants of Sir John A. Macdonald."[81] As New Zealand scholar Noel Cox observed:

> The 1978 proposals and, more particularly, their failure to be enacted, testify to the significance and complexity of the Crown in Canada. For many people there remained an emotional attachment to the Sovereign. But more importantly, *the provinces regarded the Crown as an*

important source of independent authority [our empha-
sis]. There was an appreciation of the advantages of not
going too far in Canadianising the Crown, and thereby
giving too much power to the federal government.[82]

The Trudeau government's attempt to designate the governor general effectively as head of state in 1978 flew in the face of the principle, accepted since the *Maritime Bank* case of 1892, that, through the
tripartite institution of monarch, governor general, and lieutenant
governor, the provincial Crown embodied provincial co-sovereignty
in Confederation. It was one of a series of moves by official Ottawa to
downplay the monarchy in an evident effort to cater to Quebec. A useful
corollary of this for the Trudeau government, not appreciated at the time
by the general public, was weakening one of the theoretical underpin-
nings of provincial autonomy. Eugene Forsey panned the bill as "an elab-
orate and ill-drawn measure," displaying "an ignorance of responsible
government that passes all understanding."[83] Trudeau is reported to have
replied to Forsey's complaint about the status of the governor general
that "[i]t's either the Governor General becoming more and more the
head of state or nothing."[84] Bill C-60 died a merciful death on the order
paper when the parliamentary session ended in the fall of 1978.

Republicanism at Rideau Hall

Nonetheless, during the tenures of Governors General Jules Léger (1974–
1979) and Edward Schreyer (1979–1984), the profile of the monarchy was
considerably lowered. In the term of the former, the Liberal government
made significant inroads by delegating to the governor general aspects
of the royal prerogative with respect to Canada's external affairs. From
1970, Mitchell Sharp, Trudeau's secretary of state for external affairs —
who was urging the prime minister to make Canada a republic — pressed
for the governor general to assume several functions from the Sovereign.
Among these were granting *agrément* to foreign ambassadors and the
appointment of Canadian ambassadors and signing their letters of credence. Due to the controversial nature of the changes (they were leaked

to the media in 1972) and, apparently, to the Queen's own reluctance, they were considerably delayed. Finally, in 1975, after Trudeau had met with the Queen, agreement was reached to transfer the functions *except* that of signing letters of credence. This was quietly announced by news release on December 30, 1975 — the favourite time of year in Ottawa for avoiding media scrutiny. The next step was proposed in 1977 by Governor General Léger himself. He was seriously worried about the threat of separatism in Quebec after the election of René Lévesque's Parti Québécois government and, as a former diplomat, thought that symbolic matters such as the governor general signing letters of credence would help to "Canadianize" the Crown and counter the perception of a "foreign" head of state. Once again, Trudeau met with the Queen, who gave her consent. And once again, the move was quietly announced on December 30, 1977.[85]

With the appointment of Jeanne Sauvé (1984–1990), Rideau Hall increasingly promoted the governor general as head of state, often using the euphemism "*de facto* head of state." This quasi-presidential attitude troubled Saskatchewan people on her two visits to the province:

> [t]he style of this governor general was not such as to endear her to an informal rural population. An austere classical concert sponsored by Sauvé in Regina was unenthusiastically received. Lieutenant Governor Fred Johnson was nearly apoplectic when he caught one of Sauvé's staff changing his seating plan at a dinner at Government House. Local municipalities were offended when Rideau Hall staffers attempted to ban the singing of "God Save The Queen" and replace the toast to the Queen by a "toast to the Governor General." While this was in line with current thinking in Ottawa, it was a gross misreading of prairie sensitivities.[86]

Meeting with a class of elementary school children in small-town Saskatchewan, Sauvé asked them what the governor general did. They brightly responded that she represented the Queen. This was not to Madame Sauvé's liking. She hastened to inform the students that the governor general was Canada's head of state.[87]

The republican trend was attenuated when Ramon Hnatyshyn occupied the office of governor general (1990–1995), but reappeared with vigour under Roméo LeBlanc (1995–1999), Adrienne Clarkson (1999–2005), and Michaëlle Jean (2005–2010). References to the governor general as head of state multiplied. During LeBlanc's time in office, officials in Prime Minister Jean Chrétien's office put forward a proposal that would make Canada a republic by the new millennium, although Chrétien himself never expressed support for the idea. His deputy prime minister, John Manley, was a vocal republican, calling for the end of the monarchy in a particularly ill-timed statement shortly before Queen Elizabeth's Golden Jubilee visit to Canada in 2002.

During the tenures of Roméo LeBlanc and Adrienne Clarkson, a number of portraits of members of the Royal Family were removed from Rideau Hall. Several were retrieved by Quebec senator Serge Joyal, who placed them in the Senate's collection of portraits of French and British monarchs of Canada displayed in the Parliament Buildings in Ottawa (the Senator subsequently called for the state rooms at Rideau Hall to be protected from the whims of the incumbents). The vice-regal salute (part of "God Save the Queen" and "O Canada"), played since Roland Michener's time for the official entrance at functions of the governor general and lieutenant governors, was discontinued. In 2002, Rideau Hall tried to minimize the Queen's Golden Jubilee by placing its emphasis on the fiftieth anniversary of the "Canadian governors general." On June 6, 2004, at the sixtieth anniversary of the D-Day landings on Juno Beach in Normandy, Governor General Clarkson visibly attempted to upstage the Queen. In response to questioning afterwards, Rideau Hall officials referred, disparagingly and misleadingly, to Her Majesty's presence at Juno Beach as that of the "Queen of England" — a mistake frequently made by the media, but in this case done intentionally by people who knew better.*

Then, by a press release on December 29, 2004 — as we have seen, the time of year chosen in Ottawa to surreptitiously implement manoeuvres against the Crown — Paul Martin's Liberal govern-

---

* The title Queen (or King) of England has not existed since the union of England and Scotland in 1707. The last Queen of England was therefore Queen Anne (1701–1714).

ment, apparently at the instigation of Clarkson, slipped through an announcement that the Queen's name would be removed from diplomatic letters of credence and recall. These would now be solely in the name of the governor general. The *issue* of the letters, as previously noted, had reverted to the governor general in 1977, but the letters still stated that they were in the name of and on behalf of the Sovereign. Christopher McCreery caustically commented that this change "made absolutely no sense at all [...] It was a blatant move to enhance further, then, Governor General Adrienne Clarkson's view of herself as Canada's head of state."[88] Clarkson, her husband, John Ralston Saul, and the Rideau Hall staff consistently portrayed the governor general as "number one" in Canada, downplaying the role and status of the Queen and the lieutenant governors. On a visit to Saskatchewan, this resulted in a protocol standoff between governor general and lieutenant governor, which required delicate negotiations to resolve.[89]

Senior staff at Rideau Hall mused about making the governor general "fount of honours" instead of the Queen.[90] It had been customary for a governor general–designate, before his or her installation, to visit the Queen, at which time the monarch presented him or her with the insignia of principal companion of the Order of Canada. This was not technically required, as a governor general holds the office *ex officio*, but it was a significant symbolic gesture. Adrienne Clarkson insisted on presenting the insignia to her successor, Michaëlle Jean, in 2005.* Breaking another long-time precedent, she also attended Jean's installation ceremony in the Senate Chamber — as Jean would do five years later at David Johnston's installation. These moves reflected the Clarksonian view of the national vice-regal office: one governor general passes the mantle to the next in presidential form, minimizing and preferably eliminating the role of the Sovereign.

The "head of state" manoeuvres continued with more vigour in Michaëlle Jean's time, as a personality cult increasingly characterized the media-savvy incumbent of Rideau Hall. Stephen Harper's Conservative government did insist that the Queen preside at the

---

* The practice of the Queen presenting the insignia was resumed for David Johnston in 2010, apparently over the objections of Michaëlle Jean.

Adrienne Clarkson, seen here with Queen Elizabeth in Regina in 2005, was an exceptional governor general, but considered herself Canadian head of state.

Government of Saskatchewan

ninetieth anniversary ceremonies of the Battle of Vimy Ridge in France in 2007 rather than the governor general; it was rumoured that there were strenuous objections to this from Rideau Hall. The latter continued to portray the governor general as head of state, sometimes *de facto*, sometimes not. During Michaëlle Jean's 2006 visit to Saskatchewan, her staff admitted that it was Rideau Hall policy for the governor general not to mention the Crown or the Queen in her speeches[91] — a practice evident since the time of Sauvé. During Jean's tenure, citizens afforded the opportunity to receive national honours at Rideau Hall found that references to and evidence of Canada's constitutional monarchy were conspicuously absent. The Royal Victorian Order, the Queen's personal honour for service to the Sovereign and the Crown, was viewed coolly, although it had been officially one of Canada's national honours since 1972. The governor general's office did not encourage nominations, despite having suitable candidates in their own establishment.[92] In 2007, Rideau Hall declined a request from the honours chancery in the United Kingdom to notify Canadian members of the Order's quadrennial gathering at Windsor Castle.[93]

Portraits of the Royal Family at Rideau Hall continued to be removed or downgraded. In 2007, in a newspaper feature story, Michaëlle Jean was said to be "highlighting paintings that draw less and less attention to the office's British traditions." The 1979 portrait of the Queen and the Duke of Edinburgh by Quebec artist Jean-Paul Lemieux — an odd, modernistic view of them standing in a field — was bumped from the front wall of the Rideau Hall ballroom to the back, where it became the sole portrait of the Queen on display at Rideau Hall. "That's it as far as Her Majesty is concerned," said a Rideau Hall staffer in an interview. "We really want to create a Canadian interior." Traditional portraits of the Royal Family, she said, "had become a bit of an anachronism here" and "did not fit in with the current role of the Governor-General." Some were given to the Senate, others were moved "to near the lower-level staff entrance, cloakroom and public toilets."[94] (The Queen would be rehabilitated by a new Diamond Jubilee portrait placed in the ballroom in 2012).

In 2009, controversy erupted again when Michaëlle Jean referred to herself as Canadian head of state in a speech in Paris. This time, the office of Prime Minister Harper intervened to set the record straight: "Queen Elizabeth II is Queen of Canada and Head of State," said the prime ministerial spokesman in an unprecedented public statement. "The Governor General represents the Crown in Canada." Author and journalist John Fraser, Master of Massey College, University of Toronto (founded by and named after the distinguished governor general), decried Rideau Hall's "creeping head-of-statism of governors-general."[95] The Prime Minister's Office asked Rideau Hall to correct references to the governor general as head of state in its newly revised website. A New Democratic member of Parliament and former civics teacher chimed in, "it should be cleared up real quick that the Queen is the head of state."[96]

The concept of the governor general as head of state received much media and academic attention and support. For two decades, in the 1990s and 2000s, the influential *Globe and Mail* called editorially for the governor general to become head of state after the present Queen's reign ended. In a bizarre twist, this person would be elected by the companions of the Order of Canada — "an oligarchy," as Jacques Monet put it, which "would essentially — and harmfully — change the nature of the

Order."[97] A columnist for the newspaper, Jeffrey Simpson, belaboured the theme of the uselessness of the monarchy. Typical of many academics, historian Christopher Moore considered the monarchy anomalous in modern Canada, even if it had served a useful purpose in the nineteenth century. He concluded that "an elected governor general, holding the same limited powers as the appointed one, would be more legitimate both in the exercise of those powers in a constitutional emergency and as a Canadian symbol around which the meaning of Canadian nationality could continue to be debated."[98] (This notion of an *elected* governor general, as has already been noted, is fraught with difficulties.) A prominent historian, Michael Bliss, called for the end of the monarchy, which he termed "an absurd anachronism."[99]

Some academics, while prepared to keep the Queen in a symbolic role similar to that envisaged in Bill C-60 in 1978, still proposed that the governor general be called head of state. In 2010, reacting to the Michaëlle Jean incident of the previous year, political scientist C.E.S. Franks stated — misleadingly — that, apart from two minor exceptions, "since 1947 the governor-general has exercised all the powers of the sovereign in Canada" and proposed that the governor general be designated Canada's head of state while the Queen remained Sovereign, even though he admitted that "the term 'head of state' has no constitutional or legal status or meaning in Canada." This was to "encourage Canadians to take the position of governor-general more seriously."[100]

The Letters Patent of 1947

In the equivalent of an exit interview in 2010, Michaëlle Jean reiterated the Rideau Hall mantra that the Letters Patent of King George VI of 1947 made the governor general *de facto* head of state.[101] The Letters Patent are another much cited but widely misunderstood part of Canada's constitutional history. In them, the King directed, "We do hereby authorize and empower Our Governor General, with the advice of Our Privy Council for Canada, or of any members thereof or individually, as the case requires, to exercise all powers and authorities lawfully belonging to us in respect of Canada."

This has been interpreted by some as making the governor general in effect Canadian head of state. Former governor general Adrienne Clarkson asserted that "the final authority of the state was transferred from the monarch to the Governor General in the Letters Patent of 1947, thereby making Canada's government independent of Great Britain."[102] Her spouse, John Ralston Saul, echoed her. With the Letters Patent of 1947, he said, "the powers of the Canadian head of state were fully and formally transferred from the monarch to the Governor General."[103] Yet a more nuanced view of the Letters Patent is appropriate. The Letters Patent do not assert that the governor general is head of state. Rather, they empower that person to *exercise* the powers of the Sovereign, who remains their source of legitimacy. In other words, the powers are *delegated*. As a commentator on the 2009 incident said, "The 1947 Letters Patent adjusted the office [of governor general] and downloaded remaining workaday functions of Head of State. King George VI did not, and constitutionally could not, abdicate his status or that of his heirs by such means."[104]

While the Letters Patent did authorize the governor general to exercise powers of the monarch, this was to be "on advice." And by no means were all of the royal powers immediately exercised by the governor general, nor are they to this day. The issuing and signing letters of credence for ambassadors, as we have seen, was given to the governor general thirty years later, in 1977. The prerogative of heraldry was only transferred in 1988. The Sovereign has continued to act on the direct advice of the Canadian prime minister on a number of occasions. Examples are the proclamation of the national flag in 1965, the proclamation of the *Constitution Act* in 1982, and the appointment of additional senators in 1990. The Queen formally appoints the governor general and personally approves the creation of national honours and their insignia. It is more accurate to say, in the words of a federal government publication, that the Letters Patent of King George VI "authorized and empowered the Governor General to exercise most of the royal prerogatives in right of Canada."[105] Christopher McCreery summed up the issue as follows:

> In essence, the *Letters Patent 1947* constitute the office
> of the governor general and also regulate the delegation

of the royal prerogative. They were the culmination of a long process whereby successive governors general were given increasing ability to act in the place of the Sovereign and exercise the royal prerogative without direct consultation with the king or queen of the day. [...] while much authority was delegated by the King to the governor general, this was done in the form of enabling legislation, and particular areas of the royal prerogative were outlined as being beyond the scope of the governor general's duties, except in the most exceptional circumstances such as a regency or the incapacity or capture of the Sovereign by a foreign power. Thus, the *Letters Patent* constitute a *delegation* of most powers, not a blanket abdication of the Sovereign's role in the Canadian state.[106]

McCreery sardonically remarked that during the "head of state" controversy in 2009 the Letters Patent "were held up by officials at Rideau Hall as a sort of emancipation proclamation that transformed the governor general into a person holding all the powers of the Sovereign. It was a rather imaginative development that ignored sixty years of history."[107] Finally, while the Letters Patent apply to the Sovereign in right of Canada as a whole, they do not and cannot affect the realities of the provincial Crown. The governor general does not have the power to exercise royal powers in provincial jurisdiction. The author responded as follows to the proposal from C.E.S. Franks that the governor general be called head of state: "Canada is a federal state, a compound monarchy. The governor general exercises the monarch's powers in federal jurisdiction only. She cannot do so in provincial jurisdiction — cannot substitute for the lieutenant governors, cannot name provincial premiers, swear in cabinets or sign their orders in council, give royal assent in legislatures or exercise the reserve powers of dissolution, prorogation or dismissal within the province."[108] Constitutional realities make it clear that the headship of state in Canada is tripartite.

A Lapsed Monarchy?

An option has been floated of letting the monarchy lapse at the end of the reign of Queen Elizabeth II and simply making the governor general head of state. However, this would constitutionally be very difficult to achieve, since, under the terms of the *Constitution Act, 1982*, both houses of Parliament and all ten provincial legislatures must agree on any changes to the offices of the Queen, the governor general, and the lieutenant governors.[109] Edward McWhinney, an academic and Liberal MP, proposed a way around this. By not proclaiming Charles, Prince of Wales, as King of Canada upon the death of Queen Elizabeth, the country would become a republic in all but name. A future government of Canada, could, he suggests, "sever" what he calls "the last Imperial constitutional ties" by "simply failing to proclaim any legal successor to the Queen in relation to Canada [...] The 'office of the Queen' would thus remain but remain inactive, and like very many other 'spent' sections of the Constitution Act, *presumably* wither away and lapse by convention."[110] However, the legality, let alone the desirability, of this process has been sharply challenged by other experts, with the status of the provinces playing centrally in their argument.

Ian Holloway, dean of law at the University of Western Ontario and subsequently at the University of Calgary, noted that, while section 58 of the *Constitution Act, 1867,* does not actually say that the lieutenant governor is the representative of the Queen in the province, it was something read into the *British North America Act* by the judiciary. Section 41 of the *Constitution Act, 1982,* provides that any amendment to the constitution "in relation to the office of the Queen, the Governor General and the Lieutenant Governor of a province" requires unanimity among the federal Parliament and all ten provinces. "For the federal government to try to republicanize Canada through the back door in the way McWhinney suggests," said Holloway, "would be contrary to the inferred principles underlying section 41. *The plain intent of section 41 is to signal that the Crown in Canada is owned jointly by the country and the provinces* [our emphasis]." There is, added Holloway, another reason why the McWhinney recipe for abolishing the monarchy is not feasible. Section 9 of the *Constitution Act, 1867,* provides that the executive government of

Canada is vested in the Queen. Section 17 provides that the Parliament of Canada consists of the Senate, the House of Commons, and the Queen. In other words, without a monarch, we could have neither a government nor a Parliament.[111]

Rebutting McWhinney's suggestion that failing to proclaim the new monarch on the death of the incumbent would effectively end the monarchy, Holloway had this to say:

> ... proclamation does not *make* someone the monarch. Rather, it simply declares what has already taken place by operation of the common law. In other words, it is the death of the monarch that triggers succession. And the succession is instantaneous. It does not depend upon the positive action of either the privy council or Parliament. That is why the old saying, "the king is dead; long live the king!" represents an accurate statement of the law. Barring any amendment to the constitution, the fact of succession is guaranteed by the common law. Upon the demise of Queen Elizabeth, she will automatically be succeeded by the heir to the throne. And by virtue of section 9 of the *Constitution Act, 1867*, executive authority over Canada will then be fully vested in the new king.[112]

Finally, one should not assume that replacing a monarch and vice-regal representatives by a president, elected or not, will reduce costs or cut back on pomp and circumstance. Experience in republics shows otherwise. People familiar with international diplomacy can cite chapter and verse of pretentious, ostentatious protocol in presidential regimes. Peter Boyce quotes "one of the most liberal and left-leaning High Court justices" in Australia who "argued vigorously for retention of the Crown," preferring "a head of state who could transcend national boundaries" rather than one who "catered to 'narrow nationalism,'" fearing that "a president would be less restrained in his or her use of the reserve power than a governor-general, and that a presidency would invite a more expensive, pompous and vulgar use of symbols and ceremony."[113]

FEDERALISM IN MONARCHY AND REPUBLIC

It is not only of interest to, but fundamentally important for, Canadians to assess whether republican theory and practice would lead to centralization. Historians have commented on how decentralized the *ancien régime* in France actually was compared to the republic, despite the appearance of monarchical absolutism from the time of Louis XIV. By contrast, the French Revolution and the republican (and imperial) regimes that followed were rigorously and sometimes ruthlessly centralist. It has been noted that "even the absolutist regime of the Sun King paled in comparison to the modern state that would succeed it. Born in the aftermath of the French Revolution, the unitary state became the most powerful, centralized form of political organization in the history of human societies."[114] It was only in the late twentieth century, three hundred years after the Revolution, that France introduced a modicum of decentralization, in the process encouraging a revival of local culture, language, and pride in regions such as Languedoc, Corsica, and Brittany. To this day, France has great difficulty in accommodating other cultural communities. French leaders constantly refer to "l'ordre républicain" and "la tradition républicaine." This order and this tradition are not friendly to distinctive minorities.

The English (and later British) monarchy from the sixteenth to the eighteenth centuries was culpable of endorsing oppression of the Scots and Welsh, as well as oppressing the Irish until the early twentieth century. This explains the hostility of much of the Irish diaspora towards the monarchy. Yet under its monarchy, the United Kingdom, despite being theoretically a unitary state, has in fact admitted an immense diversity, with the centuries-old separate legal and educational systems in Scotland, the linguistic and cultural identity of Wales, and repeated efforts at self-government in Northern Ireland.[115] With the establishment of the Scottish Parliament and Welsh assembly in 1999 and the revival of the Northern Ireland assembly the same year, it can be argued that the United Kingdom has evolved towards a quasi-federal state.

It would be intriguing to compare the strength of sub-national jurisdictions, and therefore the health of federalism, in monarchical and republican federal states.[116] Apart from Canada and Australia (and the tiny Caribbean realm of St. Kitts & Nevis), there are five federations in the Commonwealth, of which one is a monarchy (Malaysia) while four are republics (India, Pakistan, Nigeria, and South Africa). Malaysia is a federated monarchy; although the Queen is not its sovereign, federalism is healthy in that country. Republican India, by contrast, is an uneasy federation. David E. Smith noted, "British India was a unitary state before 1935 and the unitary assumptions from that experience persisted after independence and into a federal republic that awarded superordinate powers to the central government. Federalism [...] was viewed as a threat to national stability in India."[117] Nigeria and Pakistan, too, can be viewed as uneasy federations. South Africa, although a federal state, is characterized by a powerful central government and clearly subordinate states.

Outside the Commonwealth, Belgium is a federal monarchy with three components: Wallonie (French-speaking), Flanders (Dutch-speaking), and Brussels-Capital (bilingual), all of which are highly autonomous and co-exist in a state of tension under a constitutional monarch. Spain is a monarchical federal state with strong regional identities. On the other hand, Austria, Switzerland, and the Federal Republic of Germany can be cited as examples of republics where federalism is alive and well. The Russian Federation provides an interesting study of national/sub-national dynamics, although the primacy of the central government in Moscow is undisputed.

Canada and Australia

In Australia, hesitations about adopting a republican form of government, in addition to the issue of presidential powers already noted, revolve to a certain extent around the perceived threat to federalism. "[A]ny transition to a republic," says David E. Smith, "has immense implications for the states." He quotes a former chief justice of the High Court, Sir Harry Gibbs, as saying, "the legal complexities associated with the change to a republic involve difficult questions that go to the very heart of federation."[118] Sir Harry "argued that any amendment to the status of the Crown would be messy and require amendment of the *Australia Acts* of 1986, which in turn would require the consent of all six states."[119] Another critic held that, under a proposal by republican proponent George Winterton, "the states would have lost 'even the capacity to change or preserve their own constitutional identity.'" This played a large part in the defeat of the republican option in the 1999 referendum. In Australian referenda, "… the people have generally voted against the attempt to transfer power from the states to the centre."[120] Even republican-leaning state governors were said to be nervous about the possibility of a directly elected state equivalent of the president competing with them for power and influence.

Prime Minister Gough Whitlam, after the *Royal Styles and Titles Act* of 1973 created the title "Queen of Australia," argued that the Queen could now only be advised on state matters by him. This led the states to fear that "Mr Whitlam's design was to unravel the constitution and reduce the states to administrative regions, through manipulation of the Crown."[121] It was the status of the governors, at the time and until 1986 appointed by the Queen on the advice of British ministers, that prevented this. Also in 1973, Whitlam, without consulting the states, asked the United Kingdom to end appeals to the Judicial Committee of the Privy Council. The British government balked, citing the need for a joint request from the federal and state governments. Appeals from Australia's federal courts to the JCPC ended in 1975, but it was not until the passage of the *Australia Acts* in 1986, which resolved in the states' favour their right to advise the Queen directly on the appointment of their governors, that appeals from the state courts were also ended.* The Canadian premiers, resisting Trudeau's Bill C-60 in 1978 and the patriation of the Constitution in 1981, might well have cited the Australian experience of federal unilateralism.

Canadian federalism, in the sense of meaningful, quasi-autonomous provincial jurisdiction, was historically protected and developed by the institution of the Crown. Would genuine federalism exist today in the absence of the Crown? J.L. Granatstein, reviewing David Smith's *The Invisible Crown* in 1996, asserted that it would: "there seems no reason whatsoever that the same system could not exist even in the absence of a Canadian monarch." Perhaps. Yet current institutions stem from deep

---

* In New Zealand, appeals to the JCPC ended only in 2004, when a Supreme Court of New Zealand was established.

roots, and their continued existence is nurtured by them. Responding fifteen years later to Granatstein's comment, Smith countered, "there is no question that in the evolution of Canadian federalism the Crown and its interpretation by the courts is the turning point."[122] Although one cannot of course know what Canadian federalism would have become without the Crown, it is unlikely that it would have sustained its vigour and might even have been a shadow of its present self. Once again, Quebec should be grateful for the monarchy.

Furthermore, "[w]hether or not tension between republicanism and federalism is endemic is not the point," says David E. Smith. "For a country like Canada, where federalism is the bedrock of national existence, the possibility that the two systems are incompatible is enough to prompt unease."[123] Referring to thoughts of secession from or renegotiation of Confederation, and not only in Quebec, Smith notes that "[u]nlike the irrevocable, indissoluble, rigid republic and its federation [the United States], Canada's monarchical federation lacks definition to such an extent that its parts may periodically contemplate disengagement or re-engagement on new terms." He adds, "[t]hat perception — the idea that the terms of union may be redefined or that they are ever renegotiable — reveals an attitude toward federalism that is unrepublican in the American sense of the term."[124]

The First Nations

As First Nations seek to redefine their relationship with Canada, evolving towards what they view as a "third order of government," the role of the Crown is crucial. This evolution is palpably occurring. It is of prime concern for the Province of Saskatchewan, where the First Nations constitute a substantial and rapidly growing minority. Indeed, Merrilee Rasmussen believes that "in future, the important role of the Saskatchewan Legislature will be in its relationships with other, Aboriginal governments within the boundaries of the province."[125] She cites a 2000 court case in the British Columbia, *Campbell v. British Columbia*, where Gordon Campbell, then leader of the opposition and later to be premier, challenged the validity of the 1999 Nisga'a Agreement with Canada and British Columbia, on the grounds that it was inconsistent with the division of powers between the federal and provincial governments in sections 91 and 92 of the *British North America Act*. In rejecting this argument, Justice Williamson "held that Aboriginal rights, including an inherent right of self-government providing the jurisdiction to make laws, survived as one of the unwritten 'underlying values' of the Constitution outside of the powers distributed to Parliament and the legislatures in 1867. The federal-provincial distribution of powers in 1867 was aimed at a different issue and was a division 'internal' to the Crown."[126] Justice Wiliamson concluded that "after the assertion of sovereignty by the British Crown, and continuing to and after the time of Confederation, although the right of Aboriginal people to govern themselves was diminished, it was not extinguished."[127]

Given that the Nisga'a Agreement provides for concurrent law-making power by the First Nation, arguably it constitutes a third order of government in Canada. Concurrent law-making is one of the key concepts of federalism. Where there is conflict between two jurisdictions, the doctrine of "paramountcy" provides for constitutional recognition of which should prevail. "A crucial feature of federal states is the issue of constitutional protection of each order of government. In other words, neither order of government can unilaterally dissolve the other order of government."[128] The authors of these words, Greg Poelzer and Ken Coates, believe that, amidst the conflicting and divisive opinions about Aboriginal self-government within the Canadian confederation, the Crown offers a solution. As has already been seen, the Crown was the overarching framework for provincial co-sovereignty in the Canadian constitutional order, partly through the *British North America Act*, partly through the court interpretations that followed. A similar approach could apply to the First Nations. Indeed, the Royal Commission on Aboriginal Peoples stated pertinently in its Final Report of 1996:

> The treaties form a fundamental part of the constitution
> and for many Aboriginal peoples, play a role similar to
> that played by the *Constitution Act, 1867* [...] in relation
> to the provinces. The terms of the Canadian federation
> are found not only in formal constitutional documents
> governing relations between the federal and provincial

governments but also in treaties and other instruments establishing the basic links between Aboriginal peoples and the Crown. In brief, *"treaty federalism" is an integral part of the Canadian constitution* [our emphasis].[129]

Pelzer and Coates pursue this approach in saying "[i]nstitutions that predate Canada that Aboriginal and non-Aboriginal Canadians share, and that can serve as organizing principles for building a new future, do exist. In fact, the most elemental building block of Canadian political institutions, the Crown, may well provide the answer." Echoing and emphasizing David E. Smith's seminal work, they point out that "the existence of a divided Crown, federal and provincial, and of provinces led by their own powerful executives in possession of sovereignty in their own right, made Canada a compounded monarchy." This could be the key to finding a rightful and appropriate place for First Nations as a third order of government: "[t]he Crown may provide an integrative force that at once provides for greater autonomy for Aboriginal governments and binds these governments as essential members within the Canadian body politic."[130]

However, Poelzer and Coates assert that for such an approach to work, two things are required. First, non-Aboriginal Canadians must recognize the special relationship of the First Nations with the Crown. Second, Aboriginals must come to terms with the compound monarchy in Canada. First Nations have a history of looking to the imperial and then the federal Crown as their sole interlocutor, given that section 91 of the *British North America Act* assigned responsibility for Indians and their lands to Ottawa. In Chapter I, we mentioned the 1982 ruling of the Court of Appeal of England that the Crown of Canada, not that of the United Kingdom, was responsible for the treaty relationship. Noting the provincial dimension of the Canadian Crown, Lord Justice Kerr stated that the "rights and obligations in relation to the Indian peoples are therefore the responsibility of the Crown in right of *the Dominion or Provinces of Canada* [our emphasis], not of the Crown in right of the United Kingdom."[131] Poelzer and Coates go on to say: "First Nations leaders in many ways operate with a vision of Canada frozen in 1867," before the judicial-driven evolution to compound monarchy changed that vision. "However, much of the authority that First

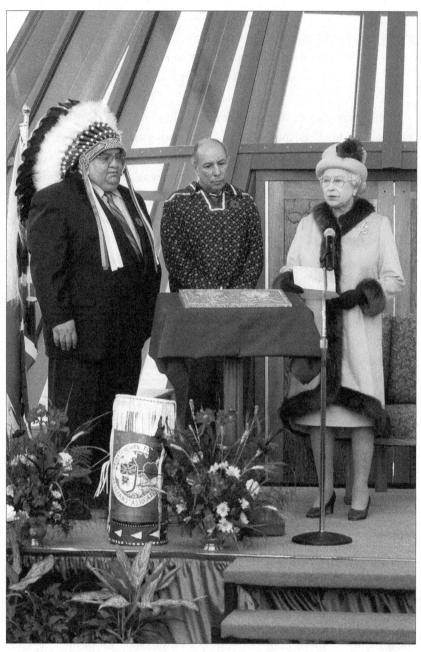

There is a special bond between the First Nations and the Crown. Queen Elizabeth II visited the First Nations University of Canada in Regina in 2005 and presented a tablet showing her royal cypher and that of Queen Victoria.

Government of Saskatchewan

Nations government seek, whether concurrent, or concurrent with paramountcy, are actually provincial powers," such as Crown lands, natural resources, health, and education. What has been called "treaty federalism" would involve "extending our current practice of federalism and of recognizing the common institution of the Crown."[132] This is a work in progress. Much more needs to be done as the federal government, the provinces, and the First Nations grapple with the implications of a third order of government.

However, the tried and proven flexibility of the compound monarchy holds much promise. Already, First Nations are paying increased attention to the lieutenant governor and the provincial Crown. The Province of British Columbia was a party to the Nisga'a Agreement, and Saskatchewan has been a party to the treaty land entitlement process in that province. "The instrumentality of the Crown," say Poelzer and Coates, "will likely play a crucial role in articulating a new, collective understanding of the divisibility of sovereignty in Canada and of the ability of the federation to accommodate Aboriginal self-government without immolating the national political and constitutional system."[133] The traditional, historic, deeply rooted relationship of the First Nations with the Crown and the Sovereign is, then, not archaic folklore or mere sentimentality. It is potentially the grounding of a dynamic future for the Aboriginal peoples in Confederation.

Individual and Community

It is indubitable that republicanism appeals to the individual's relationship with the state, rather than cultural communities. One might call it atomistic rather than communitarian. Yet from the beginning, Canada was a federation based on language and culture, as well as geographic regions. Quebec saw to that. This affected not only the initial confederation agreements, tempering Macdonald's unitary thrust, but also the legal and pragmatic evolution of the federation thereafter. Oliver Mowat, Honoré Mercier, and their colleagues based their objections to centralism, and thus their support for the provincial Crown and lieutenant governor, on the defence of the community interest.[134]

Objections to the third order of government for Aboriginal peoples are usually based on the equality of all citizens before the law and the premise of individual rights. This individualistic approach to democracy found its ultimate expression in the French Revolution and, in more moderate form, the American republic. Yet, as those supporting the "third order" point out, "[w]hile this view appeals to one model of liberal democracy, it neglects the degree to which the Canadian experiment was built on different premises, including the recognition of collective rights and federal citizenship. [...] Group rights, the centrepiece of Aboriginal aspirations for self-government, have long been hallmarks of the evolution of the Canadian polity."[135] Examples of this are, of course, language rights but also religious rights, dating back to 1867 and the *British North America Act*. In Canada, there is not an official separation between church and state. Denominational schools are protected in most provinces. "Canadians cherish individual liberties, but they also cherish Canada as a community of distinct and historically separated constituencies. This is the essence of the Canadian federal experiment."[136] Oliver Mowat, Edward Blake, David Mills, Honoré Mercier, and their counterparts in the Maritimes, although they would not have thought of applying this sentiment to the First Nations, would most assuredly have lauded its spirit. And the notion has historical roots from well before Confederation. Many of the "late Loyalists" who emigrated from the United States to Upper Canada between the American War of Independence and the War of 1812 did so because they found more tolerance under the Crown than in the republic. This was particularly the case for religious minorities such as the pacifist Mennonites. In the words of American historian Alan Taylor, "[t]he pious pacifists felt threatened by republicanism, which promoted majority rule at the expense of cultural minorities. They suffered from the American paradox, later noted by Alexis de Tocqueville, that the emphasis on individualism led to a majoritarian conformism intolerant of dissent. [...] They preferred the rule of a distant king to domination by a local majority intolerant of cultural difference."[137]

"Could it be," asks David E. Smith, "that a constitutional monarchy is more tolerant of variety and less demanding of coherence than a republican system of government?"[138] Flexibility, then, is the watchword of Canada's monarchical federalism. A republican polity would entail vast consequences for Confederation, with the risk of substituting rigidity for fluidity and upsetting a fine balance which has been achieved over a period of 150 years.

THE MONARCHY REBOUNDS

Commenting in 2011 on the Rideau Hall regimes since that of Jeanne Sauvé, Ottawa journalist Dan Gardner observed that "step by step, with an airbrushing here, a change of protocol there, republicans erased the monarchy from public consciousness [...] That was the way the game was played. Slowly erase the visible presence of the monarchy. Quietly shuffle the Queen offstage. In her place: the governor general. The idea was to effect constitutional change by the tiniest of increments so that it could ultimately be presented as a fait accompli."[139] The prime ministerial rebuff to the Rideau Hall of Michaëlle Jean in 2009 over the "head of state" issue marked a turning point, said Gardner, even before successful 2010 and 2011 royal tours. He might also have noted that in 2009 the Conservative government thoroughly reworked the anodyne citizenship study guide for immigrants to give a prominent place to the monarchy, among other Canadian institutions.[140]

The year 2009, therefore, appeared to have marked, if not a sea change in the fortunes of the monarchy, at least a tendency towards its rehabilitation. Stephen Harper's government hosted a major tour by the Prince of Wales and his new wife Camilla, Duchess of Cornwall, the first appearance of the prince in Canada in eight years. Shortly thereafter, the *Globe and Mail*, to the astonishment of many observers, reversed its twenty-year editorial stance that Canada should become a republic at the end of the Queen's reign. It called for the continuation of the monarchy, although still proposing "head of state" designation for the governor general. The newspaper supported a campaign to restore the name of the *Royal* Canadian Navy in its 2010 centennial. During the highly successful tour of the Queen and the Duke of Edinburgh that year, including a fleet review at Halifax and visits to Toronto, Winnipeg, and Ottawa, Harper's government carefully arranged for Governor General Jean and her husband to visit the Shanghai exhibition in China at the time of the Canada Day celebrations in Ottawa, over which the Queen presided. Veteran journalist Michael Valpy commented that all of this was, "if not a seismic shift in the media's agenda-setting mythology about the Canadian monarchy — at least a foundational tremor."[141]

The Queen's 2010 tour elicited an endorsement of the monarchy by Jack Layton, leader of the federal New Democratic Party. Speaking with the chair of the Monarchist League of Canada at an official dinner given for the Royal Couple by the prime minister in Toronto, Layton said, "[s]ome people think the NDP may want to get rid of the monarchy but I can assure you that that's absolutely not the case. My Dad was a big time monarchist and so am I."[142] Given the declared monarchist sentiments of the Conservative prime minister, this left only the Liberal leader in Parliament to hear from — and Michael Ignatieff remained evasive on the subject.

During their 2010 tour, the Queen and the Duke of Edinburgh took part in a fleet review in Halifax for the centennial of the Canadian Navy, which would retrieve its royal designation the following year. The Queen's personal Canadian standard shows she is aboard HMCS St. John's.

Michaëlle Jean and her husband Jean-Daniel Lafond, however, were not finished with controversy, even in the dying months of their tenure at Rideau Hall in 2010. Having commenced in October of 2005, Jean's five-year minimum appointment came to an end in the fall of 2010. Although this is only a customary mandate and not a statutory term (only the lieu-tenant governors are constitutionally guaranteed a minimum five years), Prime Minister Harper made it clear that Jean would be replaced as soon as the five years were up. But instead of the arbitrary, unilateral choice by the prime minister of the day, as had been done by Paul Martin in Jean's case, Harper appointed a committee of experts to consider and rec-ommend possible candidates as governor general.* The group conducted wide consultations, including among them Liberal opposition leader Michael Ignatieff and the NDP's Jack Layton. However, relying on her popularity and telegenic image, Michaëlle Jean is believed to have cam-paigned privately for an extension of her mandate, especially cultivating the Haitian community in Montreal. Ignatieff inexplicably succumbed to the lobbying and publicly announced his support for an extension of Jean's mandate, the only one to breach the confidential nature of the con-sultations. This partisan intervention was unprecedented and roundly criticized. And it was certainly to no avail. Soon after the Queen's 2010 tour, the prime minister announced the appointment of David Johnston, president of the University of Waterloo, as the next governor general.

No stranger to controversy himself, Michaëlle Jean's husband, Jean-Daniel Lafond, was reported to have told federal staff preparing for the Queen's 2010 visit that he did not want the royal couple accommodated as they usually were at Rideau Hall and that they should stay at a hotel (he vigorously denied the report). In an interview with the Paris-based magazine *l'Express*, where he was identified as "mari de Michaëlle Jean, Gouverneure générale (et à ce titre, chef d'État de facto) du Canada," Lafond offered his opinion that "[a]ujourd'hui, le Canada britannique est en train de s'effilocher, les liens avec la couronne sont symboliques."

---

* The committee comprised historian-authors Jacques Monet and Christopher McCreery; Sheila-Marie Cook, secretary to the governor general; Kevin MacLeod, Canadian secretary to the Queen; Christopher Manfredi, dean of arts at McGill University; and University of Calgary political scientist Rainer Knopff.

He also stated that he and his wife, "néoQuébécois" immigrants from France and Haiti, were the first real Québécois to occupy Rideau Hall. Georges Vanier was summarily dismissed: "avant nous, le seul Québécois ici était le general Vanier et on ne peut pas imaginer plus canadien que lui!" Jeanne Sauvé was ignored.[143]

David Johnston set a totally different tone. Upon the announcement of his appointment, he emphasized his role as the monarch's representative: "Je suis très honoré d'avoir été nommé le prochain Gouverneur général par sa majesté la Reine, sur la recommandation du Premier ministre [...] As the representative of the Queen of Canada, who is our country's head of state, I pledge to be a stalwart defender of our Canadian heritage, of our Canadian institutions and of the Canadian people." This was in sharp contrast to Adrienne Clarkson's description of herself as head of state in media interviews following the announcement of her appointment in 1999.

After a year in office, the governor general was the subject of a magazine interview entitled "Keep calm and carry on": "He's no Adrienne Clarkson or Michaëlle Jean," commented the writer of the article, "but Governor General David Johnston believes a quiet and steady manner suits him, and his job." Johnston said that, among his predecessors, he was especially drawn to John Buchan, Lord Tweedsmuir, "a man of many parts and [...] a quiet man [...] who derived his joy from serving well." He described the vice-regal role as follows: "First of all, it is the representative of the Queen, so it's leader as servant. Secondly, it's apolitical and non-political. It is supposed to be out of controversy. Thirdly, it's supposed to speak to and reinforce those values that are most important to Canada."[144] The first two of these traits represented a marked contrast with the approach of Johnston's immediate predecessors. The attitude of the prime minister changed too: Stephen Harper had monthly meetings with this governor general and directed that he have access to certain cabinet documents. Johnston made his mark in his "quiet and steady manner" through thoughtful speeches and in-depth newspaper articles. After representing Canada at the inauguration of the Mexican president in 2012, the governor general contributed an op-ed piece to the *Globe and Mail* on legal reform in Mexico, undertaken with Canadian help. The former dean of law said "[a]s Governor-General and as someone who cares deeply about justice and the rule of law, I am pleased that Mexico's judicial reformers are drawing insight and lessons from the criminal process used in Canada and in other Commonwealth countries."[145] The article was a fine example of a governor general using both the prestige of his office and his own personal qualifications to contribute to Canada's international standing.

Prince William and Catherine, Duke and Duchess of Cambridge and future king and queen, enjoyed a spectacularly successful tour in 2011. Their first overseas tour since their marriage earlier in the year was a major coup for the Harper government. It was masterminded by Kevin MacLeod, Usher of the Black Rod in the Senate and Canadian secretary to the Queen (and author of the educational booklet *A Crown of Maples*, whose publication was so long delayed). The Duke and Duchess participated in the Canada Day celebrations, as Prince William's grandparents had done a year earlier, drawing record crowds to Parliament Hill. They also managed the feat of popular visits to Montreal and Quebec, where

Prince William, Duke of Cambridge and eventual heir to the throne, and Catherine, Duchess of Cambridge, at the Canada Day celebrations in Ottawa in 2011. Their first Canadian tour was a resounding success.

enthusiastic spectators vastly outnumbered the inevitable groups of sovereigntist protesters. This was followed by visits to Prince Edward Island, the Northwest Territories, and Alberta for the Calgary Stampede. While their international celebrity was clearly a major factor in their public appeal, observers concluded that the Duke and Duchess had struck a chord among younger Canadians for the relevance of the monarchy.

In the wake of the tour, the Conservative government announced the restoration of the historic titles of the Canadian Armed Forces: Royal Canadian Navy, Royal Canadian Air Force, and Canadian Army. The move received much editorial praise across the country as a revival of proud traditions and the undoing of an error made in 1968. It was inevitably decried as a retrograde colonial move by the Bloc Québécois and by some academics like J.L. Granatstein. Regrettably, in the absence of an ailing Jack Layton, the spokesman for the NDP, which had become the official opposition in the 2011 general election, joined in the criticism. The death of Layton, occurring shortly afterwards, not only deprived his party of his committed monarchical voice, but led to concerns that the now overwhelmingly dominant Quebec caucus of the NDP might make common cause with republican-minded sovereigntists in that province. Indeed, there were rumblings in both the New Democratic and the Liberal parties about making the monarchy a political issue. NDP leadership candidate Nathan Cullen called for a referendum on the monarchy. A resolution for its elimination was presented by young Liberals at a party policy convention early in 2012 (the resolution was soundly defeated), and former astronaut and now MP Marc Garneau deplored the return of "royal" to the navy and air force. This was unfortunate. The Crown is by nature non-partisan. Yet any enhancements to it, such as those made by the Conservatives from 2007, have to be chosen and implemented by the government of the day, which offers a tempting political target for those opposed to that government for other reasons. It is significant that Stephen Harper himself was lukewarm at best about the monarchy when he entered politics. With experience of governing came a realization of the intrinsic value of the institution for Canada and the undesirability of the alternatives. If Harper had once favoured the Crown merely as a symbol of heritage, he now considered it an integral component of Canada's system of government.

The Conservative government announced in 2011 that Canadian diplomatic missions abroad were to display portraits of the Queen, a practice
that was long-standing but erratically applied. One commentator suggested
that Harper's government was "pursuing symbols and areas ignored" for
forty years, including "the Arctic, the military, national sports and especially the monarchy."[146] One of the prime movers in the new approach to
symbols was Calgary MP Jason Kenney. In 2007, while Secretary of State
(Multiculturalism and Canadian Identity) for the Department of Canadian
Heritage, Kenney showed his mettle by overcoming entrenched bureaucratic opposition in the department and at Rideau Hall to finally publish
A Crown of Maples. After becoming minister of Citizenship, Immigration
and Multiculturalism in 2008, Kenney oversaw publication of the new
citizenship guide for immigrants, which, unlike its bland predecessors,
included robust passages on Canada's history, institutions, military traditions, and the Crown. Jason Kenney was the prime minister's point man
in courting immigrants and cultural communities, successfully counter-
ing the impression that the Conservatives were hostile to immigration.
Observers were struck by the juxtaposition of promoting immigration
while lauding historic Canadian traditions like the monarchy. Perhaps in
the twenty-first century Canada had at last come to terms with its identity.

THE DIAMOND JUBILEE AND BEYOND

The 2012 Diamond Jubilee of Queen Elizabeth II, marking her sixty
years as Sovereign — the only other such anniversary had been Queen
Victoria's in 1897 — confirmed the monarchy's new popularity. Early in
2011, Stephen Harper's Conservative government, totally in synch with
Governor General David Johnston, announced a comprehensive Jubilee
program, with provincial participation. This included a logo, website,
events across the country, grants for community celebrations, and a
Diamond Jubilee Medal. Canada Post issued a historic series of postage
stamps commemorating the Queen's reign. Rideau Hall, in contrast with
2002, where the "fiftieth anniversary of the Canadian governors general"
vied for pride of place with the Sovereign's Golden Jubilee, added the
Diamond Jubilee logo to its letterhead, with the slogan "Vivat Regina."

And there was no vice-regal sixtieth anniversary logo on the certificate for the Diamond Jubilee Medal. Prime Minister Harper, in an appropriately non-partisan manner, named his Liberal predecessor once removed, Jean Chrétien, as Canada's representative on the Commonwealth Advisory Group of the Diamond Jubilee Trust.

The Prince of Wales and Duchess of Cornwall made a four-day Diamond Jubilee tour to New Brunswick, Toronto, and Saskatchewan. Observers were struck both by the relaxed, informal approach adopted by the Royal Couple and by the warm reception given to them in the three provinces. The tour devoted ample time to the charitable and policy interests of the Prince and Duchess, in contrast to the lacklustre program of their 2009 tour, prepared on short notice and focused mainly on military ceremonies. The trend-setting tour in 2011 by "Will and Kate," Duke and Duchess of Cambridge, seemed to have had a liberating effect on the royals and their tour organizers. The substantive side of Charles — his charities and educational and artistic initiatives — long appreciated in the United Kingdom but little known in Canada, had received a major boost in 2010. Under the auspices of former Ontario lieutenant governor Hilary Weston and her husband, grocery magnate Galen Weston, close friends of the Prince of Wales, the Prince's Charities Canada was set up to assist the Canadian charities supported by Charles, among them heritage, music, professional development for injured veterans, and business support for disadvantaged youth. On the eve of the 2012 tour of the Prince and Duchess, the *Globe and Mail* published a laudatory two-page illustrated feature on the Prince's Charities.[147] Those looking to the future of the monarchy were encouraged by Canadians' revived interest in the heir to the throne — and vice versa.

Governor General Johnston and Prime Minister Harper travelled to London with a Canadian delegation for the spectacular Jubilee celebrations in the United Kingdom. The highlight for the Canadians was the unveiling of a new state portrait of herself by the Queen. Commissioned by the federal government from Toronto artist Phil Richards to mark the Diamond Jubilee, it showed the Queen standing before a portrait of Queen Victoria at Rideau Hall. The new portrait was hung in the very place in the Rideau Hall ballroom whence its predecessor had been banished during the Michaëlle Jean years.

QUEEN ELIZABETH II
DIAMOND JUBILEE MEDAL

MÉDAILLE DU JUBILÉ DE DIAMANT
DE LA REINE ELIZABETH II

D. Michael Jackson, CVO, CD

By Command of Her Majesty The Queen,
the Diamond Jubilee Medal is presented to you
in commemoration of the sixtieth anniversary
of Her Majesty's Accession to the Throne
and in recognition of your contributions to Canada.

Par ordre de Sa Majesté la Reine,
la Médaille du jubilé de diamant vous est présentée
en commémoration du soixantième anniversaire
de l'accession de Sa Majesté au Trône et en reconnaissance
de votre contribution au service du Canada.

Governor General of Canada   Gouverneur général du Canada

1952 - 2012

On the occasion of   À l'occasion du

the fiftieth Anniversary   cinquantième anniversaire

of the accession of   de l'accession de

HER MAJESTY THE QUEEN   SA MAJESTÉ LA REINE

to the Throne   au Trône

the Golden Jubilee Medal   la Médaille du jubilé

is presented to   est remise à

Dr. Michael Jackson, L.V.O., C.D.

CANADIAN GOVERNORS GENERAL 1952-2002 LES GOUVERNEURS GÉNÉRAUX CANADIENS

Two governors general, two approaches to the Queen's jubilees. The medal certificate for the Golden Jubilee in 2002 includes the fiftieth anniversary of the "Canadian" governors general. The Diamond Jubilee certificate in 2012 focuses on the Queen's sixtieth anniversary.

Michael Jackson

The Media Changes Its Tune

Media comment on the Diamond Jubilee was refreshingly positive. On Accession Day, February 6, 2012, the *Globe and Mail* editorially praised the Queen as representing not only Canada's traditions and old virtues but also its present, its democratic institutions, and its future. The editorial concluded "[e]ven agnostics might on this occasion be tempted to say God Save the Queen."[148] While this tribute was by then not unexpected from the *Globe and Mail*, that from the traditionally republican-leaning *Toronto Star* came as a surprise. Citing opinion polls showing the monarchy more popular than ever in Canada, the newspaper said:

> Logic would suggest that as the country grew and welcomed millions of people from all parts of the world, allegiance to an ancient institution rooted in British traditions would have become tenuous at best. Instead, the monarchy is more secure than it's been in quite a while. [...] monarchy is entwined in every aspect of our system of government and laws, and in an odd reversal of history *has come to symbolize democracy itself* [our emphasis]. [...] It is hard to imagine a more successful reign than that of the Queen of Canada.[149]

Some prominent national columnists agreed. In a piece entitled "The Queen and a nationalism built on love," Andrew Coyne interpreted the resounding success of the Diamond Jubilee celebrations as "a mixture of affection for the Queen and a deep attachment to what she represents," i.e., the people and the nation. "That bedrock of popular affection is what ultimately underpins her constitutional role. A constitutional order founded on love strikes me as no bad thing." He concluded by endorsing the hereditary principle of monarchy at the head of the state as far preferable to elected and appointed officials who are by definition transitory and of whom we inevitably tire.[150] Columnist Michael Den Tandt applied the argument more specifically to Canada. Scolding Winnipeg NDP Member of Parliament Pat Martin for using the Jubilee celebrations to call for the end of the monarchy, Den Tandt contrasted the royals with politicians "grubbing for popularity, hacking away at his or her opponents on Twitter, sniping, deking and ducking whenever it is expedient to do so." The Queen and her family, he said, believe that their life mission "is to be simply, visibly decent and devoted to duty, in a way that transcends electoral politics." He asked, "Is Ottawa so firm in its foundations that we can afford to cast aside a family entirely devoted to [such values], and to our shared history?"[151]

Renewed media interest in the monarchy was demonstrated by the fact that *Maclean's* magazine published no fewer than four special commemorative editions in two years: two on the wedding of William and Kate and their Canadian tour in 2011 and two on the Queen's Diamond Jubilee in 2012.[152]

Canadian federal political leaders were on side. When Jason Kenney, on behalf of Prime Minister Harper, moved a "humble address" to the Queen for the Diamond Jubilee in the House of Commons on June 4, 2012, representatives of other parties spoke enthusiastically in support. Peter Stoffer, a Nova Scotia MP, "on behalf of all New Democrats across the country and on behalf of Her Majesty's Loyal Opposition," stated that the Queen "truly has been a symbol of hope, truth, justice, charity and love." Interim Liberal leader Bob Rae asserted, "we have a constitutional monarch who is above politics, rancor and division." Elizabeth May, first and only Green Party MP, made a telling observation: "It is very healthy that we do not turn a prime minister into a royal. In order to avoid that natural human temptation, we need the monarchy."[153]

Discordant Voices

Of course, there could scarcely be unanimity on an issue like the monarchy. During the 2012 Quebec election campaign, Parti Québécois leader Pauline Marois — soon to be premier — attacked the federal Conservatives for promoting the Crown. It "creates institutions like that of the lieutenant governor, which is useless [...] I'll trade [Harper] the royalty for Quebec sovereignty."[154] At its policy convention in April 2013, the federal New Democratic Party did not debate a resolution from a Quebec constituency that "an NDP government would pursue the objective of establishing a parliamentary republic upon the death of the present sovereign;" but MP Pat Martin introduced a private member's bill in the House of Commons to remove the Queen from the citizenship oath as a step towards "severing Canada's ties with the British monarchy."[155]

During the 2013 leadership campaign for the Liberal Party of Canada, the candidates were canvassed by Monarchist League members about their attitude to the Crown. While no candidate considered the monarchy a priority, Deborah Coyne responded that she favoured "eventually establishing a Canadian head of state with democratic legitimacy." Martha Hall Findlay said, "I'd be happy to have Canada become completely independent from Britain." However, Marc Garneau, who had regretted the return of the royal titles for the Canadian Forces, stated, "Canadians support the monarchy" and that he did "not plan to make an issue of it." The ultimate winner of the Liberal leadership, Justin Trudeau, did not respond to the survey.[156]

A discordant view on the monarchy was linked to the perceived misuse of the royal prerogative to centralize power in the executive. In the midst of Diamond Jubilee year, a movement called Your Canada — Your Constitution (YCYC) appeared, led by Duff Conacher, formerly of Democracy Watch, and Andrew Cohen, late of the Historica-Dominion Institute. The group labelled itself an "educational charity," with the objective of alerting Canadians to deficiencies in their democratic institutions. While it purported to be neutral on the question of the monarchy, at its first conference and in subsequent communications YCYC turned out to have a thinly veiled republican agenda. Taking aim at what they considered excessive executive powers, notably the exercise of prorogation, YCYC's leaders sought in effect the elimination of their constitutional source — the Crown — and those who incarnated it: the monarch, the governor general, and the lieutenant governors. One opinion poll commissioned by YCYC asked "to what extent do you agree or disagree that Canada's Constitution should be changed to make Canada a fully independent country by retiring the British monarchy as Head of Canada's federal and provincial governments?" As critics of YCYC, led by University of Ottawa graduate student James Bowden, were quick to point out, its polls were manipulative and factually wrong.[157] They ignored the history and practice of responsible government, the autonomous Canadian monarchy since the 1931 Statute of Westminster, and the key role of constitutional conventions, and they caricatured the monarch and vice-regal representatives as holding and exercising arbitrary powers.

In addition to removing Canada's "foreign" monarchy, YCYC's main thrust appeared to be the codification of the reserve powers. In a survey released early in 2013, the group claimed that "84% of Canadians want powers of Prime Minister and premiers restricted with clear, enforceable rules" when they were asked about "writing down the currently unwritten constitutional 'conventions.'"[158] YCYC appeared to conflate legitimate and long-standing concerns about constraints on executive power with the fundamental nature of Canada's monarchical, parliamentary democracy. Although pointing out that in Britain, Australia, and New Zealand, steps had been taken to make first ministers and governments more accountable, YCYC called for much more radical constitutional change. Like many critics of Canada's parliamentary democracy, YCYC failed to note that in Westminster, Canberra, and Wellington, party discipline is far less strict than in Ottawa and elected members are far more independent of the leadership. Parliament's role can and should be restored and enhanced by parliamentarians themselves.

Would the post-2006 positive attitude to the Crown turn out to be long-lasting or transitory? Would the apparent revival of favour towards the monarchy evident in 2010–2012 be durable, or just a blip in public opinion? Was the recent royal popularity attached to the institution, or was it due to the near-universal affection, respect, and admiration for Queen Elizabeth II and would not survive the succession by her eldest son? Would Canadians continue to appreciate the merits of sharing an ancient monarchy with other realms, or eventually consider having the "British" monarch as their Sovereign to be an outdated anomaly? Republican-leaning academics like historian Christopher Moore tended to the latter answers, citing the lobby group Citizens for a Canadian Republic, which calls the Queen in right of Canada "a Canadian fabrication" and proposes a head of state elected by Parliament or the people.[159] Others took the opposite tack. Carolyn Harris, an emerging scholar at Queen's University, traced the ups and downs of the Queen's reign in four phases: the Young Queen of Canada, the Controversial Queen of Canada, the Celebrity Queen of Canada, and the Jubilee Queen of Canada. Her conclusion was that Canadian public perception of the Queen had come full circle to a renewed respect and admiration. Thanks also to the new generation of royals represented by the Duke and Duchess of Cambridge, and the return to favour of the Prince of Wales, "there is every reason to believe that the revival of Canadian crown will continue for decades to come."[160] During 2012, the Canadian Museum of Civilization in Gatineau, Quebec, presented a special display on the Diamond Jubilee, with many of the artifacts loaned by Senator Serge Joyal. Attendance surpassed the museum's expectations by 50 percent. "Il y a donc, en 2012, un intérêt populaire réel pour la monarchie et pour la personne de Sa Majesté — et cela dépasse les convictions constitutionnelles / politiques; et cela dépasse *a fortiori* les convictions partisanes."[161]

New Initiatives

Expanding the positive royal news to the indigenous dimension of the Crown, Prime Minister Stephen Harper made a historic announcement late in Diamond Jubilee Year about the process of vice-regal appointments. As we have seen, this involved an advisory committee, chaired by the Canadian secretary to the Queen, to recommend candidates for provincial lieutenant governors, territorial governors, and not least the governor general, confirming and extending the process successfully used for the selection of David Johnston in 2010. The announcement was well received, with the sole of exception of the new Parti Québécois government in Quebec, which decried the move as colonial and called again for the elimination of the vice-regal offices. The first vice-regal appointment made on the recommendation of the advisory committee was that of Frank Fagan as lieutenant governor of Newfoundland and Labrador in March 2013. Another welcome feature of the prime minister's initiative was that the Canadian secretary to the Queen would become a permanent position, with the incumbent, veteran public servant Kevin MacLeod, appointed for a six-year term from 2013. He would also "be responsible for advising the Prime Minister on matters related to the Canadian Crown, including providing advice on the Government of Canada's heritage-related commemorative initiatives, high level coordination of Royal Tours to

Canada, and state ceremonial and protocol advisory functions."[162] It was one of the most positive initiatives for the Canadian Crown to emerge from the Diamond Jubilee.

Another positive development was the changed attitude of Rideau Hall towards the provincial lieutenant governors. No longer were they treated as inferiors. Instead, Governor General David Johnston spoke of Canada's "vice-regal family." At a meeting of vice-regal representatives in Ottawa in June 2012, he said, quoting *The Evolving Canadian Crown*:

> As former Lieutenant Governor of Saskatchewan Lynda Haverstock and Dr. Michael Jackson have written: "The genius of the Crown is that it balances the roles of Sovereign, governor general and lieutenant governor to incarnate Canada's federal and parliamentary polity." At the heart of this balanced system is what has been termed a "compound monarchy." I think it is quintessentially Canadian, this idea of a shared Crown. What a wonderful symbol of unity and diversity to guide us! Let us keep this image in mind during our discussions today on our evolving Crown and country. Together, as representatives of the Queen, we can strengthen Canada by strengthening our provinces and territories — and vice versa.[163]

At long last, Rideau Hall had grasped the notion of the collective Canadian Crown — what Frank MacKinnon had called "the team of governors" as early as 1976 and David E. Smith had termed Canada's "compound monarchy" in 1995.

Regardless of the vicissitudes of opinion polls and statements by politicians, the Conservative government continued its revival of Canada's royal heritage, for example by restoring historical army names in 2013: the Royal Canadian Armoured Corps, the Corps of Royal Canadian Engineers, the Royal Canadian Corps of Signals, the Royal Canadian Infantry Corps, and the Corps of Royal Canadian Electrical and Mechanical Engineers, "to honour their illustrious history of service to Canada."[164]

Governor General David Johnston adopted a more positive approach than his recent predecessors to the roles of the monarch and the lieutenant governors.

Sergeant Serge Gouin, Rideau Hall; © Her Majesty The Queen in Right of Canada, represented by the Office of the Secretary to the Governor General (2010)

There were renewed efforts to deal with the appalling ignorance of the Crown and parliamentary democracy in Canada's school systems. In 2011, Ontario teacher Nathan Tidridge, quoted in the Introduction to this book, published *Canada's Constitutional Monarchy*, a highly readable illustrated guide to the Canadian monarchy aimed at a secondary school audience. Bolstered by political scientist Peter Russell and John Fraser, Master of Massey College, Tidridge led a campaign to convince the Ontario ministry of education to reform "a curriculum that is providing no direction," resulting in "egregious errors in our textbooks."[165]

Reforming the Succession to the Throne

At the biennial conference of Commonwealth Heads of Government held in Perth, Australia, in October 2011, the governments of the United Kingdom and the Queen's fifteen other realms agreed to changes to the rules of succession to the throne proposed by British Prime Minister David Cameron. Archaic British legislation dating back to the eighteenth century, notably the *Act of Settlement* of 1701, not only limited the succession to the eldest son of the monarch (male primogeniture), but barred those married to Roman Catholics from succeeding to the throne. The *Royal Marriages Act* of 1772 also required descendants of George II to obtain the monarch's permission to marry. These discriminatory provisions, enacted for distant historical reasons, had no place in the twenty-first-century Commonwealth. In Canada, the rules of succession had been challenged under the Charter of Rights and Freedoms in the *O'Donahue* case of 2003. The Ontario Superior Court of Justice, however, ruled that the Canadian monarch was the same as that of the United Kingdom; the succession was therefore part of Canada's constitutional law, not ordinary law, and was thus not subject to charter challenges. The ruling was upheld by the Ontario Court of Appeal in 2005.[166]

The sixteen realms undertook to eliminate primogeniture, the bar to the monarch marrying a Roman Catholic, and the requirement of the monarch to approve marriages of those in the succession (other than the six people closest in line to the throne). With the process no doubt hastened by the news that the Duchess of Cambridge, wife of heir to the throne Prince William, was expecting their first child, the United Kingdom introduced its legislation in December 2012. Coordinated by New Zealand, the fifteen other realms all confirmed their agreement. The same month, the *Succession to the Crown Act 2013* was introduced in the UK Parliament; it was adopted by the House of Commons in January 2013 and by the House of Lords in April, and received royal assent on April 25, 2013.[167]

Similar legislation in Canada, however, faced complications over its constitutional status. While there was a consensus on the desirability of the changes to the succession rules, how should they be implemented? By federal legislation or by constitutional amendment? And if the latter, would it fall under section 41 (a) of the *Constitution Act, 1982*, which requires the approval of all ten provincial legislatures, as well as of both houses of Parliament, to any changes to "the office of the Queen"? Introducing bill C-63, the *Succession to the Throne Act, 2013*, at the beginning of 2013, the federal government opted for legislation, arguing that, since the United Kingdom determined the succession to the throne, Canada need only to give its assent to the British legislation. Passed unanimously and without debate by the House of Commons on February 4, the bill was debated, studied in committee, and eventually approved by the Senate on March 26, and received royal assent on March 27, 2013.

There was considerable division of opinion on the issue of process, although not the substance, of the legislation. For example, the Monarchist League of Canada vigorously supported the federal legislation,[168] while its 1994 offshoot, the Canadian Royal Heritage Trust, equally vigorously opposed it.[169] Those in support of the government's view argued that Canada cannot legislate for the succession to the throne and can assent to British legislation because the succession is a matter for the United Kingdom to decide, subject to consultation with the other realms. There are legal grounds to say that the succession to the throne in Canada changes automatically when it is changed by the United Kingdom.

Those opposed to the 2013 *Act* argued that the succession is part of the constitutional law of Canada (as stated in the *O'Donahue* case of 2003) and that since 1982 UK legislation can no longer apply to Canada. Although the United Kingdom and Canada (as well as the other realms) share the same monarch, the Crown and the Queen of Canada are separate and distinct from those of the United Kingdom (as already noted, this was clearly stated by the Court of Appeal of England in 1982 in a case brought by the First Nations). Furthermore, section 41 (a) of the *Constitution Act, 1982*, does apply, because changing the succession does indeed alter "the office of the Queen."[170]

In pragmatic terms, modernizing the succession rules by federal legislation was infinitely preferable to the perilous process of a constitutional amendment involving all ten provinces, especially with a Parti Québécois government in power in Quebec. Memories of the patriation disputes and the botched Meech Lake and Charlottetown accords of the 1980s were enough to deter federal politicians from reopening the constitution. On the other hand, might the *Succession to the Throne Act, 2013* be a dangerous precedent for unilateral federal changes to the monarchy without provincial consent? As one commentator noted, using a simple parliamentary majority for this purpose may "[render] meaningless the constitutional protection many see as the legal firewall built to preserve the monarchy in Canada."[171] Philippe Lagassé observes that if the office of the Queen is interpreted narrowly, as it appears to be in the 2013 *Act*, "then the federal Parliament could unilaterally pass a number of acts that affect the Crown, such as a regency act or an act that assents to a British decision to change royal families without provincial consent."[172]

Interestingly, Australia and New Zealand chose to pass their own succession legislation and not assent to the British law. And the Australian state of Queensland decided to pass its own law.

Robert E. Hawkins, however, while taking seriously the arguments against the Canadian legislation, maintains that it "accords with the convention of symmetry that preserves the personal unity of the British and Dominion Crowns." For Professor Hawkins, this "symmetry" is effectively a constitutionally entrenched convention. And provincial consent to changes to the succession is not required. Indeed, the 2013 Act had the merit of "avoiding the constitutional gridlock which provincial involvement could entail, especially given that there is no valid provincial interest in having different monarchs in different provinces." In pragmatic terms, asserts Hawkins, constitutional interpretation should "yield workable outcomes."[173] It remains to see if the provinces will oppose any such federal initiatives in the future. None did in 2013, and Ontario legal counsel supported the federal bill. However, Manitoba's minister of justice stated that the succession act was "not in any way a precedent."[174]

Then, in June 2013, two Laval University law professors filed a motion in Quebec Superior Court, contending that the *Succession to the Throne Act, 2013* was unconstitutional because it did not follow the amending formula in section 41 (a) of the *Constitution Act, 1982* and was therefore contrary to the Charter of Rights and Freedoms. They stated that their aim was not "to contest the political decision to amend the rules regarding the designation of the head of state, but rather to ensure that such amendments are made in compliance with the Constitution." "The office of the Queen," they said, "is the constitutional foundation for Canada's executive and legislative authority in both provincial and federal jurisdictions."[175] Here were echoes of *Hodge v. The Queen* in 1883 and *Liquidators of the Maritime Bank* in 1892! One Montreal academic saw the amendment to the succession as a way "to simply abolish the monarchy rather than modernize it,"[176] although this was not the declared intent of the plaintiffs in the case. It is likely that Quebec nationalists saw the succession as a way to assert Quebec's role in constitutional amendment. As one commentator wryly put it, "The irony is palpable: Sovereigntists are basing a challenge to the federal government, and an attempt to shore up Quebec's veto, on the argument that the monarch is 'the Queen of Quebec.'"[177]

Into the Future

A key factor in the revival, or at the least the retention, of the monarchy in Canada, barring any major, politically supported move for its abolition linked to Quebec, may well be the consequences of such an upheaval. Few Canadians have an appetite for reopening thorny constitutional issues. The question of what would replace the monarchy has never been satisfactorily answered. The alternatives, once they are closely examined, seem dubious, even unpalatable. Many Canadians feel that it best to let sleeping dogs lie. It may be preferable to stay with a system which is not perfect, having as it does the drawbacks of a non-resident monarch and the ambiguous role of the royal prerogative, yet which works well in practice and has provided Canada with two centuries of satisfactory governance. Such sentiments may not be lofty or noble, but they reflect a quiet pragmatism which is very much part of the Canadian temperament — that of the "peaceable kingdom."

Recent books on Queen Elizabeth II have emphasized her personal astuteness in adapting the monarchy to change, and consequently the resilience of this ancient institution, which regularly polls 70–80 percent support in the United Kingdom. "It has managed [to adapt] without us noticing — ever changing yet never changing," says royal commentator Robert Hardman. "And that is all down to the shrewd leadership of an innately conservative woman who had also proved to be the very model of a modern monarch."[178] The Queen's other realms have benefited from and been influenced by this monarchical success story. That customary Canadian parallel, Australia, gives cause for reflection. A major Australian tour by the Queen and the Duke of Edinburgh in 2011, on the occasion of the Commonwealth Heads of Government meeting, was an enormous success, amazing monarchists and republicans alike. Much as in Canada, opinion polls showed public support for a republic at its lowest level in two decades and support for the monarchy at its highest, notably among those aged between eighteen and thirty-five. Even more surprising was a successful Diamond Jubilee tour in Australia, New Zealand, and Papua New Guinea in 2012 by the hitherto much-maligned Prince of Wales and Duchess of Cornwall. Calling Charles "the very model of a modern heir to the throne," a republican-minded newspaper, *The Australian,* asserted that the "modest, successful royal tour sets challenges for republicans."[179] Another press organ commented, "even staunch republicans mostly admit that there is little public enthusiasm for a break from the monarchy in the short term. It seems we've come to accept that Prince Charles will eventually become our king."[180]

After the Queen's 2011 tour, an Australian newspaper admitted, "the republican flag now hangs limp in the doldrums of indifference."[181] Will this flag, and its even limper Canadian equivalent, unfurl again?

Conclusion

Our Queen is the latest link in a long golden chain that connects the Canadian story. The mystery and magic behind our constitutional arrangements are all tied to an hereditary monarchy. That is the real secret of the Crown. It is our past, which if denied will confound our future; it is our dignity, which if cast carelessly aside will make us a crasser people; it is the protection of our rights, which if abandoned could lead to demagogic manipulation or excess. Most important of all, the Crown defines our uniqueness and is evidence of a mature community that can carry forward its history and heritage and uniqueness with pride.[1]

— John Fraser

As we have abundantly seen, the Crown is of great importance to Canada and Canadians. It encapsulates the priceless heritage of a thousand-year evolution towards parliamentary democracy and the rule of law. In more specifically Canadian terms, over a period of three centuries, the Crown has been a remarkably benevolent instrument of responsible government, nation-building, Aboriginal rights, national independence, provincial autonomy, francophone identity, and a distinctive political culture in North America. It is key to the way Canadians govern themselves.

The Crown was instrumental in Canada's transition to independence. It was also crucial in the evolution of the Canadian state towards true federalism, despite the initial constraints of constitutional texts and the centralizing thrust of the first federal governments — and some subsequent ones. It is in large measure thanks to the Crown and the lieutenant governor that, through the courts, the provinces secured their jurisdictional autonomy and constitutional co-sovereignty. The same potential now exists for integrating a "third order" of Aboriginal government in Confederation. Since "the Queen transcends and encompasses both the central and the provincial governments, the Canadian headship of state is not a creature of either jurisdiction. Through the offices of the Governor General and the Lieutenant Governor, the Queen reigns impartially over Confederation as a whole."[2] This point was well made by Frank MacKinnon when he wrote:

> The sovereignty of provincial governments [...] is not passed on to them either by the Parliament of Canada, which has not the power to do it in a federal system, or by the Governor General, who is not himself a source of supreme power on his own, and who heads a government which is sovereign only in federal matters. The constitutional status of the provinces is therefore greatly enhanced by the practice of keeping the Crown and headship of state separate from the Governor General.[3]

Canadians should, then, be extremely cautious about removing or even diminishing Canada's monarchical culture and institutions — a change which would be much more fundamental than it appears on the surface and holds the risk of far-ranging, unintended consequences to the political order. The advantages of the present system of constitutional monarchy far outweigh its defects. The alternatives are dubious at the best and in all likelihood would be injurious to Canada's best interests. Certainly, given past history, Canadian provinces, like the Australian states, should be very wary indeed of the centralizing implications of a republic. Indeed, the most telling aspect of efforts to downplay or remove the monarchy in Canada has been the failure to take into account the provincial Crown and the lieutenant governor who embodies it. This is a misreading of the pragmatic and emotional reality of the provincial vice-regal office. Those pushing for elimination of the monarchy have usually ignored not only the implications for federalism but also the interests of the Aboriginal peoples. The First Nations instinctively understand the powerful moral, social, and political resonances of the Crown as symbol and realize its potential for their own status in the Canadian confederation.

The revival of interest in and support for the constitutional monarchy in the twenty-first century is welcome. New Canadians have become far more favourable to the Crown. In addition, the younger generations (roughly Canadians under forty) have also grown supportive. The more widespread anti-monarchism of the early Baby Boomers is starting to look like an aberration in Canadian history rather than the establishment of new republican norms. The academy has also experienced a renaissance in the study of the Crown, particularly since the prorogation-coalition controversy of 2008, and a new generation of students has engaged seriously with the topic. However, some caution is in order. It is true that the Crown in Canada has never been better promoted in terms of the Royal Family itself. Yet the welcome reforms that have been implemented were relatively easy, such as restoring the royal prefix to the navy and air force, increasing the frequency of royal tours, celebrating the Diamond Jubilee, and publishing better government literature on the Crown.

The other, underlying aspects of the Crown — including our approach to history and our institutions themselves — need to be reinforced. If the "dignified" dimension of the Crown is again valued, its "efficient" side must also be treated with more respect and more transparency. Governments that — rightly — enjoy the symbolism of constitutional monarchy must pay more than lip service to the conventions of parliamentary democracy which the Crown represents. The entire institution of responsible government, of which the Crown is such an integral part, is largely misunderstood by the population and is criticized by those seeking a republican political order. The importance of the Crown for responsible government in its sub-national dimension is not always sufficiently appreciated by those closest to it: the premiers and governments of the provinces. They should see Quebec sovereigntist hostility to the office of lieutenant governor for what it is: an attack on Canadian federalism and parliamentary government.

Yet constitutional monarchy and its concomitant responsible government have proven themselves to be immensely successful, both nationally and provincially. In Canada, as in Australia and New Zealand, the Crown has underlined the distinction between polity and executive, between head of state and head of government, and has provided a factor of dignity and trust to political institutions. The monarch and her representatives have superbly fulfilled the roles of community leadership and promotion of voluntarism. While conservative in nature, the Crown has enabled "[i]deological radicalism [...] to find a peaceful expression,"[4] as shown by the early rise of social democratic parties in all three realms. Common elements are the sheer adaptability of the Crown and the Westminster system of government and their evolution to the point where the surrogate governors embody the Crown, transcend its British origins, and, in the cases of Australia and Canada, exemplify federalism.

But the Crown is not only about legal matters like constitutions and governments and courts and legislatures. It is a symbol of values and traditions and heritage, of loyalty, identity, and ethos. Former Saskatchewan premier Allan Blakeney once said that a role of the Queen, governor general, and lieutenant governors is "to embody, without too much clarity or precision, the few values we hold in common."[5] Imprecision can be a virtue, because it allows for flexibility, adaptation, and evolution. An Australian legal scholar published a book about the constitutional monarchy in that country called *The Chameleon Crown*.[6] The fluidity and nuance of the Crown, far from being a liability, have been an unequivocal asset to our federal, bilingual, multicultural, immigrant country. With its ideals of community solidarity and inclusion, the Crown has been and is key to our thriving civil society, our tolerance, our openness, and, in the words of the *Constitution Act, 1867*, "peace, order and good government." Jacques Monet said, "la monarchie [...] est fondée sur la dignité et l'égalité des personnes, sur la promotion des cultures, et, pour les Canadiens français en particulier, sur la défense et l'illustration de la langue française. De plus, et de par sa nature même, elle rebute les étroitesses nationalistes et s'entoure de notions plus larges, telles que celle de la famille et de la fraternité universelle."[7]

Is it not remarkable that in Canada we have been able to create a viable, healthy, prosperous, inclusive nation with such a sparse population scattered across such an enormous northern landmass? That we have not only survived as an independent country but flourished next door to the most powerful nation on earth? That we continue to attract immigrants from around the world who seek to share our good fortune? Is it a coincidence that constitutional monarchies like Canada are among the most stable, free, and peaceful countries in the world?

We suggest that it is no coincidence at all. The Crown is not just a question of legality and constitutional constructs, however important they are. It speaks to the heart as well as the mind. The Crown focuses our gaze on who we are and whence we come, on what values we hold dear and how we will pursue our future. This is why it is vitally important in the twenty-first century to understand and appreciate the Crown, a remarkable institution that Canadians, for half a millennium, have inherited, adapted, and shaped into one of the pillars of Canada's identity as a nation.

Notes

PREFACE

1. Rudyard Griffiths, *Who We Are: A Citizen's Manifesto* (Vancouver/Toronto: Douglas & McIntyre, 2009), 48.
2. Nathan Tidridge, *Canada's Constitutional Monarchy* (Toronto: Dundurn, 2011), 19.
3. Ian Holloway, "The Law of Succession and the Canadian Crown," presented at the conference "The Crown in Canada: A Diamond Jubilee Assessment," Regina, October 2012.
4. *Ibid.*
5. John Ralston Saul, *A Fair Country: Telling Truths About Canada* (Toronto: Viking Canada, 2008).
6. Hilary M. Weston, *No Ordinary Time: My Years as Ontario's Lieutenant Governor* (Toronto: Whitfield Editions, 2007), 8.
7. Lowell Murray, "Which Criticisms Are Founded?" in Serge Joyal, ed., *Protecting Canadian Democracy: The Senate You Never Knew* (Montreal & Kingston: McGill-Queen's University Press, 2003), 135–36.
8. Calgary: Glenbow-Alberta Institute and McClelland and Stewart West, 1976.
9. Toronto/Vancouver: Clarke Irwin & Company, 1979.
10. Ottawa: Le Cercle du livre de France, 1979.

11. David E. Smith, *The Invisible Crown: The First Principle of Canadian Government* (Toronto: University of Toronto Press, 1995; reprinted with a new preface, Toronto: University of Toronto Press, 2013).

INTRODUCTION

1. Hugh Segal, "Royal Assent: A Time for Clarity," in Jennifer Smith and D. Michael Jackson, eds., *The Evolving Canadian Crown* (Montreal & Kingston: McGill-Queen's University Press, 2012), 217–18.
2. Quoted in David Dilks, *The Great Dominion: Winston Churchill in Canada, 1900–1954* (Toronto: Thomas Allen Publishers, 2005), 83.
3. Department of Foreign Affairs & International Trade, The Skelton Lecture, 2004, 4–5 (*www.dfait-maeci.gc.ca/department/skelton*).
4. John G. Diefenbaker, *Those Things We Treasure* (Toronto: Macmillan of Canada, 1972), 14.
5. *The Invisible Crown*, 176, 182.
6. Noel Cox, *A Constitutional History of the New Zealand Monarchy: The Evolution of the New Zealand Monarchy and the Recognition of an Autochthonous Polity* (Saarbrücken: Verlag Dr. Müller, 2008), 35–36.
7. *Ibid.*, 46.
8. *Ibid.*, 45.
9. *The Invisible Crown*, 11.

CHAPTER I
CANADA — HISTORICALLY A CONSTITUTIONAL MONARCHY

1. Eugene Forsey, *Freedom and Order* (Toronto: McClelland and Stewart, The Carleton Library, 1974), 21.
2. Frédéric Lemieux, Christian Blais, Pierre Hamelin, *L'histoire du Québec à travers ses lieutenants-gouverneurs* (Québec: Les Publications du Québec, 2005), 5.
3. Hereward Senior and Elinor Kyte Senior, *In Defence of Monarchy* (Toronto: Fealty Enterprises, 2009), 27.

4. Hugh Segal, *The Right Balance: Canada's Conservative Tradition* (Vancouver/Toronto: Douglas & McIntyre, 2011), 15.
5. For a concise and lucid explanation of the role of these three leaders and the achievement of responsible government, see John Ralston Saul, *Louis-Hippolyte LaFontaine and Robert Baldwin* (Toronto: Penguin Canada, Extraordinary Canadians Series, 2010).
6. See on this subject Donald Creighton, *The Road to Confederation: The Emergence of Canada, 1863–1867* (Toronto: Macmillan of Canada, 1964), Chapter Two, "The Astonishing Agreement."
7. Quoted in Janet Ajzenstat, Paul Romney, Ian Gentles, and William D. Gairdner, eds., *Canada's Founding Debates* (Toronto: University of Toronto Press, 2003), 203–04, 281.
8. *Ibid.*, 185.
9. *Ibid.*, 72.
10. *Ibid.*, 19.
11. Quoted in Donald Creighton, *The Road to Confederation*, 128.
12. Frances Monck, *My Canadian Leaves: An Account of a Visit to Canada in 1864–5* (London: 1891).
13. Richard Gwyn, *John A., The Man Who Made Us. The Life and Times of John A. Macdonald*, Volume I: 1815–1867 (Toronto: Vintage Canada, 2008), 396.
14. *Ibid.*, footnote.
15. Arthur Bousfield and Garry Toffoli, *Royal Observations: Canadians & Royalty* (Toronto: Dundurn, 1991), 128.
16. Quoted in Donald Creighton, *The Road to Confederation*, 421–22.
17. *Ibid.*, 422.
18. *Ibid.*, 423.
19. *Ibid.*, 424.
20. W.L. Morton, *The Kingdom of Canada: A General History From Earliest Times* (Toronto: McClelland and Stewart, 1963), 324. Richard Gwyn expresses similar sentiments (*John A., The Man Who Made Us*, 397).
21. "How the Dominion Ceased to Be," in *A Fair Country*, 250–59.
22. See David E. Smith, *Federalism and the Constitution of Canada* (Toronto: University of Toronto Press, 2010), 52, 66, 156–57.
23. *The Kingdom of Canada*, 494.

24. This is the view of Richard Gwyn, in the second volume of his biography, *Nation Maker: Sir John A. Macdonald: His Life, Our Times,* Volume Two: 1867–1891 (Toronto: Random House Canada, 2011), 323.

25. Noel Cox, *A Constitutional History of the New Zealand Monarchy,* 167.

26. P.B Waite, *In Search of R.B. Bennett* (Montreal & Kingston: McGill-Queen's University Press, 2012), 204, quoting Mackenzie King's diaries.

27. According to Eugene Forsey, however, Lord Bessborough persuaded Bennett and King to agree on John Buchan's appointment ("The Role of the Crown in Canada Since Confederation," *The Parliamentarian* 60, no. 1 (1979), 15).

28. *A Constitutional History of the New Zealand Monarchy,* 127–28.

29. *Ibid.,* 139–41.

30. *The Queen v. The Secretary of State for Foreign and Commonwealth Affairs* [1981] 4 C.N.L.R.

31. *A Constitutional History of the New Zealand Monarchy,* 61.

32. Jacques Monet, *La Monarchie au Canada,* 27–29.

33. Hereward Senior and Elinor Kyte Senior, *In Defence of Monarchy,* 17.

34. Arthur Bousfield and Garry Toffoli, *Royal Observations,* 165.

35. See Phillip Buckner and John G. Reid, eds., *Revisiting 1759: The Conquest of Canada in Historical Perspective* and *Remembering 1759: The Conquest of Canada in Historical Memory* (Toronto: University of Toronto Press, 2012). In the latter, a good summary and synthesis are found in Jocelyn Létourneau, "What Is to Be Done With 1759?"

36. See Donald Fyson, "The Conquered and the Conqueror: The Mutual Adaptation of the *Canadiens* and the British in Quebec, 1759–1775," in *Revisiting 1759.*

37. John Diefenbaker commented, "[i]t will ever be the pride of Canadians that the first success of the overseas adventure of British parliamentary government among Commonwealth nations took place in Canada. Many years in advance of its acceptance in the United Kingdom, religious freedom was given to Canada by the British Parliament in 1774." (*Those Things We Treasure,* 110–11.)

38. Arthur Bousfield and Garry Toffoli, *Royal Observations,* 165.

39. Hugh Segal, *The Right Balance,* 24.

40. Arthur Bousfield and Garry Toffoli, *Royal Observations*, 166.

41. Stanley Ayling, *George the Third* (London: Collins, 1972), 200, quoted in Robert M. Stamp, *Kings, Queens & Canadians* (Toronto: Fitzhenry & Whiteside, 1987), 57.

42. Arthur Bousfield and Garry Toffoli, *Home to Canada: Royal Tours 1786–2010* (Toronto: Dundurn, 2010), 33.

43. Nathan Tidridge, *Prince Edward, Duke of Kent: Father of the Canadian Crown* (Toronto: Dundurn, 2013).

44. Janet Ajzenstat, *The Canadian Founding: John Locke and Parliament* (Montreal & Kingston: McGill-Queen's University Press, 2007), 128, 140.

45. For the close relationship between the de Salaberry family and Prince Edward, see Nathan Tidridge, *Prince Edward, Duke of Kent*.

46. Alan Taylor, *The Civil War of 1812* (New York: Alfred A. Knopf, 2010), 152.

47. "La Couronne et le Canada francophone," presented at the conference "The Crown in Canada: A Diamond Jubilee Assessment," Regina, October 2012.

48. Janet Ajzenstat, "Constitutionalism," in Janet Ajzenstat and Peter J. Smith, eds., *Canada's Origins: Liberal, Tory, or Republican?* (Ottawa: Carleton University Press, 1995, 1997), 224.

49. Cited in Jacques Monet, *The Last Cannon Shot: A Study of French-Canadian Nationalism, 1837–1850* (Toronto: University of Toronto Press, 1969), 3.

50. Hector Langevin, *Les Mélanges*, May 4, 1849; cited in *ibid.*, 355.

51. Jacques Monet, "La Couronne du Canada," *Journal of Canadian Studies / Revue d'études canadiennes* 11, no. 4 (1976), 30.

52. Quoted in Frank MacKinnon, *The Crown in Canada*, 31.

53. *Ibid.*, 30.

54. *Le Devoir*, Montréal, 17 mai 1939, p. 12 (quoted by Serge Joyal in "La Couronne et le Canada francophone").

55. *Le Devoir*, Montréal, 10 octobre 1951, p. 3 (quoted in *ibid.*).

56. See Robert Speaight, *Vanier: Soldier, Diplomat and Governor General* (Toronto: Collins, 1970), Chapter 23, "A Critical Visit."

57. See Mary Francis Cody, *Georges and Pauline Vanier: Portrait of a Couple* (Montreal & Kingston: McGill-Queen's University Press, 2011), 238–41.

58. Margaret MacMillan, *The Uses and Abuses of History* (Toronto: Penguin Canada, 2008), 71.

59. Christian Dufour, *Le défi québécois: Essai* (Montréal : Éditions de l'Hexagone, 1989), 42–43.

60. We owe this observation to Dr. Jacques Monet, SJ.

61. David Arnot, "We Are All Treaty People," in Howard A. Leeson, ed., *Saskatchewan Politics: Crowding the Centre* (Regina: Canadian Plains Research Center, University of Regina, 2009), 226.

62. See in particular Alan Taylor, *The Civil War of 1812*.

63. *Ibid.*, Chapter Fifteen, "Peace."

64. David Arnot, "We Are All Treaty People," 236.

65. L. James Dempsey, *Warriors of the King: Prairie Indians in World War I* (Regina: Canadian Plains Research Center, University of Regina, 1999), 7.

66. *Ibid.*, 19.

67. J.R. (Jim) Miller, "Petitioning the Great White Mother: First Nations' Organizations and Lobbying in London," in Phillip Buckner, ed., *Canada and the End of Empire* (Vancouver, Toronto: UBC Press, 2005), 299.

68. *Ibid.*, 301–15.

69. Quoted in Regina *Leader-Post*, July 6, 1973.

70. David Arnot, "The Honour of the First Nations — the Honour of the Crown," in Jennifer Smith and D. Michael Jackson, eds., *The Evolving Canadian Crown*, 161.

71. There is a good explanation of the honour of the Crown and the Supreme Court's reasoning by John Ralston Saul in *A Fair Country* (66–80). Saul's view, however, is that the Crown is an abstraction, whose "underlying idea of the Crown has nothing to do with monarchy" (70); this does not square with the First Nations' perception, nor indeed with that of most others.

72. Quoted in David Arnot, "The Honour of the First Nations — the Honour of the Crown," 161–62.

73. *A Constitutional History of the New Zealand Monarchy*, 86.

74. John D. Whyte, "The Australian Republican Movement and Its Implications for Canada," in *Constitutional Forum constitutionnel* 4, no. 3 (1993), 91.

75. Greg Poelzer and Ken Coates, "Aboriginal Peoples and the Crown in Canada: Completing the Canadian Experiment," in Hans Michelmann and Cristine de Clercy, eds., *Continuity and Change in Canadian Politics: Essays in Honour of David E. Smith* (Toronto: University of Toronto Press, 2006), 164.

CHAPTER II
CROWN, PARLIAMENTARY DEMOCRACY, AND THE ROYAL PREROGATIVE

1. David E. Smith, *The People's House of Commons: Theories of Democracy in Contention* (Toronto: University of Toronto Press, 2007), 120.
2. Kevin S. MacLeod, *A Crown of Maples: Constitutional Monarchy in Canada* (Ottawa: Department of Canadian Heritage, 2012), 16–17.
3. *Roach v. Canada (Minister of State for Multiculturalism and Citizenship)* (C.A.) [1994] 2 F.C. 406; *Chainnigh v. Attorney General of Canada*, 2008 FC 69. We thank Philippe Lagassé and John Whyte for their comments on these rulings.
4. Vernon Bogdanor, *The Monarchy and the Constitution* (Oxford University Press, 1995), 66.
5. A.V. Dicey, *Law of the Constitution*, 10th ed. (London: Macmillan, 1956), 424.
6. Philippe Lagassé, "Parliamentary and Judicial Ambivalence Toward Executive Prerogative Powers in Canada," *Canadian Public Administration / Administration publique du Canada* 55, no. 2 (2012), 159.
7. *Canada (Prime Minister) v. Khadr*, 2010 SCC 3, [2010] 1 S.C.R. 44.
8. Philippe Lagassé, "Parliamentary and Judicial Ambivalence," 168.
9. *Ibid.*, 177.
10. *The Invisible Crown*, 179.
11. D. Michael Jackson, "Political Paradox: The Lieutenant Governor in Saskatchewan," in Howard A. Leeson, ed., *Saskatchewan Politics: Into the Twenty-First Century* (Regina: Canadian Plains Research Center, University of Regina, 2001), 51.

12. For a summary of these decisions, see Brian Slattery, "Why the Governor General Matters," in Peter Russell and Lorne Sossin, eds., *Parliamentary Democracy in Crisis* (Toronto: University of Toronto Press, 2009).

13. *Reference re Resolution to Amend the Constitution*, [1981] 1 SCR 753 at 884, 125 DLR (3d) 1.

14. Nicholas A. MacDonald and James W.J. Bowden, "The Manual of Official Procedure of the Government of Canada: An Exposé," *Constitutional Forum constitutionnel* 20, no. 1 (2011), 34.

15. "Why the Governor General Matters," 87–88.

16. Ajzenstat, Romney, Gentles, Gairdner, *Canada's Founding Debates*, 39.

17. Janet Ajzenstat, *The Once and Future Canadian Democracy. An Essay in Political Thought* (Montreal & Kingston: McGill-Queen's University Press, 2003), 64.

18. See Donald Creighton, *The Road to Confederation*, 54–62.

19. Allan Levine, *King. William Lyon Mackenzie King: A Life Guided by the Hand of Destiny* (Vancouver/Toronto: Douglas & McIntyre, 2011), 147.

20. *Ibid.*, 156.

21. See Eugene A. Forsey, *The Royal Power of Dissolution of Parliament in the British Commonwealth* (Toronto: Oxford University Press, 1943, 1968).

22. R. McGregor Dawson, "The Constitutional Question," *Dalhousie Review* VI, No. 3 (1926).

23. Thomas Crerar, quoted in Allan Levine, *William Lyon Mackenzie King*, 158.

24. Canada, Privy Council Office, Henry F. Davis and André Millar, *Manual of Official Procedure of the Government of Canada* (Ottawa: Government of Canada, 1968), 149–50.

25. Mary Frances Coady, *Georges and Pauline Vanier: Portrait of a Couple*, 230–32.

26. Robert Speaight, *Vanier: Soldier, Diplomat and Governor General*, 403–04.

27. Denis Smith, *Rogue Tory: The Life and Legend of John G. Diefenbaker* (Toronto: MacFarlane, Walter & Ross, 1995), 510.

28. Peter Neary, "The Morning After a General Election: The Vice-Regal Perspective," *Canadian Parliamentary Review* 35, no. 3 (2012), 26.

29. James Ross Hurley, "The Royal Prerogative and the Office of Lieutenant Governor: A Comment," *Canadian Parliamentary Review* 23, no. 2 (2000), 18–19.

30. Robert E. Hawkins, communication to the author, November 2012.

31. Patrick Monahan, "The Request She Can't Refuse," *Globe and Mail*, August 30, 2008.

32. *Conacher v. Canada (Prime Minister)* 2009 FC 920 [2010] 3 F.C.R 411.

33. Adrienne Clarkson, *Heart Matters: A Memoir* (Toronto: Viking Canada, 2006), 192.

34. *Globe and Mail*, August 30, 2008.

35. Andrew Heard, "The Governor General's Suspension of Parliament," in Peter Russell and Lorne Sossin, eds., *Parliamentary Democracy in Crisis*, 52–53.

36. Patrick Monahan, "The Constitutional Role of the Governor General," in Jennifer Smith and D. Michael Jackson, eds., *The Evolving Canadian Crown*, 80.

37. *Manual of Official Procedure of the Government of Canada*, 408–09.

38. *Globe and Mail*, December 2, 2008, A14. Robert E. Hawkins comments that "there is no doubt that a coalition government might have been proper. The issue is whether it would have been proper for the governor general to call upon such a possible coalition had the prime minister recommended dissolution" (communication to the author, November 2012).

39. Tom Flanagan, "Only Voters Have the Right to Decide on the Coalition," *Globe and Mail*, January 9, 2009.

40. For example, Andrew Heard, "The Governor General's Suspension of Parliament," and Graham White, "The Coalition That Wasn't: A Lost Reform Opportunity," in *Parliamentary Democracy in Crisis*. Andrew Heard reiterates his position in "The Reserve Powers of the Crown: The 2008 Prorogation in Hindsight," in Jennifer Smith and D. Michael Jackson, eds., *The Evolving Canadian Crown*, 87–97.

41. C.E.S. Franks, "To Prorogue or Not to Prorogue: Did the Governor General Make the Right Decision?" in *Parliamentary Democracy in Crisis*, 45.

42. *Manual of Official Procedure of the Government of Canada*, 150.

43. Barbara J. Messamore, *Canada's Governors General, 1847–1878: Biography and Constitutional Evolution* (Toronto: University of Toronto Press, 2006), 148.

44. There is a good description of this episode in Richard Gwyn's *Nation Maker*, Chapter Seventeen.

45. "Prorogation, Then and Now," *National Post*, December 8, 2008, A11.

46. C.E.S. Franks, "To Prorogue or Not to Prorogue," 46.

47. *Ibid.*, 45.

48. Patrick Monahan, "The Constitutional Role of the Governor General," 81.

49. *Ibid.*, 82–83.

50. "The Morning After a General Election," 27.

51. "The Royal Prerogative and the Office of Lieutenant Governor," *Canadian Parliamentary Review* 23, no. 1 (2000), 19.

52. *The Royal Power of Dissolution in the British Commonwealth*, 7.

53. Frank MacKinnon, *The Crown in Canada*, 122.

54. For a strong view in favour, see Sir David Smith, *Head of State: the Governor-General, the Monarchy, the Republic and the Dismissal* (Sydney: Macleay Press, 2005). For the opposing view, see George Winterton, *Parliament, the Executive and the Governor-General* (Melbourne University Press, 1983), and *Monarchy to Republic* (Melbourne: Oxford University Press, 1986).

55. Edward McWhinney, *The Governor General and the Prime Ministers: The Making and Unmaking of Governments* (Vancouver: Ronsdale Press, 2005), 70.

56. Norman Ward, *Dawson's Government of Canada* (Toronto: University of Toronto Press, 1987), 191.

57. Dennis Baker, *Not Quite Supreme: The Courts and Coordinate Constitutional Interpretation* (Montreal & Kingston: McGill-Queen's University Press, 2010), 72–73.

58. In the video "On Behalf of Her Majesty: The Story of British Columbia's Government House and the Lieutenant Governor" (Victoria: British Columbia Government House Foundation, 1991).

59. Eugene Forsey, *The Royal Power of Dissolution in the British Commonwealth*, 259.

60. For the history of Canadian honours see Christopher McCreery, *The Order of Canada: Its Origins, History and Development* (Toronto: University of Toronto Press, 2005), and *The Canadian Honours System* (Toronto: Dundurn, 2005). See also John Blatherwick, *Canadian Orders, Decorations and Medals*, Fifth Edition (Toronto: The Unitrade Press, 2003); and his *Canadian Knighthoods* (self-published, 1996), which lists all Canadian recipients of imperial honours from the grade of Companion/Commander and above.

61. Quoted in Robert Hardman, *Her Majesty: Queen Elizabeth II and Her Court* (New York: Pegasus Books, 2012), 220.

62. Christopher McCreery, *The Order of Canada*, 7.

63. For the Royal Victorian Order in Canada, see Christopher McCreery, *On Her Majesty's Service: Royal Honours and Recognition in Canada* (Toronto: Dundurn, 2008).

64. For a detailed explanation of this convoluted story, see Christopher McCreery, *The Order of Canada*, 24–48, and, for a summary, *The Canadian Honours System*, 35–38.

65. Christopher McCreery gives a description and appraisal of the Bennett honours revival in *The Order of Canada*, 51–56.

66. P.B. Waite, *In Search of R.B. Bennett* (Montreal & Kingston: McGill-Queen's University Press, 2012), 182.

67. Quoted in *ibid.*, 221–22.

68. *The Order of Canada*, 56.

69. P.B. Waite, *In Search of R.B. Bennett*, 207.

70. *Ibid.*, 272.

71. See Christopher McCreery, "The Crown and Honours: Getting It Right," in Jennifer Smith and D. Michael Jackson, eds., *The Evolving Canadian Crown*, 140–42.

72. See Christopher McCreery, *The Canadian Forces' Decoration / La Décoration des Forces canadiennes* (Ottawa: Department of National Defence, 2010).

73. See Christopher McCreery, *The Canadian Honours System*, Chapter 3, for a succinct explanation of these developments.

74. See Christopher McCreery, *The Order of Canada*, 80–102.

75. *Ibid.*, Chapter Five.

76. Personal conversation with Sir Conrad Swan.

77. See Christopher McCreery, *The Order of Military Merit / l'Ordre du mérite militaire* (Ottawa: Department of National Defence, 2012).

78. Christopher McCreery, *On Her Majesty's Service*, 40–42.

79. See Stanley Martin, *The Order of Merit: One Hundred Years of Matchless Honour* (London: I.B. Tauris, 2000), 147–49 for Penfield and 394–97 for Pearson.

CHAPTER III
THE PROVINCIAL CROWN IN CANADA —
FROM SUBORDINATE TO COORDINATE

1. Jacques Monet, "Reflections on the 'Canadianization' of the Crown," in Jennifer Smith and D. Michael Jackson, eds., *The Evolving Canadian Crown*, 206–07.

2. David E. Smith, *Federalism and the Constitution of Canada*, 62.

3. The *Constitution Act, 1867*, Section 90.

4. *Ibid.*

5. Letter of September 26, 1864, to Edward Cardwell, Colonial Secretary, commenting on the Charlottetown Conference, quoted in G. P. Browne, ed., *Documents on the Confederation of British North America* (Toronto: McClelland and Stewart, Carleton Library Series no. 40, McGill-Queen's University Press, Carleton Library Series 215, 2009), 48.

6. Donald Creighton, *The Road to Confederation*, 1–9.

7. Christopher Moore, *1867: How the Fathers Made a Deal* (Toronto: McClelland & Stewart, 1997), 36–37.

8. G. P. Browne, ed., *Documents on the Confederation of British North America*, 115.

9. *Ibid.*, 76.

10. *Ibid.*, 117.

11. *Ibid.*, 173.

12. *Ibid.*, 170.

13. *Ibid.*, 188.

14. *Ibidem.*

15. *Ibid.*, 223.

16. *Ibid.*, 237.

17. *Ibid.*, 239.

18. *Ibid.*, 240.

19. *Ibid.*, 256.

20. *Ibid.*, 275.

21. *Ibid.*, 289.

22. *Ibid.*, 315.

23. Christopher McCreery, presentation on "The Provincial Crown: How Effective Is It?" at the conference "The Crown in Canada: A Diamond Jubilee Assessment," Regina, October 2012.

24. Goldwin Smith, *Canada and the Canadian Question* (first published in 1891 by Hunter Rose Co. of Toronto; edited by Carl Berger, University of Toronto Press, 1971), 118.

25. *Ibid.*, 125.

26. J.R. Mallory, in David Butler and D.A. Low, eds., *Sovereigns and Surrogates* (London: Macmillan, 1991), 43.

27. Lemieux, Blais, Hamelin, *L'histoire du Québec à travers ses lieutenants-gouverneurs*, 43. See also Jacques Monet, *The Canadian Crown*, 42.

28. "Empire, Crown and Canadian Federalism," *Canadian Journal of Political Science* 24, no. 3 (1991), 471.

29. *Federalism and the Constitution of Canada*, 55.

30. *The People's House of Commons*, 27.

31. *A Constitutional History of the New Zealand Monarchy*, 138.

32. John T. Saywell, *The Lawmakers: Judicial Power and the Shaping of Canadian Federalism* (Toronto: University of Toronto Press, 2002), 114.

33. Paul Romney, *Getting It Wrong: How Canadians Forgot Their Past and Imperilled Confederation* (Toronto: University of Toronto Press, 1999), 154.

34. Saywell, *The Lawmakers*, 95.

35. *Ibid.*, 98.

36. *Ibid.*, 99.

37. Paul Romney, *Getting It Wrong*, 111.

38. *The Lawmakers*, 50.

39. This issue is thoroughly explored in Robert C. Vipond, *Liberty and Community: Canadian Federalism and the Failure of the Constitution* (Albany, NY: State University of New York Press, 1991), especially in Chapter 4, "Provincial Autonomy and Imperialism."

40. W.L. Morton, *The Kingdom of Canada*, 374.

41. Robert Vipond, *Liberty and Community*, 66.

42. *Ibid.*, 68.

43. Cited in Saywell, *The Lawmakers*, 52.

44. *A.G. Quebec v. A.G. Canada.*

45. *A.G. Ontario v. O'Reilly.*

46. Saywell, *The Lawmakers*, 341, note 94.

47. *Ibid.*, 54–55.

48. *Ibid.*, 125.

49. *Ibid.*, 127–28.

50. Paul Romney, *Getting It Wrong*, 148.

51. *A.G. of Canada v. A.G. of Ontario*, 1898

52. Saywell, *The Lawmakers*, 173.

53. *Ibid.*, 174.

54. *Ibid.*, 175. Saywell points out that Lord Watson, in the *Liquidators* decision cited by Haldane, did not say that the lieutenant governor "directly" represented the Sovereign (388, note 139).

55. *Ibid.*, 176.

56. *Ibid.*, 177.

57. Robert E. Hawkins notes that "the term 'civil rights' in section 92(13) of the *BNA Act* does not have exactly the same meaning that we ascribe to it today. It really means property rights, contract and tort, in other words the rights of the individual protected by common law — not so much the rights of citizens against interference by the state — the Charter idea." Communication to the author, November 2012.

58. *Liberty and Community*, 3. See also his Conclusion, especially 194–96.

59. David E. Smith comments that as "a result of *Snider*, labour became for most purposes a provincial matter" (*Federalism and the Constitution of Canada*, 96).

60. Saywell, *The Lawmakers*, 161.

61. *Ibid.*, 192.

62. *Ibid.*, 199–201.

63. P.B. Waite, *In Search of R.B. Bennett*, 56–57.

64. Quoted in Saywell, *The Lawmakers*, 211.

65. Gerald Baier, *Courts and Federalism: Judicial Doctrine in the United States, Australia, and Canada* (Vancouver: UBC Press, 2006), 55.

66. Cited in Saywell, *The Lawmakers*, 229.

67. For example, John Ralston Saul takes a dim view of the JCPC's rulings, which, in his opinion, "made form, not content, the driving force of Canadian politics" and did much damage to the public good (*A Fair Country*, 162). Gordon DiGiacomo has a similar view of the JCPC's work in "Ottawa's Deferential Approach to Intergovernmental Relations," in Gordon DiGiacomo and Maryantonett Flumian, eds., *The Case for Centralized Federalism* (Ottawa: University of Ottawa Press, 2010).

68. Cited by Janet Ajzenstat in "Bicameralism and Canada's Founders: The Origins of the Canadian Senate," in Serge Joyal, ed., *Protecting Canadian Democracy: The Senate You Never Knew*, 17.

69. Donald Creighton, *Canada's First Century* (Toronto: Macmillan, 1970), 46.

70. Christopher Moore, *1867: How the Fathers Made a Deal*, 116.

71. Janet Ajzenstat, *The Once and Future Canadian Democracy*, 171. See also G.P Browne, *Documents on the Confederation of British North America*, Introduction, xix–xv.

72. Peter H. Russell, *Constitutional Odyssey: Can Canadians Become a Sovereign People?*, Third Edition (Toronto: University of Toronto Press, 2004), 45.

73. Thomas J. Courchene, "Federalism, Decentralization and Canadian Nation Building," in Ruth Hubbard and Gilles Paquet, eds., *The Case for Decentralized Federalism* (Ottawa: University of Ottawa Press, 2010), 21–22.

74. *Ibid.*, 23.

75. *Federalism and the Constitution of Canada*, 74.

76. We owe this paragraph to Christopher McCreery, presentation on "The Provincial Crown: How Effective Is It?" at the conference "The Crown in Canada: A Diamond Jubilee Assessment," Regina, October 2012.

77. Gerald Baier, *Courts and Federalism*, 50.

78. Edwin R. Black, *Divided Loyalties: Canadian Concepts of Federalism* (Montreal & London: McGill-Queen's University Press, 1975), 48.

79. Quoted in John English, *Citizen of the World: The Life of Pierre Elliott Trudeau*, Volume One: 1919–1968 (Toronto: Alfred A. Knopf

Canada, 2006), 226. "By the mid-1950s Trudeau had become a close student of Canadian federalism and a defender of provincial rights" (286). Trudeau would move in a centralist direction from the 1960s.

80. Michael M. Atkinson, Daniel Béland, Gregory P. Marchildon, Kathleen McNutt, Peter W.B. Phillips, and Ken Rasmussen, *Governance and Public Policy in Canada: A View from the Provinces* (Toronto: University of Toronto Press, 2013), xviii, 23.

81. John Ralston Saul, *Reflections of a Siamese Twin: Canada at the End of the Twentieth Century* (Toronto: Penguin Books Canada, 1997), 420.

82. *Ibid.*, 419, 422.

83. See Saywell, *The Lawmakers*, 231–32.

84. *Courts and Federalism*, 127–28.

85. *Globe and Mail*, December 23, 2011, A8.

86. "Beware of Ottawa Bearing Gifts," *Globe and Mail*, January 17, 2012, A13.

87. Neil Reynolds, "Lord Atkin Knew Who was Boss," *Globe and Mail*, June 4, 2012, A11.

88. For opposing points of view on Canadian federalism, see Ruth Hubbard and Gilles Paquet, eds., *The Case for Decentralized Federalism*, and Gordon DiGiacomo and Maryantonett Flumian, eds., *The Case for Centralized Federalism* (Ottawa: University of Ottawa Press, 2010).

89. "Saskatchewan and Canadian Federalism," 298–99.

90. February 8, 1952 (Saskatchewan Archives, R192.3, Proclamation 607).

91. Quoted in Anne Twomey, *The Chameleon Crown: The Queen and Her Australian Governors* (Sydney: The Federation Press, 2006), 266.

92. Leslie Zines, quoted in John Williams, "'The Blizzard and Oz': Canadian Influences on the Australian Constitution Then and Now," in Linda Cardinal and David Heaton, eds., *Shaping Nations: Constitutionalism and Society in Australia and Canada* (University of Ottawa Press, 2002), 9.

93. Quoted in *ibid.*, 8.

94. Peter Boyce, *The Queen's Other Realms*, 145.

95. See Anne Twomey, *The Chameleon Crown*, especially Chapter 19, "Direct Access to the Queen."

96. Peter Boyce, *The Queen's Other Realms*, 146.
97. Gerald Baier, in *Courts and Federalism*, provides an account of the Australian court cases.

IV
LIEUTENANT GOVERNORS —
PRESTIGE, OBSCURITY, AND REVIVAL

1. John T. Saywell, *The Office of Lieutenant Governor* (Toronto: University of Toronto Press, 1957; Revised Edition, Toronto: Copp Clark Pitman, 1986), 221–23.
2. Saywell gives a detailed discussion of the power of reservation, in *ibid.*, Chapter Eight, "Provincial Legislation."
3. Edwin R. Black, *Divided Loyalties*, 36.
4. Alfred Thomas Neitsch, "A Tradition of Vigilance: The Role of the Lieutenant Governor in Alberta," *Canadian Parliamentary Review* 30, no. 4 (2007), 20.
5. *Ibid.*, 22.
6. Interview with Allan Blakeney, 1999.
7. See Evelyn Eager, *Saskatchewan Government: Politics and Pragmatism* (Saskatoon: Western Producer Prairie Books, 1980), 127–29, and John Saywell, *The Office of Lieutenant-Governor*, 267.
8. Interview.
9. Personal source.
10. See Lemieux, Blais, Hamelin, *L'histoire du Québec à travers ses lieutenants-gouverneurs*, 83, for a vivid description of this "*coup d'État.*" For details, see Saywell, *The Office of Lieutenant Governor*, 113–19.
11. *Ibid.*, 147–49.
12. Saywell, *The Office of Lieutenant Governor*, 119–30.
13. *Ibid.*, 131–40.
14. *Ibid.*, 140–43.
15. *Ibid.*, 271–73.
16. *Ibid.*, 149–50.
17. *Ibid.*, 150.
18. *Ibid.*, 156–58.

19. *Ibid.*, 273–74.
20. For the controversy over the Scott appointment, see John Saywell, *The Office of Lieutenant-Governor*, 104–07; Evelyn Eager, *Saskatchewan Government: Politics and Pragmatism*, 125–26; and Gordon L. Barnhart, *"Peace, Progress and Prosperity": A Biography of Saskatchewan's First Premier, T. Walter Scott* (Regina: Canadian Plains Research Center, University of Regina, 2000), 44–45.
21. Kenneth Munro, *The Maple Crown in Alberta: The Office of Lieutenant-Governor, 1905–2005* (Victoria: Trafford Publishing, 2005), 94–96.
22. Alfred Thomas Neitsch, "A Tradition of Vigilance," 23.
23. Edward McWhinney, *The Governor General and the Prime Ministers*, 63.
24. Peter Boyce, "Reserve Powers," *The Queen's Other Realms*, 160–64.
25. *The Office of Lieutenant-Governor*, 257.
26. *Ibid.*, 21.
27. Edwin R. Black, *Divided Loyalties*, 35.
28. Lemieux, Blais, Hamelin, *L'histoire du Québec à travers ses lieutenants-gouverneurs*, 84.
29. See Saywell, *The Office of Lieutenant-Governor*, 234–48, for a detailed account.
30. *Ibid.*, 254.
31. See *ibid.*, 228–32.
32. Philippe Doré, clerk of the executive council at the time, gave an account of this incident (typescript, Saskatchewan Legislative Assembly, 1978). Premier Allan Blakeney suggested that the *Constitution Act, 1867,* be amended to allow the administrator to function for ninety days following the death of a lieutenant governor, but no such action was ever taken by the federal government.
33. *The Office of Lieutenant-Governor*, 260–61.
34. Kenneth Munro, *The Maple Crown in Alberta*, 61–63.
35. *Ibid.*, 100, 159–60.
36. Margaret Hryniuk and Garth Pugh, *"A Tower of Attraction": An Illustrated History of Government House, Regina, Saskatchewan* (Regina: Government House Historical Society / Canadian Plains Research Center, 1991), 106.

37. Stephen LaRose, "Dr. Lynda Haverstock Touring Saskatchewan," *Pink Magazine Saskatchewan*, no. 5, April 2012, 16.

38. Peter Boyce, *The Queen's Other Realms*, 97.

39. Christopher McCreery, "The Provincial Crown: How Effective Is It?"

40. Interview with Allan Blakeney, 1999.

41. *Ibid.*

42. Confidential information.

43. Stephen LaRose, "Dr. Lynda Haverstock Touring Saskatchewan," 15–16.

44. In addition to his biography of Walter Scott, Gordon Barnhart authored *Building for the Future: A Photo Journal of Saskatchewan's Legislative Building* (2002) and edited *Saskatchewan's Premiers of the Twentieth Century* (2004), both published by Canadian Plains Research Center, University of Regina.

45. The story of Government House is well told in Margaret Hryniuk and Garth Pugh, "*A Tower of Attraction.*" See also Robert H. Hubbard, *Ample Mansions: The Viceregal Residences of the Canadian Provinces* (Ottawa: University of Ottawa Press, 1989), 172–89.

46. See Margaret Hryniuk and Garth Pugh, "*A Tower of Attraction,*" 68–71.

47. From the Regina *Leader-Post*, quoted in "*A Tower of Attraction,*" 106.

48. *Ibid.*, 106–07.

49. Interview, 1999.

50. Personal sources.

V

THE CONTEMPORARY PROVINCIAL CROWN

1. Lemieux, Blais, Hamelin, *L'histoire du Québec à travers ses lieutenants-gouverneurs*, 34.

2. Ken Tyler, quoted in D. Michael Jackson, "Political Paradox: The Lieutenant Governor in Saskatchewan," 49.

3. Lemieux, Blais, Hamelin, *L'histoire du Québec à travers ses lieutenants-gouverneurs*, 33.

4. David E. Smith commented that this rationale was in error. "If there was arrogance in the Liberal stand, it was in this rejection of the crown's prerogative power to find advisers." *Prairie Liberalism:*

The Liberal Party in Saskatchewan, 1905–71 (Toronto: University of Toronto Press, 1975), 197.

5. Patrick Kyba, "J.T.M. Anderson," in Gordon L. Barnhart, ed., *Saskatchewan Premiers of the Twentieth Century* (Regina: Canadian Plains Research Center, University of Regina, 2004), 121.

6. For descriptions of this episode, see Edward McWhinney, *The Governor General and the Prime Ministers*, 108–10, and Peter Neary, "The Morning After a General Election," 27–28.

7. This section relies mainly on confidential sources.

8. Dr. Lam revealed this in an interview with the *South China News*, an Asian newspaper, as an illustration of the role of the lieutenant governor, not expecting it to go any further. However, the story was picked up by the Vancouver *Sun*, which widely publicized it. See Ronald L. Cheffins, "The Royal Prerogative and the Office of Lieutenant Governor," 15.

9. Edward McWhinney, Vancouver *Sun*, May 3, 1991, quoted in Peter Boyce, *The Queen's Other Realms*, 107.

10. Edward McWhinney, *The Governor General and the Prime Ministers*, 70.

11. Merrilee D. Rasmussen, "The Decline of Parliamentary Democracy in Saskatchewan" (unpublished M.A. thesis, University of Regina, 1994), 86.

12. *Ibid.*, 65–66. The words in quotation marks are from Frank MacKinnon.

13. *Ibid.*, 91–92.

14. Interviews with Sylvia Fedoruk.

15. Merrilee Rasmussen was also critical of the New Democratic government of Roy Romanow for using special warrants inappropriately in 1992, "fundamentally the same as their use by the Conservative government in 1987" ("The Decline of Parliamentary Government in Saskatchewan," 132–33).

16. Saywell, *The Office of Lieutenant-Governor*, 276–77.

17. Peter Milliken, "Appropriation Acts and Governor General's Special Warrants," *Canadian Parliamentary Review* 13, no. 2 (1990).

18. Alfred Thomas Neitsch, "A Tradition of Vigilance," 23–24.

19. *Ibid.*, 25.

20. *Ibid.*

21. Kenneth Munro, *The Maple Crown in Alberta*, 107.

22. *Ibid.*, 108–09.
23. "A Tradition of Vigilance," 27.
24. Robert E. Hawkins, communication to the author, November 2012.
25. *No Ordinary Time*, 46.
26. *Ibid.*, 46–49.
27. Robert E. Hawkins, communication to the author, November 2012.
28. For the views of prime ministers Tony Blair and Gordon Brown, see Robert Hardman, *A Year with the Queen* (New York: Simon & Schuster, 2007), 168–70. For the views of James Callaghan, John Major, and David Cameron, see, by the same author, *Her Majesty: Queen Elizabeth II and Her Court*, 153–55.
29. *Ibid.*, 220.
30. Source: correspondence from the official secretaries to the governors, 2009–10.
31. Information was not available from New Brunswick and Newfoundland and Labrador.
32. Kenneth Munro, *The Maple Crown in Alberta*, 104.
33. Interview with Grant Devine, 2008.
34. Interview with Roy Romanow, 2008.
35. Interview with Lorne Calvert, 2008.
36. Interview with Brad Wall, 2008.
37. *The Crown in Canada*, 47, 136.
38. *The Invisible Crown*, x–xi, 181.
39. *Constitutional Law in Canada*, Second Edition (Toronto: Carswell, 1985), 91.
40. Christopher McCreery, "The Provincial Crown: How Effective Is It?"
41. *Ibid.*
42. See Paul Benoit, "State Ceremonial: The Constitutional Monarch's Liturgical Authority," in Jennifer Smith and D. Michael Jackson, eds., *The Evolving Canadian Crown*.
43. For an illustrated account of the visit of the Prince of Wales, see *Saskatchewan, Royal Reflections: The Prince of Wales in Saskatchewan* (Regina: Government of Saskatchewan, 2001).
44. Conversation with the author.
45. Christopher McCreery, *The Order of Canada*, 117, 123.
46. *The Canadian Honours System*, 124.

47. Saskatchewan and Ontario also convened the first conference on Commonwealth Honours and Awards in Regina, in 2006. See Michael Jackson, ed., *Honouring Commonwealth Citizen: Proceedings of the First Conference on Commonwealth Honours and Awards* (Toronto: Ontario Ministry of Citizenship and Immigration, 2007).

48. D. Michael Jackson, "Political Paradox," 67–68; and ed., *Honouring Commonwealth Citizens*, in particular Michael Jackson, "Honours in the Federal State," and Lynda Haverstock, "Bestowing Honours — the Other Side."

49. D. Michael Jackson, "The Development of Saskatchewan Honours" (unpublished research paper for the Senior Management Development Program of the Saskatchewan Public Service Commission, 1990), 13–14.

50. *Ibid.*, 15–16.

51. Christopher McCreery, *The Canadian Honours System*, 124.

52. For the history of Australian honours and an explanation of the honours system in Australia, see Stanley Martin, "Perspectives on the Honours of Australia," and Malcolm Hazell, "The Australian Honours System: An Overview," in Michael Jackson, ed., *Honouring Commonwealth Citizens.*

53. *From Palace to Prairie: the Crown and Responsible Government in Saskatchewan* (Regina: Saskatchewan Intergovernmental Affairs and Saskatchewan Communications Network, 1997).

54. See Lynda Haverstock, "Bestowing Honours — the Other Side," in Michael Jackson, ed., *Honouring Commonwealth Citizens.*

55. Announcement from Office of the Prime Minister, November 4, 2012.

56. Lemieux, Blais, Hamelin, *L'histoire du Québec à travers ses lieutenants-gouverneurs*, 44.

57. *No Ordinary Time*, 108.

58. *The Queen's Other Realms*, 113.

59. "Canada," in David Butler and D.A. Low, eds., *Sovereigns and Surrogates*, 45.

60. *Canadian Monarchist News / Les Nouvelles monarchiques du Canada*, Special Issue, March 2013, no. 34, "The Cost of Canada's Constitutional Monarchy / Le coût de la monarchie constitutionnelle au Canada."

61. Serge Joyal, "The Crown and Prime Ministerial Government," in Jennifer Smith and D. Michael Jackson, eds., *The Evolving Canadian Crown*, 223.
62. *Heart Matters*, 193.
63. Lemieux, Blais, Hamelin, *L'histoire du Québec à travers ses lieutenants-gouverneurs*, 295. The opposition Liberals did not support the motion.
64. *Ibid.*, 338–39.
65. Rhéal Seguin, "Quebeckers Feel Short-Changed by Lieutenant-Governor's Coin," *Globe and Mail*, February 5, 2010.
66. *No Ordinary Time*, 51.
67. Letter to the author from Anne Parker, Official Secretary to the Governor of Tasmania, December 9, 2009.

VI
CANADA: FEDERAL MONARCHY — OR FEDERAL REPUBLIC?

1. Eugene Forsey, *Freedom and Order*, 23.
2. See David E. Smith, *The Republican Option in Canada, Past and Present*. Citizens for a Canadian Republic only began in 2002 (*www.canadian-republic.ca*), whereas the Monarchist League of Canada had been founded as early as 1970 (*www.monarchist.ca*).
3. In his preface to Eugene Forsey's *Freedom and Order*, 8.
4. C.P. Champion calls this "a bloodless *coup d'état* by neo-nationalists, overthrowing a symbolic order grounded in centuries of history," *The Strange Demise of British Canada* (Montreal & Kingston: McGill-Queen's University Press, 2010), 165.
5. See *ibid.* and Gregory A. Johnson, "The Last Gasp of Empire: The 1964 Flag Debate Revisited," in Phillip Buckner, ed., *Canada and the End of Empire* (Vancouver: University of British Columbia Press, 2005).
6. C.P. Champion, *The Strange Demise of British Canada*, 226, 231.
7. Jonathan F. Vance, *Maple Leaf Empire: Canada, Britain, and Two World Wars* (Toronto: Oxford University Press, 2012), 3–4.
8. Jonathan F. Vance, *A History of Canadian Culture* (Toronto: Oxford University Press, 2009), 153.

9. See Robert M. Stamp, *Royal Rebels: Princess Louise & the Marquis of Lorne* (Toronto: Dundurn, 1988).

10. See Kevin Shea and John Jason Wilson, *Lord Stanley: The Man Behind the Cup* (Bolton ON: Fenn Publishing Company, 2006).

11. Sandra Gwyn, *The Private Capital: Ambition and Love in the Age of Macdonald and Laurier* (Toronto: McClelland and Stewart, 1984), 278.

12. *Ibid.*, 298–99.

13. Jonathan F. Vance, *A History of Canadian Culture*, 373.

14. See J. William Galbraith, *John Buchan: Model Governor General* (Toronto: Dundurn, 2013).

15. Arthur Bousfield and Garry Toffoli, *Royal Observations*, 190.

16. Duff Hart-Davis, ed., *King's Counsellor: Abdication and War. The Diaries of Sir Alan Lascelles* (London: Phoenix, 2007), 333–34.

17. Michael Bliss, *Right Honourable Men* (Toronto: HarperCollins Publishers, 1994, 2004), 237.

18. Peter Boyce, *The Queen's Other Realms*, 71.

19. Claude Bissell, *The Imperial Canadian: Vincent Massey in Office* (Toronto: University of Toronto Press, 1986).

20. Peter Stursburg, *Roland Michener, The Last Viceroy* (Toronto: McGraw-Hill Ryerson, 1989).

21. See Corinna A.W. Pike and Christopher McCreery, *Canadian Symbols of Authority* (Toronto: Dundurn, 2011), 260–67.

22. Personal source.

23. See Christopher McCreery, *The Canadian Honours System*, 152–55.

24. See Christopher McCreery, "The Crown and Honours: Getting it Right," in Jennifer Smith and D. Michael Jackson, eds., *The Evolving Canadian Crown*, 145, where McCreery refers to "regular attempts to marginalize" the Queen's role in the honours system.

25. Personal source.

26. *A Crown of Maples* was originally proposed in 1993 as a national complement to *The Canadian Monarchy in Saskatchewan*, published in 1989 and 1990. Canadian Heritage and Rideau Hall tenaciously resisted its publication until finally succumbing to ministerial pressure in 2008 (personal sources).

27. See Eugene Forsey, "The Role of the Crown in Canada since Confederation," 16.

28. David Smith, *The Invisible Crown*, 46, 59.

29. Jacques Monet, "Reflections on the 'Canadianization' of the Crown," in Jennifer Smith and D. Michael Jackson, eds., *The Evolving Canadian Crown*, 212.

30. For positive comments on this practice by Prime Ministers Pearson and Trudeau, see Frank MacKinnon, *The Crown in Canada*, 103, and Jacques Monet, *The Canadian Crown*, 67–70.

31. Quoted in J.R. Mallory, "Canada," in Butler and Low, eds., *Sovereigns and Surrogates*, 51–52.

32. Peter Boyce, *The Queen's Other Realms*, 74. See Jacques Monet, "Reflections on the 'Canadianization' of the Crown," 208, for an anecdote about how Schreyer's name was drawn to Trudeau's attention.

33. *The Queen's Other Realms*, 196.

34. "Republican Tendencies," in *Policy Options politiques*, May 1999, 11.

35. *Heart Matters*, 200–01.

36. *Ibid.*, 195–97, 201.

37. Personal source.

38. See Margaret MacMillan, Marjorie Harris, and Anne L. Desjardins, *Canada's House: Rideau Hall and the Invention of a Canadian Home* (Toronto: Alfred A. Knopf Canada, 2004).

39. See Gerda Hnatyshyn and Paulette Lachapelle-Bélisle, *Rideau Hall: Canada's Living Heritage* (Ottawa: Friends of Rideau Hall, 1994).

40. "The Right to Warn, but Not to Leak," *Globe and Mail*, September 27, 2008.

41. Christopher McCreery, "The Crown and Honours: Getting It Right," in Jennifer Smith and D. Michael Jackson, eds., *The Evolving Canadian Crown*, 147.

42. Hans J. Michelmann, "Introduction," in Hans J. Michelmann and Cristine de Clercy, eds., *Continuity and Change in Canadian Politics*, 6.

43. "Imagining Constitutional Crises," 186–87.

44. Robert Hardman, *Her Majesty: Queen Elizabeth II and Her Court*, 30–31.

45. *A Constitutional History of the New Zealand Monarchy*, 14–15.

46. Janet Ajzenstat, *The Canadian Founding: John Locke and Parliament* (Montreal & Kingston: McGill-Queen's University Press, 2007), xiii, 26–27. Ajzenstat disagrees on this point with Peter Russell, who, in

Constitutional Odyssey, asserts that the Fathers of Confederation did not consider or accept popular sovereignty. Christopher Moore is of the same view as Ajzenstat, in *1867: How the Fathers Made a Deal*, 28–29.

47. *Ibid.*, 27.

48. Walter Bagehot, *The English Constitution* (London: 1867; Fontana edition, 1963), 94.

49. Ralph Heintzman, "The Meaning of Monarchy," *Journal of Canadian Studies / Revue d'études canadiennes*, 12, no. 2 (1977).

50. *Sovereigns and Surrogates*, 9, note 1.

51. *Head of State*, 86.

52. Correspondence with the author.

53. *The Queen's Other Realms*, 29.

54. See also on this subject Sean Palmer, "The Ramifications of Sharing a Head of State: A Study in the Implications of a Structure," unpublished PhD thesis, Auckland University of Technology, 2010.

55. Graham Barnes, *National Post*, October 9, 2009, A11.

56. The official website of the British Monarchy, *www.royal.gov.uk*.

57. *Her Majesty: Queen Elizabeth II and Her Court*, 15–18.

58. Glenn A Palmer and John D Whyte, "Imagining Constitutional Crises," 189, 190.

59. The supposed convention of the *removal* of the governor general on advice of the prime minister has, however, been challenged by D.P. O'Connell: if this were the case, he says, "the constitution is destabilized at its heart. Any Governor-General is liable to intimidation by a Prime Minister, and the two offices of Head of State and Head of Government are apt, in practical terms, to coalesce" ("Canada, Australia, Constitutional Reform and the Crown," *The Parliamentarian* 60, no. 1 (1979), 9).

60. Glenn A Palmer and John D Whyte, "Imagining Constitutional Crises."

61. *The Republican Option in Canada*, 219.

62. *The People's House of Commons*, 28.

63. See Noel Cox, *A Constitutional History of the New Zealand Monarchy*, 238–39.

64. Noel Cox, "'The Crown Down Under': Issues and Trends in Australia and New Zealand," in Jennifer Smith and D. Michael Jackson, eds., *The Evolving Canadian Crown*, 199.

65. *Evatt and Forsey on the Reserve Powers* (Sydney: Legal Books, 1990), xc.

66. *The Queen's Other Realms*, 232.

67. Peter Russell, "Educating Canadian on the Crown — A Diamond Jubilee Challenge," presented at the conference "The Crown in Canada: A Diamond Jubilee Assessment," Regina, October 2012.

68. Robert E. Hawkins, "Written Reasons and Codified Conventions in Matters of Prorogation and Dissolution," in Jennifer Smith and D. Michael Jackson, eds., *The Evolving Canadian Crown*, 113.

69. Peter Neary, "The Morning After a General Election," 28.

70. *The reasons of the Governor of Tasmania, the Honourable Peter Underwood AC, for the commissioning of the Honourable David Bartlett to form a government following the 2010 House of Assembly election* (Government House, Hobart, Tasmania, April 9, 2010), 4.

71. For the Tasmanian episode, see Peter Boyce, "The Australian Monarchy in the Twenty-First Century," in Jennifer Smith and D. Michael Jackson, eds., *The Evolving Canadian Crown*, 184. Dr. Boyce elaborated on the episode in a personal communication to the author in December 2011.

72. Peter Neary, "The Morning After a General Election," 24.

73. Robert Hardman, *Her Majesty: Queen Elizabeth II and Her Court*, 164–66.

74. Patrick Monahan, "The Constitutional Role of the Governor General," in *The Evolving Canadian Crown*, 84.

75. Nicholas A. MacDonald and James W.J. Bowden, "Manual of Official Procedure of the Government of Canada: An Exposé," 38.

76. Robert E. Hawkins, communication to the author, November 2012.

77. David Flint, *On Line Opinion*, January 7, 2012.

78. John Fraser, *The Secret of the Crown: Canada's Affair with Royalty* (Toronto: House of Anansi Press, 2012), 69–71.

79. See D.P. O'Connell, "Canada, Australia, Constitutional Reform and the Crown," 8; and Eugene Forsey, "The Role of the Crown in Canada since Confederation," 17–19. For the "Canadianization" of the Crown, see David E. Smith, *The Invisible Crown*, Chapter 3, "Canadianizing the Crown," and Peter Boyce, "Canadianising the Royal Prerogative," in *The Queen's Other Realms*, 70–71.

80. "The Role of the Crown in Canada since Confederation," 18.
81. *The Invisible Crown*, 55.
82. *A Constitutional History of the New Zealand Monarchy*, 193–94.
83. *A Life on the Fringe*, 157–58.
84. Peter Boyce, *The Queen's Other Realms*, 71.
85. Christopher McCreery, "Myth and Misunderstanding: The Origins and Meaning of the Letters Patent Constituting the Office of the Governor General, 1947," in Jennifer Smith and D. Michael Jackson, eds., *The Evolving Canadian Crown*, 46–50.
86. D. Michael Jackson, "Political Paradox," 70.
87. Personal experience of the author.
88. "Myth and Misunderstanding," 51.
89. Personal experience of the author.
90. Personal source.
91. Personal source.
92. See Christopher McCreery, *On Her Majesty's Service*, 45–48, 78.
93. Personal source.
94. "Rideau Hall's New Look," *National Post*, April 7, 2007, A3.
95. *Globe and Mail*, October 10, 2009.
96. *National Post*, October 10, 2009, A10.
97. "Reflections on the 'Canadianization' of the Crown," in Jennifer Smith and D. Michael Jackson, eds., *The Evolving Canadian Crown*, 209.
98. Christopher Moore, *1867: How the Fathers Made a Deal*, 243.
99. Michael Bliss, *Right Honourable Men*, 305.
100. C.E.S. Franks, "Keep the Queen and Choose Another Head of State," *Globe and Mail*, April 10, 2010.
101. A spokesperson for Jean had said that "as the representative of the Crown in Canada, the Governor-General carried out the duties of the head of state and therefore is de facto head of state," *Globe and Mail*, October 10, 2009.
102. *Heart Matters*, 189.
103. *A Fair Country*, 258.
104. Graham Barnes, *National Post*, October 9, 2009, A11.
105. Kevin S. MacLeod, *A Crown of Maples*, 35.
106. "Myth and Misunderstanding," 32.

107. *Ibid.*, 34.
108. Michael Jackson, "Crown and Country," *Globe and Mail*, April 12, 2010.
109. Section 41 (a).
110. *The Governor General and the Prime Ministers*, 125.
111. Ian Holloway, personal communication to the author, November 2009.
112. Ian Holloway, "The Law of Succession and the Canadian Crown," presented at the conference "The Crown in Canada: A Diamond Jubilee Assessment," Regina, October 2012.
113. *The Queen's Other Realms*, 218.
114. Greg Poelzer and Ken Coates, "Aboriginal Peoples and the Crown in Canada," 150.
115. David E. Smith notes that the 1870 description of Canada as "three kingdoms" alluded to the unity in diversity of England, Scotland, and Ireland in the United Kingdom — "the paradigm of a successful nation" (*Federalism and the Constitution of Canada*, 52).
116. The Forum of Federations lists twenty-five countries as federal states; these make up 40 percent of the world's population: Argentina, Australia, Austria, Belgium, Bosnia & Herzegovina, Brazil, Canada, Comoros, Ethiopia, Germany, India, Malaysia, Mexico, Micronesia, Nepal, Nigeria, Pakistan, Russia, St. Kitts & Nevis, South Africa, Spain, Switzerland, United Arab Emirates, United States of America, and Venezuela. In addition, Iraq and Sudan are "in transition to federalism" (*www.forumfed.org*).
117. *The Republican Option in Canada*, 221.
118. *Ibid.*, 220–21.
119. Peter Boyce, citing Anne Twomey, in "The Australian Monarchy in the Twenty-First Century," in Jennifer Smith and D. Michael Jackson, eds., *The Evolving Canadian Crown*, 180.
120. John Williams, "'The Blizzard and Oz,'" 20.
121. D.P. O'Connell, "Canada, Australia, Constitutional Reform and the Crown," 12.
122. David E. Smith, "The Crown and the Constitution: Sustaining Democracy?" in Jennifer Smith and D. Michael Jackson, eds., *The Evolving Canadian Crown*, 64.
123. *The Republican Option in Canada*, 221.

124. *Ibid.*, 172. See also his "Saskatchewan and Canadian Federalism," 303–04.

125. Merrilee Rasmussen, "Legislatures in Saskatchewan: A Battle for Sovereignty," in Howard A. Leeson, ed., *Saskatchewan Politics: Crowding the Centre*, 54.

126. *Ibid.*, 49.

127. *Campbell v. British Columbia (2000) B.C.S.C. 1123*, para. 179.

128. Greg Poelzer and Ken Coates, "Aboriginal Peoples and the Crown in Canada," 151. The Supreme Court stated in *Reference re. Secession of Quebec* 1998 that the purpose of the constitutional division of powers "would be defeated if one of these democratically elected levels of government could usurp the powers of the other simply by exercising its legislative power to allocate additional power to itself unilaterally" (50).

129. Quoted in David Arnot, "The Honour of the First Nations — the Honour of the Crown," in Jennifer Smith and D. Michael Jackson, eds., *The Evolving Canadian Crown*, 165–66.

130. Poelzer and Coates, 162, 163, 164.

131. *The Queen v. The Secretary of State for Foreign and Commonwealth Affairs* [1981] 4 C.N.L.R

132. Poelzer and Coates, 165, 166.

133. *Ibid.*, 167.

134. See again *Liberty and Community* by Robert Vipond.

135. Poelzer and Coates, 155–56.

136. *Ibid.*, 157.

137. Alan Taylor, *The Civil War of 1812*, 62–63.

138. *The Republican Option in Canada*, 64.

139. Dan Gardner, "Fighting the Dangerous Creep of Republicanism," *Ottawa Citizen*, 8 July 2011.

140. *Discover Canada: The Rights and Responsibilities of Citizenship / Découvrir le Canada: Les droits and responsabilités lies à la citoyenneté* (Ottawa: Department of Citizenship & Immigration / Ministère de la Citoyenneté & de l'Immigration, 2009 — revised editions 2011).

141. Remarks at the conference "The Crown in Canada: Present Realities and Future Options," Ottawa, June 9, 2010.

142. Quoted in *Canadian Monarchist News* 32 (Spring 2011), 3.

143. *L'Express*, 23 juin 2010.

144. *Maclean's*, October 10, 2011, 18–19.

145. David Johnston, "Partners in the Pursuit of Justicia," *Globe and Mail*, December 17, 2012, A11.

146. Jane Taber, "Harper Spins a New Brand of Patriotism," *Globe and Mail*, August 20, 2011, A3.

147. Kim Mackrael, "Royal Philanthropy: Prince Charles Rallies Top Level Support for His Canadian Causes," *Globe and Mail*, May 19, 2012, A8–9.

148. *Globe and Mail*, February 6, 2012.

149. *Toronto Star*, May 26, 2012.

150. Andrew Coyne, Regina *Leader-Post*, June 5, 2012.

151. Michael Den Tandt, "The Queen and Her Family Deserve a Closer Look," Regina *Leader-Post*, June 6, 2012.

152. *William and Kate: The Royal Wedding* (May 2011); *The Royal Tour: Canada Welcomes William and Catherine* (July 2011); *Queen Elizabeth II. The Diamond Jubilee: Celebrating 60 Remarkable Years* (2012); *The Diamond Jubilee: Special Collector's Edition* (July 2012).

153. Quoted in *Canadian Monarchist News* 33 (Summer 2012), 12.

154. *Globe and Mail*, August 8, 2012, A4.

155. Tobi Cohen, Postmedia News, "MP Says Drop Queen from Oath," Regina *Leader-Post*, April 18, 2013, A11.

156. "Message board" on *monarchist.ca*, accessed April 21, 2013.

157. *www.parliamentum.org*.

158. YCYC media release, January 23, 2013.

159. Christopher Moore, "Maple Leaf Crown," *Canada's History* (formerly *The Beaver*), June–July 2012, 29–34.

160. Carolyn Harris, in the Kingston *Whig-Standard*, June 2, 4 & 6, 2012. See her blog *www.royalhistorian.com*.

161. Communication to the author by Senator Serge Joyal, September 2012.

162. Announcement from Office of the Prime Minister, November 4, 2012.

163. Rideau Hall, June 27, 2012.

164. Carolyn Alphonso, "Incorrect Textbooks Being Used to Teach Civics," *Globe and Mail*, April 15, 2013.

165. Announcement by Hon. Peter MacKay, Minister of National Defence, April 19, 2013.

166. *O'Donohue v. Her Majesty The Queen In Right of Canada and Her Majesty The Queen In Right of Ontario.*

167. For the rationale of the UK legislation, see its Explanatory Notes, *www.publications.parliament.uk/pa/bills/cbill/2012-2013/0110/en/130110en.htm.*

168. See *www.monarchist.ca.*

169. See *www.crht.ca.*

170. For summarizing the complex issue of the succession, we are grateful to Philippe Lagassé (communication to the author, April 2013). For opposing points of view, see Rob Nicholson, "Changing the Line of Succession to the Crown," and Paul Benoit and Garry Toffoli, "More Is Needed to Change the Rules of Succession for Canada," *Canadian Parliamentary Review* 36, no. 2 (2013).

171. Lee Ward, "Succession Rules: Complicated Path to Doing the Right Thing," Regina *Leader-Post*, April 2, 2013, A6.

172. Communication to the author, April 2013.

173. Robert E. Hawkins, "'The Monarch is Dead; Long Live the Monarch': Canada's Assent to Amending the Rules of Succession." *Journal of Parliamentary and Political Law* 7, no. 3 (2013).

174. Letter from Andrew Swan, Attorney General and Minister of Justice, to the Committee Clerk of the Senate, March 6, 2013.

175. Motion by Geneviève Motard and Patrick Taillon, Quebec Superior Court, June 6, 2013, 2.

176. Rhéal Séguin, "Changes to Royal Succession Face Legal Fight in Quebec," *Globe and Mail*, June 7, 2013, A5.

177. Antonia Maioni, "Can Succession Affect Secession?" *Globe and Mail*, June 14, 2013, 15.

178. Robert Hardman, *Her Majesty: Queen Elizabeth II and Her Court*, 32.

179. *The Australian*, November 12, 2012.

180. *The Sunday Canberra Times*, November 11, 2012.

181. Quoted by Sir David Smith in "Royal Homecoming Down Under," *Canadian Monarchist News* 33 (2012), 15–16.

Conclusion

1. *The Secret of the Crown*, 204.
2. D. Michael Jackson, *The Canadian Monarchy in Saskatchewan*, Second Edition (Regina: Government of Saskatchewan, 1990), 14.
3. *The Crown in Canada*, 91.
4. Peter Boyce, *The Queen's Other Realms*, 246.
5. D. Michael Jackson, "Political Paradox," 78.
6. Anne Twomey, *The Chameleon Crown: The Queen and Her Australian Governors*. David E. Smith has said something similar: "Being infinitely malleable, the Crown can adapt to almost any constitutional change" (*The Republican Option in Canada*, 172).
7. "La Couronne du Canada," 31.

Bibliography

Ajzenstat, Janet. *The Canadian Founding: John Locke and Parliament*. Montreal & Kingston: McGill-Queen's University Press, 2003.

———. *The Once and Future Canadian Democracy. An Essay in Political Thought*. Montreal & Kingston: McGill-Queen's University Press, 2003.

Ajzenstat, Janet, Paul Romney, Ian Gentles, and William D. Gairdner. *Canada's Founding Debates*. Toronto: Stoddart, 1999; Toronto: University of Toronto Press, paperback edition, 2003.

Ajzenstat, Janet and Peter J. Smith, eds. *Canada's Origins: Liberal, Tory, or Republican?* Ottawa: Carleton University Press, 1997.

Arnot, David. "We Are All Treaty People," in Howard A. Leeson, ed., *Saskatchewan Politics: Crowding the Centre*. Regina: Canadian Plains Research Center, University of Regina, 2009.

Atkinson, Michael M., Daniel Béland, Gregory P. Marchildon, Kathleen McNutt, Peter W.B. Phillips, and Ken Rasmussen. *Governance and Public Policy in Canada: A View from the Provinces*. Toronto: University of Toronto Press, 2013.

Bagehot, Walter. *The English Constitution*. London: Oxford University Press, 1961.

Baier, Gerald. *Courts and Federalism: Judicial Doctrine in the United States, Australia, and Canada*. Vancouver: UBC Press, 2006.

Baker, Dennis. *Not Quite Supreme: The Courts and Coordinate Constitutional Interpretation*. Montreal & Kingston: McGill-Queen's University Press, 2010.

Barnhart, Gordon L. *"Peace, Progress and Prosperity." A Biography of Saskatchewan's First Premier, T. Walter Scott.* Regina: Canadian Plains Research Center, University of Regina, 2000.

———. ed. *Saskatchewan Premiers of the Twentieth Century.* Regina: Canadian Plains Research Center, University of Regina, 2004.

Benoit, Paul and Garry Toffoli. "More is Needed to Change the Rules of Succession for Canada," *Canadian Parliamentary Review* 36, no. 2 (2013).

Blatherwick, John. *Canadian Orders, Decorations and Medals,* Fifth Edition. Toronto: The Unitrade Press, 2003.

Bogdanor, Vernon. *The Monarchy and the Constitution.* Oxford University Press, 1995.

Bousfield, Arthur and Garry Toffoli. *Fifty Years the Queen: A Tribute to Elizabeth II on Her Golden Jubilee.* Toronto: Dundurn, 2002.

———. *Home to Canada: Royal Tours 1786–2010.* Toronto: Dundurn, 2010.

———. *Royal Observations: Canadians and Royalty.* Toronto: Dundurn, 1991.

———. *The Royal Tour of 1939: Royal Spring and the Queen Mother in Canada.* Toronto: Dundurn, 1989.

Bowden, James W.J. and Nicholas A. MacDonald. "Writing the Unwritten: The Officialization of Constitutional Conventions in the Core Commonwealth," *Journal of Parliamentary and Political Law* 6, no 1 (2012).

Boyce, Peter. *The Queen's Other Realms: The Crown and Its Legacy in Australia, Canada and New Zealand.* Sydney: The Federation Press, 2008.

Browne, G.P., ed. *Documents on the Confederation of British North America.* Toronto: McClelland and Stewart, Carleton Library Series no. 40, 1969; republished with an Introduction by Janet Ajzenstat, Montreal & Kingston: McGill-Queen's University Press, Carleton Library Series no. 215, 2009.

Buckner, Phillip, ed., *Canada and the End of Empire.* Vancouver, Toronto: UBC Press, 2005.

Buckner, Phillip and John G. Reid, eds. *Remembering 1759: The Conquest of Canada in Historical Memory.* Toronto: University of Toronto Press, 2012.

———. *Revisiting 1759: The Conquest of Canada in Historical Perspective.* Toronto: University of Toronto Press, 2012.

Butler, David and D.A. Low, eds. *Sovereigns and Surrogates*. London: Macmillan, 1991.

Canada. Privy Council Office. *Manual of Official Procedure of the Government of Canada*, Henry F. Davis and André Millar. Ottawa: Government of Canada, 1968. Source: Library and Archives Canada/ National Archives of Canada, Subject files, vol. 516.

The Canadian Press. *Canada's Queen. Elizabeth II: A Celebration of Her Majesty's Friendship with the People of Canada*. Toronto: John Wiley & Sons, 2008.

Champion, C.P. *The Strange Demise of British Canada: The Liberals and Canadian Nationalism, 1964–1968*. Montreal & Kingston: McGill-Queen's University Press, 2010.

Cheffins, Ronald. "The Royal Prerogative and the Office of Lieutenant Governor," *Canadian Parliamentary Review* 23, no. 1 (2000).

Clarkson, Adrienne. *Heart Matters. A Memoir*. Toronto: Viking Canada, 2006.

Coady, Mary Frances. *Georges and Pauline Vanier: Portrait of a Couple*. Montreal & Kingston: McGill-Queen's University Press, 2011.

Cox, Noel. *A Constitutional History of the New Zealand Monarchy: The Evolution of the New Zealand Monarchy and the Recognition of an Autochthonous Polity*. Saarbrücken: VDM Verlag Dr. Müller, 2008.

Creighton, Donald. *The Road to Confederation: The Emergence of Canada, 1863-1867*.

Dawson, R. McGregor. *The Government of Canada*, 5th ed., revised by Norman Ward. Toronto: University of Toronto Press, 1970.

Découvrir le Canada. Les droits et responsabilités liés à la citoyenneté. Guide d'étude. Ottawa : Ministre des Approvisionnements et Services Canada, 2011.

Dempsey, L. James. *Warriors of the King: Prairie Indians in World War I*. Regina: Canadian Plains Research Center, University of Regina, 1999.

Dicey, A.V. *Law of the Constitution*, 10th ed., intro. E.C.S. Wade. London: Macmillan and Co., 1962.

Diefenbaker, John G. *Those Things We Treasure*. Toronto: Macmillan of Canada, 1972.

DiGiacomo, Gordon and Maryantonett Flumian, eds. *The Case for Centralized Federalism*. Ottawa: University of Ottawa Press, 2010.

Dilks, David. *The Great Dominion: Winston Churchill in Canada, 1900–1954*. Toronto: Thomas Allen Publishers, 2005.

Discover Canada. The Rights and Responsibilities of Citizenship. Study Guide. Ottawa: Minister of Public Works and Government Services Canada, 2011.

Dufour, Christian. *Le défi québécois*. Montréal: Éditions de l'Hexagone, 1989.

Eager, Evelyn. *Saskatchewan Government: Politics and Pragmatism*. Saskatoon: Western Producer Prairie Books, 1980.

English, John. *Citizen of the World: The Life of Pierre Elliott Trudeau*, Volume One, 1919–1968. Toronto: Alfred A. Knopf Canada, 2006.

Evatt, H.V. *The Royal Prerogative*. Sydney: Law Book Company, 1987.

Evatt and Forsey on the Reserve Power. A complete and unabridged reprint of H.V. Evatt, *The King and His Dominion Governors* (2nd edition, 1967), and E.A. Forsey, *The Royal Power of Dissolution in the British Commonwealth*, 1968 reprint together with a new introduction by Dr Forsey. Sydney: Legal Books, 1990.

Farthing, John. *Freedom Wears a Crown*. Toronto: Kingswood House, 1957.

Forsey, Eugene A. *Freedom and Order: Collected Essays*. Toronto: McClelland and Stewart, 1974.

———. *A Life on the Fringe: The Memoirs of Eugene Forsey*. Toronto: Oxford University Press, 1990.

———. "The Role of the Crown in Canada since Confederation," *The Parliamentarian* 60, no. 1 (1979).

———. *The Royal Power of Dissolution of Parliament in the British Commonwealth*. Toronto: Oxford University Press, 1943. Reprinted with corrections as an Oxford in Canada paperback, 1968.

Fraser, John. *The Secret of the Crown: Canada's Affair with Royalty*. Toronto: House of Anansi Press, 2012.

Galbraith, J. William. *John Buchan: Model Governor General*. Toronto: Dundurn, 2013.

The Governors General of Canada from Viscount Monck to David Johnston. Ottawa: New Federation House, 2013.

Griffiths, Rudyard. *Who We Are: A Citizen's Manifesto*. Toronto: Douglas & McIntyre, 2009.

Gwyn, Richard. *John A. The Man Who Made Us: The Life and Times of John A. Macdonald. Volume One: 1815–1867*. Toronto: Vintage Canada, 2008.

———. *Nation Maker: Sir John A. Macdonald, His Life, Our Times. Volume Two: 1867–1891.* Toronto: Random House Canada, 2011.

Gwyn, Sandra. *The Private Capital: Ambition and Love in the Age of Macdonald and Laurier.* Toronto: McClelland and Stewart, 1984.

Hardman, Robert. *A Year with The Queen.* New York: Simon & Schuster, 2007.

———. *Her Majesty: Queen Elizabeth II and Her Court.* New York: Pegasus Books, 2012.

Hart-Davis, Duff, ed. *King's Counsellor. Abdication and War: The Diaries of Sir Alan Lascelles.* London: Phoenix, 2007.

Hawkins, Robert E. "'The Monarch is Dead; Long Live the Monarch': Canada's Assent to Amending the Rules of Succession." *Journal of Parliamentary and Political Law* 7, no. 3 (2013).

Heintzman, Ralph. "The Meaning of Monarchy," *Journal of Canadian Studies / Revue d'études canadiennes* 12, no. 2 (1977).

Hnatyshyn, Gerda and Paulette Lachapelle-Bélisle. *Rideau Hall: Canada's Living Heritage.* Ottawa: Friends of Rideau Hall, 1994.

Hogg, Peter. *Constitutional Law in Canada,* Second Edition. Toronto: Carswell, 1985.

Hryniuk, Margaret and Garth Pugh. *"A Tower of Attraction": An Illustrated History of Government House, Regina, Saskatchewan.* Regina: Government House Historical Society / Canadian Plains Research Center, University of Regina, 1991.

Hubbard, R.H. *Ample Mansions: The Viceregal Residences of the Canadian Provinces.* Ottawa: University of Ottawa Press, 1989.

Hubbard, Ruth and Gilles Paquet, eds. *The Case for Decentralized Federalism.* Ottawa: University of Ottawa Press, 2010.

Hurley, James Ross. "The Royal Prerogative and the Office of Lieutenant Governor: A Comment," *Canadian Parliamentary Review* 23, no. 2 (2000).

Jackson, D. Michael. *The Canadian Monarchy in Saskatchewan,* Second Edition. Regina: Government of Saskatchewan, 1990.

———. "The Crown in Saskatchewan: An Institution Renewed," in Howard A. Leeson, ed., *Saskatchewan Politics: Crowding the Centre.* Regina: Canadian Plains Research Center, University of Regina, 2009.

———. "The Development of Saskatchewan Honours." Unpublished research paper for the Senior Management Development Program, Saskatchewan Public Service Commission, 1990.

———, ed. *Honouring Commonwealth Citizens: Proceedings of the First Conference on Commonwealth Honours and Awards, Regina, 2006.* Toronto: Ontario Ministry of Citizenship and Immigration, 2007.

———. *Images of a Province: Symbols of Saskatchewan / Images d'une province: les symboles de la Saskatchewan.* Regina: Government of Saskatchewan, 2002.

———. "Political Paradox: The Lieutenant Governor in Saskatchewan," in Howard A. Leeson, ed., *Saskatchewan Politics: Into the Twenty-First Century.* Regina: Canadian Plains Research Center, University of Regina, 2001.

———. *Royal Saskatchewan: The Crown in a Canadian Province.* Regina: Government of Saskatchewan, 2007.

Joyal, Serge, ed. *Protecting Canadian Democracy: The Senate You Never Knew.* Montreal & Kingston: McGill-Queen's University Press, for Canadian Centre for Management Development / Centre canadien de gestion, 2003.

Lagassé, Philippe. "Parliamentary and Judicial Ambivalence Toward Executive Prerogative Powers in Canada," *Canadian Public Administration / Administration publique du Canada* 55, no. 2 (2012).

Lemieux, Frédéric, Christian Blais, and Pierre Hamelin. *L'histoire du Québec à travers ses lieutenants-gouverneurs.* Quebec: Les Publications du Québec, 2005.

Levine, Allan. *King. William Lyon Mackenzie King: A Life Guided by the Hand of Destiny.* Vancouver/Toronto: Douglas & McIntyre, 2011.

Low, Anthony. *Constitutional Heads and Political Crises.* London: Macmillan, 1988.

MacDonald, Nicholas A. and James W.J. Bowden. "No Discretion: On Prorogation and the Governor General," *Canadian Parliamentary Review* 34, no. 1 (2011).

———. "The Manual of Official Procedure of the Government of Canada: An Exposé," *Constitutional Forum constitutionnel* 20, no. 1 (2011).

MacKinnon, Frank. *The Crown in Canada.* Calgary: Glenbow Alberta Institute / McClelland and Stewart West, 1976.

MacLeod, Kevin S. *A Crown of Maples: Constitutional Monarchy in Canada*. Ottawa: Department of Canadian Heritage, 2008, Revised Edition 2012.

MacMillan, Margaret, Marjorie Harris, and Anne L. Desjardins. *Canada's House: Rideau Hall and the Invention of a Canadian Home*. Toronto: Alfred A. Knopf Canada, 2004.

———. *The Uses and Abuses of History*. Toronto: Penguin Canada, 2008.

Martin, Stanley. *The Order of Merit: One Hundred Years of Matchless Honour*. London: I.B. Tauris, 2007.

McCreery, Christopher. *The Canadian Forces' Decoration / La Décoration des Forces canadiennes*. Ottawa: Department of National Defence, 2010.

———. *The Canadian Honours System*. Toronto: Dundurn, 2005.

———. *Commemorative Medals of the Queen's Reign in Canada, 1952–2012*. Toronto: Dundurn, 2012.

———. *On Her Majesty's Service: Royal Honours and Recognition in Canada*. Toronto: Dundurn, 2008.

———. *The Order of Canada: Its Origins, History and Development*. Toronto: University of Toronto Press, 2005.

———. *The Order of Military Merit / L'Ordre du mérite militaire*. Ottawa: Department of National Defence, 2012.

McWhinney, Edward. *The Governor General and the Prime Ministers: The Making and Unmaking of Governments*. Vancouver: Ronsdale Press, 2005.

Messamore, Barbara J. *Canada's Governors General, 1847–1878: Biography and Constitutional Evolution*. Toronto: University of Toronto Press, 2006.

Michelmann, Hans J. and Cristine de Clercy, eds. *Continuity and Change in Canadian Politics: Essays in Honour of David E. Smith*. Toronto: University of Toronto Press, 2006.

Milliken, Peter. "Appropriation Acts and Governor General's Warrants," *Canadian Parliamentary Review* 13, no. 2 (1990).

Monet, Jacques. *The Canadian Crown*. Toronto/Vancouver: Clarke Irwin & Company, 1979.

———. "La Couronne du Canada," *Journal of Canadian Studies / Revue d'études canadiennes* 11, no. 4 (1976).

———. *The Last Cannon Shot: A Study of French-Canadian Nationalism, 1837–1850*. Toronto: University of Toronto Press, 1969.

———. *La Monarchie au Canada.* Ottawa: Le Cercle du livre de France, 1979.

Moore, Christopher. *1867: How the Fathers Made a Deal.* Toronto: McClelland & Stewart, 1997.

———. "Maple Leaf Crown," *Canada's History* (formerly *The Beaver*), June–July 2012.

Morton, W.L. *The Kingdom of Canada: A General History From Earliest Times.* Toronto: McClelland and Stewart, 1963.

Munro, Kenneth. *The Maple Crown in Alberta: The Office of Lieutenant-Governor, 1905–2005.* Victoria: Trafford Publishing, 2005.

Neary, Peter. "The Morning After a General Election: The Vice-Regal Perspective," *Canadian Parliamentary Review* 35, no. 3 (2012).

Neitsch, Alfred Thomas. "A Tradition of Vigilance: The Role of Lieutenant Governor in Alberta," *Canadian Parliamentary Review* 30, no. 4 (2007).

Nicholson, Rob. "Changing the Line of Succession to the Crown," *Canadian Parliamentary Review* 36, no. 2 (2013).

O'Connell, D.P. "Canada, Australia, Constitutional Reform and the Crown," *The Parliamentarian* 60, no. 1 (1979).

Olmsted, Richard A., ed. *Decisions of the Judicial Committee of the Privy Council relating to the British North America Act, 1867, and the Canadian Constitution, 1867–1854.* Three volumes. Ottawa: Queen's Printer, 1954.

Palmer, Sean. "The Ramifications of Sharing a Head of State: A Study in the Implications of a Structure," unpublished PhD thesis, Auckland University of Technology, 2010.

Patmore, Glenn A. and John D. Whyte. "Imagining Constitutional Crises: Power and (Mis)behaviour in Republican Australia," *Federal Law Review* 25 (1997).

Pike, Corinna A.W. and Christopher McCreery. *Canadian Symbols of Authority: Maces, Chains, and Rods of Office.* Toronto: Dundurn, 2011.

Rasmussen, Merrilee D. "The Decline of Parliamentary Democracy in Saskatchewan," unpublished M.A. thesis, University of Regina, 1994.

———. "Legislatures in Saskatchewan: A Battle for Sovereignty?" in Howard A. Leeson, ed., *Saskatchewan Politics: Crowding the Centre.* Regina: Canadian Plains Research Center, University of Regina, 2009.

Romney, Paul. *Getting It Wrong: How Canadians Forgot Their Past and Imperilled Confederation.* Toronto: University of Toronto Press, 1999.

Russell, Peter H. *Constitutional Odyssey: Can Canadians Be a Sovereign People?* Third Edition. Toronto: University of Toronto Press, 2004.

———. "Discretion and the Reserve Powers of the Crown," *Canadian Parliamentary Review* 34, no. 2 (2011).

———. *Two cheers for minority government: The evolution of Canadian parliamentary democracy.* Toronto: Emond Montgomery Publications, 2008.

Russell, Peter H. and Lorne Sossin, eds. *Parliamentary Democracy in Crisis.* Toronto: University of Toronto Press, 2009.

Saskatchewan: Royal Reflections: The Prince of Wales in Saskatchewan, April 2001 / Réflexions royales sur la Saskatchewan: Le prince de Galles en Saskatchewan, avril 2001. Regina: Government of Saskatchewan, 2001.

Saul, John Ralston. *A Fair Country: Telling Truths About Canada.* Toronto: Viking Canada, 2008.

———. *Louis-Hippolyte LaFontaine & Robert Baldwin.* Toronto: Penguin Books, Great Canadians Series, 2010.

———. *Reflections of a Siamese Twin: Canada at the End of the Twentieth Century.* Toronto: Penguin Books, 1997.

Saywell, John T. *The Lawmakers: Judicial Power and the Shaping of Canadian Federalism.* Toronto: University of Toronto Press, for The Osgoode Hall Law Society, 2002.

———. *The Office of Lieutenant Governor.* Toronto: University of Toronto Press, 1957; Revised Edition, Toronto: Copp Clark Pitman, 1986.

Segal, Hugh. *The Right Balance: Canada's Conservative Tradition.* Vancouver/Toronto: Douglas & McIntyre, 2011.

Senior, Hereward and Elinor Kyte Senior. *In Defence of Monarchy.* Toronto: Fealty Enterprises, 2009.

Shea, Kevin and John Jason Wilson. *Lord Stanley: The Man Behind the Cup.* Bolton, ON: Fenn Publishing Company, 2006.

Smith, David E. "Bagehot, the Crown and Canadian Constitutionalism," *Canadian Journal of Political Science* 28, no. 4 (1995).

———. *The Canadian Senate in Bicameral Perspective.* Toronto: University of Toronto Press, 2003.

————. "Empire, Crown and Canadian Federalism," *Canadian Journal of Political Science* 24, no. 3 (1991).

————. *Federalism and the Constitution of Canada.* Toronto: University of Toronto Press, 2010.

————. *The Invisible Crown: The First Principle of Canadian Government.* Toronto: University of Toronto Press, 1995; reprinted with a new preface, Toronto: University of Toronto Press, 2013.

————. *The People's House of Commons: Theories of Democracy in Contention.* Toronto: University of Toronto Press, 2007.

————. *Prairie Liberalism: The Liberal Party in Saskatchewan, 1905–71.* Toronto: University of Toronto Press, 1975.

————. *The Republican Option in Canada, Past and Present.* Toronto: University of Toronto Press, 1999.

————. "Republican Tendencies," in *Policy Options / Options politiques,* May 1999.

————. "Re: The Royal Prerogative and the Office of Governor General," *Canadian Parliamentary Review* 23, no. 3 (2000).

————. "Saskatchewan and Canadian Federalism," in Howard Leeson, ed., *Saskatchewan Politics: Crowding the Centre.* Regina: Canadian Plains Research Center, University of Regina, 2009.

Smith, Sir David. *Head of State: the Governor-General, the Monarchy, the Republic and the Dismissal.* Sydney: Macleay Press, 2005.

Smith, Denis. *Rogue Tory: The Life and Legend of John G. Diefenbaker.* Toronto: MacFarlane, Walter & Ross, 1995.

Smith, Goldwin. *Canada and the Canadian Question.* Toronto: Hunter Rose Co., 1891; new edition, edited by Carl Berger, University of Toronto Press, 1971.

Smith, Jennifer and D. Michael Jackson, eds. *The Evolving Canadian Crown.* Montreal & Kingston: Institute of Intergovernmental Relations, School of Policy Studies, Queen's University, McGill-Queen's University Press, 2012.

Speaight, Robert. *Vanier: Soldier, Diplomat and Governor General.* Toronto: Collins, 1970.

Stamp, Robert M. *Kings, Queens and Canadians: A Celebration of Canada's Infatuation with the British Royal Family.* Toronto: Fitzhenry & Whiteside, 1987.

———. *Royal Rebels: Princess Louise & the Marquis of Lorne*. Toronto: Dundurn, 1988.

Stanley, George F.G. *The Role of the Lieutenant Governor / Le role du lieutenant-gouverneur*. Fredericton: Legislative Assembly of New Brunswick / l'Assemblée legislative du Nouveau-Brunswick, 1992.

Swan, Conrad. *Canada: Symbols of Sovereignty*. Toronto: University of Toronto Press, 1977.

Taylor, Alan. *The Civil War of 1812: American Citizens, British Subjects, Irish Rebels & Indian Allies*. New York, Toronto: Alfred A. Knopf, Random House, 2011.

Tidridge, Nathan. *Canada's Constitutional Monarchy*. Toronto: Dundurn, 2011.

———. *Prince Edward, Duke of Kent: Father of the Canadian Crown*. Toronto: Dundurn, 2013.

Twomey, Anne. *The Chameleon Crown: The Queen and Her Australian Governors*. Sydney: The Federation Press, 2006.

Vance, Jonathan F. *A History of Canadian Culture*. Toronto: Oxford University Press, 2009.

———. *Maple Leaf Empire: Canada, Britain, and Two World Wars*. Toronto: Oxford University Press, 2012.

Vipond, Robert C. *Liberty and Community: Canadian Federalism and the Failure of the Constitution*. Albany, NY: State University of New York Press, 1991.

Waite, P.B. *In Search of R.B. Bennett*. Montreal & Kingston: McGill-Queen's University Press, 2012.

Ward, Norman. *Dawson's Government of Canada*. Toronto: University of Toronto Press, 1987.

Weston, Hilary M. *No Ordinary Time: My Years as Ontario's Lieutenant-Governor*. Toronto: Whitfield Editions, 2007.

Whyte, John D. "The Australian Republican Movement and Its Implications for Canada," *Constitutional Forum constitionnel* 4, no. 3 (1993).

Williams, John. "'The Blizzard and Oz': Canadian Influences on the Australian Constitution, Then and Now," in Linda Cardinal and David Heaton, eds., *Shaping Nations: Constitutionalism and Society in Australia and Canada*, 2002.

Winterton, George. *Monarchy to Republic*. Melbourne: Oxford University Press, 1986.

———. *Parliament, the Executive and the Governor-General*. Melbourne University Press, 1983.

Index